Lucille Taylor
In Christian love,

Bernice Gerard.

SUPERNATURAL

BERNICE GERARD:
Today and for Life

BERNICE GERARD:
Today and for Life

Bernice Gerard

WELCH PUBLISHING COMPANY INC.
Burlington, Ontario, Canada

DEDICATION
With thanks to God for
Velma Chapman
and the gift of her friendship
and partnership in ministry.

ISBN: 1-55011-071-3

© 1988 by Bernice Gerard

Welch Publishing Company Inc.
960 The Gateway
Burlington, Ontario
L7L 5K7   Canada

Printed in Canada

CONTENTS

1

TWICE WITHOUT A MOTHER

My first loss in life was irretrievable. I lost my mother when I was a baby. Born December 24 in New Westminster, British Columbia, Canada, I lay in the Royal Columbian Hospital, kicking, squalling, and gurgling, completely unaware that I was an orphan.

Among the patients at the hospital where I was left was Annie Gerard, who was suffering an illness that later caused her death. Since her husband was a fisherman, Mrs. Gerard was brought down the Fraser River in a fishing boat and rushed to the hospital from the docks at New Westminster. In the days of her recovery her heart went out to the wee baby whose only home was the hospital. A full-blooded Indian, of what tribe I was never to learn, Annie Gerard had borne three sons already and yet desired a daughter. In these days of adoption controls, when prospective parents have to meet all kinds of requirements and face a paper inquisition, it is hard to imagine the circumstances that conspired to join the dying woman and the orphan baby who had been for some months at the hospital. Once the adoption papers were drawn up, mother and child bade farewell to the hospital and travelled home by boat fifty miles up the mighty Fraser River. At the hospital, the nurses had called me Peggy, a name that stuck until my thirteenth year — my year of crisis over identity.

Like other fisherfolk of the Fraser, the Gerards lived in a scow house, a cedar-shingled, three-room shanty built over the water, with an outhouse perched on the downstream edge. A number of cedar logs cut from British Columbia's magnificent forests, were bound together to make the raft on which sat the house. The floating home was moored to a poplar tree on the steep but sandy banks of the river. Alongside lay a second, even larger raft on which nets were racked up, and beside it bluestone tanks, necessary equipment for the gill net fisherman.

These floating homes had all the amenities, with a walkway around one side and a railing to prevent the children from falling overboard. We also had flower boxes, beautiful beyond what one would expect, with sweet peas and nasturtiums. The iron kitchen range was kept going with firewood cut at the chopping block nearby on the river bank. During the winter the stove burned all day long, serving both for heating and cooking.

How could I forget the old cook stove? One winter's day, when I was two, the boys, arriving home from a hunting trip, brought me some cat-tails. Somehow baby Peggy managed to get one of the cat-tails caught in the heavy oven door, which, when it fell open, caused a severe burn and plenty of screaming. To this day I have on my right wrist the scar left by the nasty burn I received when I tried to put the cat-tail where it ought not to go.

The Fraser River is mighty, boisterous and nearly eight hundred miles long. One hundred and thirty miles from its mouth is the Fraser Canyon, a narrow rock-bound gorge through which the water tumbles with such turbulence and force that the river, grey from so much sand and silt, maintains its identity as far as thirty miles into the Pacific Ocean. We drank the grey, sandy water and trusted its purity but nobody trusted the river itself. The swift, eddying waters continually worked their strange patterns on the sandy banks, building up a peninsula here, carrying away an island there, changing the course of an inlet somewhere else. By the time I was old enough to be adept at handling the skiff and the dugout canoe, there was instilled in me a strong, healthy fear of the river. To be seen standing up in the canoe in midstream meant a sound thrashing on return to shore, all in the interest of warning against future foolhardiness.

Ignorance of the ways of the river cost two Japanese girls their lives when I was twelve. What they took to be a quiet bathing beach with a delightful sand bar, was, owing to the mysterious workings of the river, really a treacherous eddy. Once caught in the current's downward pull, they were unable to free themselves from the river's power. Since it all happened on the waterfront of our own residence, the authorities asked my brothers to search for the bodies, with the result that the incident was indelibly sketched upon my childhood memories.

Treacherous and unfaithful, relentless and unsympathetic, with periodic bursts of anger expressed in raging floods, the Fraser, Queen of the Valley, still held extraordinary power over the men of the river, most of whom were gill net fishermen like Leo Gerard and his sons. Toiling on the water all hours of the night and day in all kinds of weather, their strength and skills were too often inadequate for the might and craft of the river. In spite of hardships, the river brought out in them a lust for gambling.

I often heard the fishermen say that after "this" season, they'd be leaving the river, with all its uncertainties. But on opening day of the new season, when men gathered in their boats at the head of the drift to draw numbers to decide each man's turn, they would be there with the rest, dreaming that this time Fortune would favor them and give them the biggest catch ever. When the gun went off, signaling the opening of the season, they would sally forth to cast their nets, knowing that though the river guaranteed prosperity for only a few, at least the winter's debts to the packing company collector, as well as today's bread, beans and coffee were as sure as that the waters flowed seaward.

Each man had a small boat, sometimes powered by a marine engine or sometimes by an engine from a wrecked car. The boat would be built right on the river by men who had followed the boat-building craft all their lives. The cabin housing the engine, sleeping quarters, kitchen and pilot's perch occupied the forward part of the boat, the fish box was in the center at deck level, and piled in the stern were several hundred feet of fishing net.

Rigged with surface floats and sinkers, the net hangs like a curtain in the water, so that the salmon swim into the mesh and are caught behind the gills; hence the name gill net. Different nets are used at different times, as the size of the mesh determines the size of the fish most likely to be caught. Having run his boat off shore and upstream sufficiently, the fisherman throws his net over the wooden roller at the stern until the right amount of net is out of the boat. By controlling the speed of the engine and keeping a hand on the rudder, he skillfully lines his net out across the current. On one end of the net is the buoy, the first item thrown overboard, on the other is the fisherman in his boat. He must cast the net skillfully to avoid known underwater snags, and at the same time stay close enough to the sand bars to be in contact with the schools of fish running upwards to the spawning grounds. As he drifts with the current, he watches the net for strikes, or any indication of snagging on underwater hazards like sunken stumps or submerged dead heads.* "There's a strike," says he when he sees the floats begin to bob up and down in one spot, and knows a salmon has hit the net and is struggling to get free. Most of the time he is already counting his catch on the basis of how many "strikes" he has seen, and whether or not certain floats remain partially submerged with a few bobs up and down every once in a while.

Perhaps the fisherman drifts for a mile, then he cuts the engine and begins hauling the net over the roller into the boat, piling it in orderly fashion, getting ready for the next drift. Fishing people of years ago did it all by hand: throwing out, hauling in, stacking the net, pulling the fish free from entanglement in the meshes, and tossing them into the fish box up ahead to thrash around the box in one last struggle for life. At regular intervals the big collector's boat came from the fish packers down river to take the fisherman's catch to be marketed.

Of all the edible fish caught in the Fraser, the cohoe, steelhead, jack salmon, spring salmon, humpback, and sockeye, among others, the sockeye is the greatest treasure. This red-fleshed fish travels upstream in great schools so that when a "run" is on it is bonanza time for the fishermen. How these splendid salmon overcome so many obstacles while ascending the river in late summer to spawn at a place where they were born four years before is one of nature's great

*A soggy, almost submerged log.

romances. Each spring the young fish run downstream to disappear into the Pacific and then return four years later to the Fraser, as some unknown power brings them back to their birthplace to spawn and die.

Annie Gerard was a woman who knew the ways of the river. Though I was scarcely three years old when she died, and only vaguely remember her, I know her well from her picture. I have seen the boat she used for commercial fishing. It was a big unpainted skiff with clumsy oars, and the customary roller on the stern. The neighbors used to say she would have been a good mother to me had she lived. After her death her body was taken down the river on a fishing boat and put away in the Langley Prairie Cemetery.

Though I have no memory of my adoptive mother in life, I believe I remember her in death, lying in a handmade coffin already actually in the grave. I seem to remember Maggie Patterson, a neighbor, holding my hand, saying, "Look, and say 'Good-bye,' because you will never see your mother again."

2

I REMEMBER

We bring nothing into this world, and we have nothing to say about the circumstances of our birth or the events of early childhood. Eventually, the time comes when we take our lives in our own hands for better or worse. But before any decision-making opportunities arrived for me, there were many unhappy, fear-filled hours, and the darkness threatened to destroy me.

Never had I seen anything so funny! The "old man," as the Gerard boys called their father, was down at the river bank trying to push his boat off the sandbar where it had been left when the tide went out. The more he struggled and cursed, the funnier it seemed to me, and the louder I laughed. Whereupon he took time out from his difficulties to deal with my glee. Up the bank he strode, mouth full of hair-raising oaths, turned me over his knee and gave me as sound a whipping as was ever administered by hand. Sobered and almost convinced that I had got what was coming to me, I beat a retreat to the house. "Why did he spank me for laughing at something funny?", I asked the housekeeper. The spanking had been administered without explanation, although there was plenty of exclamation! "Because it is not right to laugh at other people's troubles," she explained. I heard later that my brothers were also highly amused at the incident.

By the time I was five, we no longer lived in a scow house, but in a large family home on the River Road overlooking the Fraser. Leo Gerard was building it when Annie died. Moored out front, tied to an immense cottonwood tree, was a large covered raft on which nets were racked for drying, mending or storage. Alongside were the bluestone tanks and a variety of boats, including a dugout canoe. For a poor gill net fisherman in the Depression, the big house was too ambitious an undertaking. The house was not completed; in fact, we lived in only part of it. The Gerards had always made their living from fishing but, in common with the rest of the neighbors, kept a cow. Some of our neighbors up and down the River Road gave the appearance of doing well at dairy farming; each night we could hear the chug chug of the Sullivans' milking machine. The rest of the community eked out an existence by mixing interests in farming, lumbering, logging, and fishing. With fish and game so plentiful it took little to live, but it was hard to make even that little.

Childhood memories — what do they bring back to me? The echoing wail of a distant train blowing at a country crossing makes me think of nights alone in the big, dreary house on the river. On a warm and friendly day, having the Canadian National tracks only fifty yards from our back door gave me windows into another world to wonder at, and unfailingly friendly engineers, caboose men and conductors to return my wave.

Underneath us was quicksand, so when the train was still two miles away, the house would begin to shake and every window and door in the place would rattle. As if that was not eerie enough, when the engineer blew the whistle for the crossing, every one of our six dogs would howl. Off and on we had housekeepers, but there were times when I had to be left alone all night, since the men had to fish whenever they could. Countless times I pleaded with my father to take me on the boat with him rather than leave me in the big house alone. Through the long hours of the night he would travel up and down the mist-laden river, casting his net again and again. Sometimes, curled up in a blanket on the open deck over the fish box, lay the sleeping form of his adopted child.

At times I was boarded with the neighbors, such as the Kuzunskis, the Gerards in Bellingham, the Pattersons, or the Edwards at Hatzic, but other times we had housekeepers, and I stayed at home. Some of them were heavy on the bottle and none too careful of their language. One of our "hired girls" wore a straw hat all the time, and swore up a storm, while one of my brothers undertook systematically to teach me to swear. Having put some vulgar word forward for me to pronounce, the boys would roar heartily to see their protegée coming along so well. "Say it again! Say it with more feeling!", they would shout, and I would work away at trying to please and amuse them just as if I were earning entrance to some famous school.

There were good and pleasant memories of course: the joy of catching brook trout in a nearby stream, the expeditions to the marsh on cranberry hunts and the devotion of Tricksy, my own cocker spaniel puppy. But the good memories are clouded over by recollections of an abusive alcoholic foster father whose dreadful drunken brawls filled my heart with terror. True enough, the "old man" later laid off the bottle almost entirely on account of the fits he began taking, but not before putting me and whoever else was around through some frightening experiences. It was impossible to tell how much of his strange behavior was due to jealous rage or drunkenness, and how much to the nervous seizure in which he lost his equilibrium, both physically and mentally. It is hard to say which I feared most, the drunkenness, the sickness, or his insane jealous rage.

One housekeeper in particular he railed at continually, accusing her of having sex with whoever came along. Once, just at sundown a man stopped by our place by chance to ask directions. As we heard his boat coming down the river, she asked in sheer panic that he please hurry away. But it was too late; the "old man" had seen the visitor and as Gerard staggered through the kitchen door, he began to rail against our housekeeper, accusing her of lewd conduct with the stranger. He seemed insane with jealousy, and I noticed that his eyes were wild. Just as he was moving to strike her, he was taken with a seizure and fell to the floor making a strange noise.

Immediately, the scene changed and the child and the housekeeper were there to help when he came out of the spell. He seemed to be normal again, and even unaware of his violent, abusive conduct; as for me, the terror lingered on inside.

Once, when I was about twelve years of age I actually saved his life. We had been north of Silverdale fishing. He took in the net and headed the boat full-engine downstream. My back was to him as he sat in the bow of the boat behind the wheel. I was looking out over the stern at the pattern of the waves our boat was making, when suddenly I was aware that the boat was going crazy, zig-zagging this way and that. As I turned I saw Leo Gerard looking wild in the face and pointing madly to the sun; then he slumped over the side, and his head and arms dropped down to the water. Quickly I ran forward to shut off the motor, and grabbed his braces and clothing to stop his slipping over the side, all the while shouting, "Help! Help!" at the top of my voice, hoping the Indians camped on the south side of the nearby island could hear me.

After the Indians came and helped him onto the center deck, I ran the boat back to Silverdale where May Morgan put him to bed, and I played ordinary children's games with her son, Vernon. A touch of ordinary life with normal people always made me sorry to have to return to the unhappy circumstances of life in our lonely house by the riverside; but this time was even worse. After the terrifying experience of watching him have the seizure in the lonely spot up river, he subjected me to a stream of cursing and accusations concerning things which had never crossed my mind. He imagined that the young friend at the scow house and I were doing something sexual together. And this was on the very day when I had saved his life. Now that I was growing up, people were talking of what a good little housekeeper I would make but my fear of him was increasing day by day.

Most little girls play with dolls — I played with dogs, several of them. Fuzz, the three-legged terrier, had skillfully nursed herself back to health after losing one leg when she was run over by a railroad train. She was no good for hunting, but she was good for me as an example of bravery. All bloody with a mangled leg, she was carried off the railroad track and left under the porch to die. To everyone's surprise she gnawed the protruding leg bone smooth and licked the flesh until it healed over. Also among my closest and most loyal friends were Daisy, the water spaniel who was such a good bird dog, and a couple of lanky bloodhounds that the boys had trained for tracking deer. Besides the regular adult dog population, which included a variety of mongrels, batches of puppies arrived regularly, most of which were put in a gunny sack weighted with a rock and thrown into the river when I was not looking.

These dogs were fed irregularly on big pots of fish cooked especially for them and on what was left of the deer and bear carcasses after the humans finished with them. Feeding time for the dogs was often "teasing" time for me as my brothers pretended to leave one dog out, or failed to take care of Fuzz who was weaker and could not easily push in to get her fair share. It was an emotional crisis for me as I stood guard, demanding that each dog be given a fair share. The dogs, my playmates, unfailingly followed me to school every day. I often shared a sandwich with them along the way, which no doubt did a lot to encourage their loyalty to me. The teacher did not like dogs on the school grounds so at a certain spot along the three-mile journey through the woods I would turn and wave the dogs home. They did not always go home straight away but could be heard yelping through the woods, hot on the trail of a rabbit.

In the years before I turned thirteen, dressed in gumboots and jeans (decades before they were fashionable), I learned how to run a trap line, how to make a sling shot or a whistle from green alder, and how to load and fire a rifle or shotgun. Oh yes, not to neglect mechanical skills, my brothers taught me to run the gas boat, as well as to paddle the dugout canoe noiselessly, Indian style. So far no one cared whether I learned the things girls my age were supposed to be learning, such as sewing and housekeeping.

3

THE GROWING UP OF NOBODY'S CHILD

Every member of the Gerard family except me had jet black hair and dark, swarthy skin, due of course to their French-Indian background. It was not uncommon to hear even strangers comment on how unusual it was that little sister should be so fair when the brothers were so dark. One day, as we were on our way to the country store, Harold, the youngest of my brothers, stopped the car and offered a woman a ride. No sooner had she got into the car than she inquired in a nosey way who the little blonde was. "Oh, that's our sister," answered Harold. "Well," replied the woman, "she certainly doesn't look like your sister; she is so blonde and you are so dark. How did that happen?" Harold shrugged his shoulders rather foolishly and said the only thing he could think of, "Oh, it just happened, that's all." My ears always perked up whenever my name came into the conversation but this woman and her questions made no sense to me at that time.

Of course I loved my brothers. They teased me unmercifully, but I loved every minute of it, except when they put me down the basement stairs into pitch darkness and yelled, "The boogie man is coming!" In teasing they often called me "the little tow-headed Swede." I grew to quite an age before I learned that it was nothing bad to be a Swede. Even the Swedes in the railroad repair gang who talked a language strange to me put the question to me, "Svenska?"* Confused, I shyly replied in the negative. Whatever it was they thought was different about me from the others in my house, I was sure I was not different.

*"Are you a Swedish girl?"

19

Had Annie Gerard lived, my experience of growing up an adopted child likely would have been very different. For me her death was a severe personal loss, and life was showing me daily how tough it was to be motherless. At the Parent Teachers' Association, when mothers got together, I imagined, they talked about their own children as if they were angels; it was reported to me that one of them had said the little Gerard girl would come to no good.

When they discussed the Christmas concert and gifts to be given, one thrifty woman offered the suggestion that they should purchase gifts for all but the Gerard girl, the reason being that no one from the Gerard household belonged to the P.T.A., so there was no one to pay for the gift. "But," objected another neighbor, "to leave one child out while others got gifts would be most cruel. Anyway, the Gerard men are always generous in giving their share whenever a collection is taken to buy refreshments for the twenty-fourth of May."

When the night finally came for the concert to be presented in the school house, all had reached a high pitch of excitement, especially me, as the teacher had appointed me mistress of ceremonies. The program went off well and the teacher told me she was proud of me. Then the time came for the gifts to be taken off the tree and given out. When they handed me mine, seething with resentment, I called out in the same loud voice the teacher had told me to use for announcing, "No thank you, I don't want your old gift. I heard you didn't really want to give it." My angry reply did not make me feel one bit better and I was too upset to notice what their reaction was. But I was determined that if they did not care about me, I did not care about them.

What I really needed was a mother — especially at affairs like that. Every one of the children that attended the one-room school had a mother, except Helen and me. Her mother had died shortly after mine and her father and brothers were also fishermen. Being of the same age and having so much in common, we were born to be pals and we kept in touch over the years. In each other we confided our childish hopes and problems and between the two of us managed to stir up an extraordinary amount of trouble. No doubt she told at home what I told her about the goings-on at our house.

On one occasion, during a brawl between my adoptive father and our housekeeper, Mrs Huston, paralyzed with fear, I hid as long as I could behind bales of hay in the yard, listening in fear to Gerard's shouting and cursing and the terrified woman's response. She had told me that, due to an operation on her nose, if she were ever struck a severe blow on the head, it might mean her death. When he began beating her, it seemed to me I was the only one who could save her life. Terrified, I stole up the back steps onto the porch, and into the kitchen to the foot of the stairway leading to the attic. Stretching upward, I grasped the butt of a gun in the rack that held firearms for hunting pheasants and ducks, bear and deer. The Gerards had shown me how to handle a rifle and a shotgun, and the "old man" had recently given me my own .410 gauge shotgun. In the panic of the moment, nothing was clear to me except that someone had to help the woman; perhaps it was his life against hers.

Just as I prepared to take down the gun for action, something inside me seemed to say "No!" Immediately I turned and ran from the house toward Patterson's farm, screaming at the top of my voice, "Help — please — Daddy is killing the cook!" My screams were heard by one of our homesteading neighbors, but he, the only one that could have helped, did not feel it wise to interfere. He said later that he was afraid the quarrelers would make peace with each other and turn on him.

This particular woman, receiving low wages with much abuse for a bonus, was living far below her former estate. She had a fine English background and could tell fascinating stories about England and Spain. She also told me about Bluebeard and his murdered wives, so that when rats went thumping across the floor in the attic of our house it always made me think of Bluebeard — probably he had hung his wives from just such rafters as protruded in our upstairs.

In spite of the big crock of homebrew she kept behind the kitchen door and the terror I felt on account of the brawls, I looked to this housekeeper as my protector. I understood the domestic troubles to be mostly my father's fault; she seemed ashamed to tell her own family that she was involved with Gerard sexually. One night as I was sleeping in a double bed with her, he forced himself upon her in the bed, while the two discussed the issue of "What if the kid wakes up?"

It seemed at times as if she never really consented to being his common-law wife but wanted only to be his housekeeper. But on one of their drinking days when I walked into the kitchen from school they were busy having sex on the kitchen floor.

After one terrible drinking party when I was twelve, when I had been scared almost out of my wits, my usually ravenous appetite left me completely for three days. The housekeeper, realizing how upset I was, said accusingly to Gerard, "It is your fault." It was this Mrs. Huston to whom I went a few months later when faced with the biggest question that ever troubled me — "Who am I, really?" Here's how it all happened:

Most of the year the road from our house to the school was ankle-deep in mud in those days. The men used to complain that the politicians did not care about us except at voting time when they made big empty promises to do road repairs. Every school day I walked the three miles alone except for my dogs, wading through as many mud puddles as possible, exploring alongside the road long enough to build a dam in the fast-flowing ditch, or chasing off into the woods to gather trilliums or bluebells for the teacher. What a quaint little figure I must have been. As I said earlier, long before Levis became fashionable, they sent me off to school in a boy's shirt and jeans, and gum boots. Sometimes I was comfortable in real long stockings, and sometimes my feet were wrapped with rags for a foot covering. It is not a bad system, which I learned from a Russian family nearby: you wrap the foot tightly in a cloth and deftly shove it down into the boot, making a good substitute for socks. My favorite shoes were leather hiking boots which came three-quarters of the way up my leg, ideal for playing football but not good in the heavy rainy season for general wear. Softball was my first love but the boys considered me a fair football player also. When spring came and the girls played jacks, I changed my social circle and played football with the boys.

One particular day the lonely road to school seemed shorter than usual, as I was excited about taking a live sturgeon to school. Many of the children from farming families had never seen a sturgeon, a shark-like fish, entirely different from salmon. In preparation for eating, it must first be skinned, but even then the pieces, when dropped into the frying pan, show signs of life, as though they are dead but won't lie down. Smoked sturgeon is very tasty, so many of the river dwellers hung sturgeon strips, as well as salmon and oolichans in the home-built smokehouses. The green alderwood fires were kept burning continually until the fish was properly cured. One of our Dutch neighbors kept a few pieces of dry smoked fish in his back pocket and regularly reached for a chew as though it were snuff or chewing tobacco.

Government regulations forbade the fishermen to keep a sturgeon under three feet long, but much smaller ones showed up on our dinner table. The little fellow I had in the pail was scarcely twelve inches long. Hard as it was to carry a pail of water with a live fish in it all that distance, I had my reward in a feeling of real importance when, on reaching the school, the sturgeon was giving lively swishes of his tail, and we could begin our nature study. After all, was I not working in collaboration with the teacher?

When a farmer's kid dipped the end of his pen in the dish pan that was our fish bowl, and turned the water blue, I felt as if he was trying to poison my best friend. Of course he got lectured on how to take care of a fish. The water was changed and the fish breathed on.

Besides the sturgeon though, the main talk of the school that morning was the incident at the dance held the night before in the school house: one of my brothers had come home with a black eye. Hashing over the events, we felt it necessary to blame and justify, and soon the entire school was divided into two camps. Henry, a small, skinny, freckle-faced boy, said my brother Howard got what was coming to him. But I was sure my brother was right, whatever he was doing, and felt that somebody ought to give the *other* fellow a black eye. Back and forth we harangued, never once admitting that we knew nothing at all about what we were discussing for we hadn't been there.

"My brother was right!"

"He was not!"

"Well, prove it then!"

"You don't even know what you're talking about!"

"I do too. My brother was at the dance last night and he saw every bit of the fight."

"Anyway," I said, as though bringing up some startling new evidence, "The other fellow used brass knuckles and that's not fair."

Then Henry struck the telling blow, when he asked in sarcastic tones, "What are *you* sticking up for him for? He is not your brother. You are adopted!" Quickly I shouted, "I am not." Defiantly Henry answered, "You are." I screamed back, "I am not. Who told you I was?"

At this Henry's high-pitched voice rang out, "My father told me," and the crowd burst into gales of laughter.

We had nicknamed Henry "My father" because he so often said, "My father said so." I let him know I did not care two pins about what his father said or what anybody said — I was not adopted! Hoping to prove his accusation false, I asked, "What does it mean to be adopted?" (The word was new to me.)

"It means," said Henry, "that your own mother and dad didn't love you; they just threw you out and let somebody else take you."

Now I knew for sure! That settled it! If there had been any doubt before it was gone now. With an air of finality I roared at Henry for all the world to hear, "I am *not* adopted!" Persistent, I pressed on with him, hoping to taste victory. "All right, Smarty, you know so much, who else around here is adopted?" The motley group of boys and girls were breathless. Nobody else knew whose name would be called next.

With the air of one who really knew, Henry said, "Nobody." He was making me out to be the only one, and I could not stand the pain. Terribly angry and upset, I rushed at Henry with the intention of beating a little sense into his head. Henry wisely judged violence to be no solution and beat a retreat to the boys' toilet. Wanting badly to hurt him, I stood outside screaming, "Come on out and prove it." By the time the teacher arrived, both Henry and I were crying, and he was claiming bodily injuries. I was wild with anger and hurting deep inside. I knew that the fist fight was my fault as I had attacked him. That meant that now the teacher would get the strap and give it to us for fighting on the school grounds.

She asked me what the trouble was — why the fight? I explained with no little sense of self-righteousness that Henry had said I was adopted, which was a lie, and I was trying to make him take it back. To my surprise she did not punish me and told me to sit at my desk until I was quiet and then go and wash my face and straighten my hair. She then added that it was not lady-like for girls to fight with fists, especially with boys. She must have felt my frustration and decided that the truth, which she probably guessed, was hurtful enough without her laying on the strap as well.

In the next few weeks I made a big effort to ignore the facts of my life as disclosed by Henry, so that not one word about adoption passed my lips. The question of "belonging" had come up once before when I was a preschooler and I had put up a good fight against the facts then too. At that time Leo Gerard had no housekeeper and was handing me around to others to look after. I was living with the Edwards family on their land which, from a marvelous vantage point on the hillside, overlooks Hatzic Lake. Patrick and Josephine Edwards, who had been among the first students at the Roman Catholic Indian Mission School, were blessed with a large family, including grandchildren. At the time Grandma took me in, her husband Pat was piecing together a living by fishing and mixed farming, the best part of which was his acres of raspberry bushes.

Even now that wonderful Indian woman, Josephine Edwards, lives in memory as my Grandma; certainly I never had another. I remember her as beautiful when I was a preschooler. Years later, at over one hundred years of age, still possessed of classic features, she was proudly a representative of her own people. It took years for me to understand why she often said to her children, "We are proud to be Indian." It was she who sent me off to my first day of school with an apple in my hand for the teacher. On family picnics we all swam in Hatzic Lake, had campfires and played hide and seek among the tall timbers. Grandma was a good flower and vegetable gardener, and I was her eager-beaver helper. Digging up the ground the first time around, or hoeing, raking or even weeding was good if Grandma and I could talk as we worked, and she would hand out a little praise to her husky digger.

The family in general had some problems with liquor, but Grandma had none. I myself have only been drunk once and that was at Grandma's. Somehow my attention was fixed on a bottle of grape wine which had been left high on a kitchen shelf. The forbidden drink pleased me well, so I kept on sampling until my head began to swim. Just when the wine was getting to me, somebody called, "Peggy, go get some tomatoes from the garden for supper." Grandma did not whip me when they found me "drunk in the tomato patch" but she took time to point out that too many of her adult children were ruining their lives with liquor.

At the Edwards' place a good part of living was the pleasure of watching so many people come and go. Besides Grandma's sons and daughters and grandchildren, there were regular visitors from Harrison Lake and Chemainus. In the berry season pickers and helpers ate in a common dining room. It felt good to be on the receiving end of so much playful affection. Even Joe the Crow, who lived in the immense walnut tree in the back yard, was a regular part of the scolding and fun.

Auntie from Chemainus gave sloppy "hello" kisses but Grandma said it was the love behind it that counted, not how dry or wet. Grandma was also heard to loudly lecture Uncle from Chemainus that it was not right to pee out of his upstairs bedroom window at night; he should keep a can in his room, or go downstairs to the outhouse. "We are civilized you know; we are not living in the bush."

Grandma believed in corporal punishment, but hers was no hasty rough-hewn justice; rather, without getting into a hurry, she proceeded carefully to see that the punishment suited the crime, and that the offender shared in the decision as to how hard the spanking should be. One of my unforgettable experiences took place on a day when my adoptive father and friends arrived to visit us with chocolate bars for me and beer for everyone else, just as Grandma was about to punish me for wrong-doing. Before making the visitors welcome, Grandma turned to me and in a rough whisper said, "Never mind, you'll get yours, but not now; wait until after the company goes!"

When at last the company departed, Grandma set about to determine what my delayed judgment should be. "Now you go to the woodshed and pick out a stick for me to use on you. Bring it to the house so I can see it, and when you find the right one I will come to the shed and use it on you," were her instructions. The woodshed was at least one hundred yards from the house and my feet were leaden so it took some time for me to return with a small stick. Then

Grandma asked, "Do you think, considering how bad you have been, that your stick is anywhere big enough?" So back she would send me, again and again, until at last the bodily punishment that fell from her loving hand was almost nothing as measured against the heavy lessons she handed out.

Grandma had knowledge about which fungi were mushrooms and which were toadstools, what greens growing wild could be eaten, and what medicine could be found in the wilds. Often she would send me to the nettle patch by the horse barn with gloves and scissors so that we could have a feed of nettle greens. We regularly ate wild watercress, and dandelion greens, and once, I remember, the lot of us went picking flowers for dandelion wine. Nobody let me taste it but they talked about how powerful it was. I noticed that nobody had patience to let it be until it was ready, and nearly everyone got drunk, but not Grandma.

Her brown-skinned, dark-eyed grandchildren and I played together, roaming in total freedom over the original homestead and the nearby lands of sons Clem and Art, all Edwards territory. Then somehow we got to quarreling about whose Grandma she really was. "She's not *your* Grandma," Myrtle said, and when she would not take it back and several little Edwards chimed in, I ran home, burst into the house and demanded her reassurance: "You *are* my real Grandma aren't you?", I pleaded.

She patted me affectionately and assured me that though she wasn't really Grandma to me the way she was to Myrtle and the others, she loved me just as much as if I were a real Indian like the rest. Consoled, I returned triumphantly to the playground and assured them that even though things were not quite the same with Grandma and me as with them, she loved me too. When my adoptive father decided to take me home again I said a very sad "Good-bye, Grandma" with many tears. Had she not told me that maybe someday I could come back and live with her, the parting would have been even more painful.

If the subject of adoption was taboo with me, it certainly wasn't with the other pupils at the Jubilee School who had now found my sore spot. In our frequent quarrels during the playground games they found that just the mention of the word "adoption" riled me terribly and put me at a great disadvantage. The final blow came when Helen, my best friend, casually added, "We all know you are adopted." Stunned, I hurried home from school that day, determined to settle the question forever.

I approached Mrs. Huston the housekeeper with the question, "Am I adopted?" Very much surprised, she asked in turn, "Who told you?" "The kids at school are saying it and I want to tell them it is not true." At that point she made some seemingly irrelevant remark. But there was only one thing I wanted to know, so I repeated the question — "Am I adopted?" "Yes," she replied, "you are adopted." I objected, "No, I am not! It isn't true! I won't believe it!"

"Then," she said, "there is only one thing to do. Don't tell anyone I told you to do it but go to the storeroom beside the kitchen and look in the bottom shelf of the cupboard for a small wicker basket with a lid on it. Inside the basket are the adoption papers which you might as well see for yourself so you can know the truth."

At the first opportunity, I stealthily approached the little wicker basket, took out the paper she had described and noted with horror that my name was on the front. What Henry said was true! Whoever my own father and mother were, they had not loved me enough to keep me. My name had been Bernice Nielsen and now it was Peggy Gerard. Whoever my own father and mother were — I hated them! Dramatically, I imagined myself one of the last born into a large family like the Murphys who homesteaded nearby. They had many children but, poor as they were, at least they had not given any of their babies away. If only I had my own mother and dad, I would not mind being poor or even hungry.

The adoption papers went back into the little basket but things were never the same again. The housekeeper must have told Leo Gerard that now I knew I was adopted, so whenever I was bad, which unfortunately was quite often, the "old man" would say, "We should send you to an orphanage. You really don't belong here anyway, we just took you in."

4

A CHANCE TO CHOOSE LIFE

When two Roman Catholic nuns came as house guests a few months after this, everyone was on good behavior including the "old man," who was brother to Elizabeth, the Sister Superior. He had often rudely acknowledged that when Elizabeth announced to her French Catholic family her desire to give her life to God as a nun, he would rather have seen her hit on the head with a baseball bat. During the entire week of the visit, the Sisters were wonderfully cheerful, and unruffled by our crudities. My brothers and father, whose normal conversation had a lot of "irregularities" in it, were on "good behavior" but they had not taught me much about nuns.

At the special turkey dinner, when asked which piece I would like, I called out, innocent as the angels, "The Pope's nose, please." It was the tail end of the turkey, but nobody had shared anything with me concerning the Pope himself, spiritual leader of millions of Roman Catholics.

The Sisters showed themselves to be very good sports on fishing expeditions and sightseeing ventures, but there was a veil of mystery and secrecy about them. To me the dark robes and cowl were frightening and yet it was hard to be really afraid because their words and faces were very kind. Sister Elizabeth discussed with her irreligious brother the possibility of my being brought up in a Catholic convent, but he stoutly refused to give consent. The matter came up again for discussion several times after the Sisters departed and he repeated several times over, "If any priest sets foot on this property, I'll fill him full of salt." They used to take buck shot out of a shotgun shell and fill the shell with coarse salt. I have seen stray dogs get the salt treatment. It was really just big talk against the priest but all the noise apparently expressed his true sentiments on religion.

There was no church on our side of the river for several miles; in the main our country district was void of Christian influence. Only one of the fishermen was religious and he was regarded as something of an oddity. Another neighbor, Maggie Patterson, attended the Roman Catholic church on the Donatelli's property on the north side of the river. She talked to me about joining the CCF political party when I grew up, but never mentioned any need to join a church.

At thirteen years of age I had never seen a Bible, never heard a hymn sung, nor anyone talk to me about God. He was completely unknown to me except to the extent that I heard His name mentioned frequently in profanity. Many of the men in the district were masters in the use of vile and filthy language, and in all too many instances their deeds matched their words.

In the months before my thirteenth birthday I was wrestling with two difficult questions. One concerned my abusive adoptive father, "Should I run away, and if so, to where?" The other was, "What is death?" As I mentioned earlier, two Japanese girls had been drowned a year earlier in the channel just below our house, and I was myself motherless because Mrs. Gerard had died. Now my favorite aunt, Aunt Sina, who sent me flower seeds from California, had just died. The great idea of death was forcing its way into my consciousness.

On the way to Aunt Sina's funeral in Bellingham, Washington, my father and brothers stopped for a beer at a tavern and left me sitting in the car, thinking my own thoughts. By the time we arrived at the church, I too was thirsty and much relieved to see a fountain in the hallway at the church entrance. It was not flowing fresh, and did not taste nearly as good as I expected, but it was quenching my thirst. How surprised I was when Harold, turning around to see if I was following, grabbed me by the arm and said, "Silly, that's not for drinking, that's holy water." Poor religious illiterate that I was, I fearfully asked, "Will I die because I drank holy water?"

"No," muttered Harold, "but the priest won't think much of you."

Aunt Sina who, along with Aunt Stella, another of Leo's sisters, had spent her last days doing tapestries for the Roman Catholic Church, had been very kind to me. She wrote me letters, and sent California poppy and sweet pea seeds each spring for me to plant. Now she lay cold and white in the coffin at the front of the large ornate church amidst chanting priests who were waving censers of smoke about. The funeral, the incense, the mournful chanting and the sight of Auntie dead made me sick to my stomach. It was a great relief when the funeral was over.

After the funeral on the way home I tried hard to find out what happened to Auntie, and where she had gone. My father and brothers said they knew nothing at all about it. To them she was just gone — that's all — never to return again. In the weeks following the funeral, the buzzing of a fly or the drone of a bumblebee on the window sill filled me with a sense of dread because it reminded me of the drone of the funeral service.

Added to what I had seen happen to others was the knowledge that sooner or later all of us must die. The grownups said as we played cards in the evening, that if the Stave Falls Dam ever broke we would all be washed away, even though an island was between us and the mouth of the Stave River. Particularly in early summer and late spring the tremendous roar could be heard miles away as the water plunged past the hydroelectric plant through the floodgates of the dam. In connection with these fearful thoughts was always a terrible uncertainty about the hereafter. There was small consolation in the thought that all of the people in the world were in the same predicament — brought into this world to live, love and laugh for just a while and then sent out to nobody knows where. Little did I know that what was going on in me was an awakening to deep questions about life and death, and whether or not Somebody is behind all this. This is said by Bible-believing people to be the work of the Holy Spirit bringing conviction. I also did not know that the Lord was about to take up my cause.

At first things went on as usual in the little red Jubilee school house on Bradner Road. The teacher was going through her daily routine, giving lessons to each grade level in turn. Some of us had finished our own assignments and were listening as she taught the Grade Four class, and soon we would get a break for morning recess. Then all forty of us would fly screaming down the school steps, intent on making the most of fifteen minutes of freedom.

Just before she signaled recess the teacher called us to attention to hear an announcement: "Beginning Sunday, there will be gospel meetings here in the Jubilee School. The preachers are Miss Frances Layden and Miss Clara Manary. Everyone is welcome. Boys and girls, please tell your parents about this."

It sounded interesting but what was a preacher? Up went my hand. "Please, Miss, what is a preacher?" A little amused, the teacher replied, "A preacher is one who speaks from the Bible." Still in the dark, I followed with a logical question, "What is a Bible?" In response, she drew from her desk a mysterious black book with "Holy Bible" in letters of gold on its front cover, and gave us a few words of explanation on what the Bible was. Our curiosity having been satisfied, in a few minutes we were all happily playing in the schoolyard, completely unaware of the effect the coming meeting would have on some of us.

Somehow I managed to be there for the opening meeting that first Sunday night, not out of love of the gospel, because I had not the slightest idea what it was, but simply because it was somewhere to go. Side by side in the same double desk we used in the daytime school hours sat my pal Helen and I.

Never will I forget that first gospel meeting! The preacher chose someone to give out the hymn books, which the greener among us regarded with curiosity. When we began to sing, the words were more or less the same stream of thought as had been coming to me recently:

Life at best is very brief,
Like the falling of a leaf,
Like the binding of a sheaf,
Be in time!

And there was more of the same:

We are fading too like the flowers,
That but yesterday were in their bloom,

Oh how many pass with the hours,
O'er our path falls the shadow of the tomb.

There was something soul-stirring about the plaintive melodies, and the solemn words — the logic of which it was impossible to escape. Had I not so recently seen Aunt Sina lying in the coffin? She had faded like the flowers and been cut down like the grass.

Out came the mysterious book — the Bible. The preacher read a few lines and then started to tell the most wonderful story I had ever heard. Spellbound, I drank in every word. It was about a Man who was so wonderful that even His enemies could find no fault in Him. He took the little children in His arms and blessed them. He healed the blind and gave the lame power to walk. He even loved the unlovely Mary Magdalene, out of whom were cast seven demons (Luke 8:2). He cared for people no one else loved. Thirteen years of age, mature beyond my years, I was for the first time hearing of the marvelous Man of Galilee. The meeting was quiet, the singing poor (nobody knew the hymns), but the preaching moved me deeply.

Jesus Christ was everything wonderful that one could imagine and much more. The lady with the book pictured His sufferings in the Garden of Gethsemane and then in the judgment hall before Pilate; then dramatically we walked the way of sorrow with Him, feeling His anguish, wanting to share the load of His heavy cross. When the procession reached the summit of the hill they called Calvary, I felt certain that the story would soon be ending. Some kind of rescue must be on its way. I was sure that some person of authority would arrive at the last moment and set free the innocent one.

To my surprise and horror His persecutors threw Him roughly to the ground, nailed Him to a cross, and lifted Him up to die. Everything inside me was churning in revolt against this unspeakable injustice. Then the preacher looked down at me, right into my eyes so it seemed, and asked, "Do you know why He died?" Breathlessly I waited for the answer. She continued, "He didn't have to die. He was the Son of God and could have brought judgment on His enemies. At the crucifixion legions of angels stood alert, awaiting His command. He died because He loved you. For God so loved the world, that He gave His only begotten Son, that whosoever believes in Him should not perish, but have everlasting life." (John 3:16).

Could it be that He loved me? Why, nobody had ever loved me. I was the little Gerard girl who would never come to any good, the black sheep who was always leading the other little lambs astray. In thirteen years I had lived in many households, sometimes with relatives in the United States, sometimes with neighbors and sometimes at home. In none of the places had I really belonged. I was nobody's child. Always I was the girl "just taken in" either for pity or for a tiny margin of profit. Now the preacher was telling me that the Man Jesus loved me enough to die for me!

Cautiously I pulled myself together to face the facts. It was possible that this woman was just telling a story, to serve some purpose of her own. "Preacher," thought I, "You wouldn't stand up there looking so pretty and tell a beautiful story like that if it were not true?" If that was what she was doing, it was the meanest thing I could think of. In any case, I could not take my eyes off her.

I wanted the story to be true, and Jesus to be real. If what she said was true, if God really did love me so much that He gave His Son to die for me, I would give myself to Him and follow Him all the days of my life. The thought of rejecting the Gospel never occurred to me, but I was plenty worried that He might not want me. Had the preacher asked us that first night to go forward and take a stand for the crucified One, I would have done it. Nothing in me was saying "No." My heart was painfully tender and without a single prejudice against Him.

My own unworthiness overwhelmed me. I was old enough to know that my adoption was a failure. Knowing nothing about my natural parents I feared I had been born out of wedlock. What little information I had gleaned on that subject had been from questionable sources and filled me with a sense of shame. But worst of all was the burden of my own sin that had nailed Christ to the cross. I longed for the purity and pardon that the preacher said would come when I confessed my guilt. She quoted, "If we confess our sins, He is faithful and just to forgive us our sins, and to cleanse us from all unrighteousness." (1 John 1:9)

As we got out into the fresh air at the meeting's end, Helen and I heaved a sigh of relief. She said, "I am no sissy but do you know if they had kept on with the meeting, I would have been crying?" Relieved to find that she too had been shaken up I said, "I am no sissy either but I could have cried too. I felt very funny inside when the preacher told that story."

It was not the number of meetings I attended that made the impact, as I had the opportunity to get to only a few. One night, having begged my father to allow me to go, I walked alone through the woods about three miles to the meeting. The blobs of phosphorus casting an eerie glow in strange formation along the wooded trail usually terrified me but now they seemed insignificant. The sound of the gospel had become sweet music to my ears.

When the school house series came to a close, the meetings moved to the Monsons' house where on the first Sunday the preachers planned to "test" the meeting. In a whisper someone asked me if I had made up my mind whether or not I wanted to follow Jesus Christ, adding, "We will be asked to make known our decision on the last hymn." My decision was already made.

At a shivaree the night before, a few of us had gathered in a corner to talk and were soon into a big discussion on the gospel meetings. The neighbors, having deposited coats and babies in the bedroom, were expressing their good wishes to the newlyweds by dancing until the rafters trembled. Most of the participants had drunk quite a lot and the housewarming was turning into a rough party. Sitting on a large wooden barrel in the corner with a few others around me, I voiced my disapproval of the celebration, and to my own surprise spoke out loudly in favor of the gospel meetings: "When I grow up I am going to give my life to God like the preacher women have done." In the face of a flurry of comments, favorable and unfavorable, I stood my ground.

For days I had been able to think of nothing else but the gospel meetings and the possibility of new life; now my secret thoughts were spoken. "If you desire to confess Jesus Christ as your personal Savior, please signify your decision by standing during the singing of this hymn," said the preacher. Not knowing what to expect but determined to be obedient, I stood up along with a couple of others. "God, if there is a God, I'm giving my life to you. Please wash away my sins and make me clean as snow," I prayed earnestly, silently. To my astonishment a great peace came over me, and I knew something good had happened inside me. My knees felt weak, and tears began to flow unbidden down my cheeks. The meeting now ended, the preacher came smiling to put her arms around me and commend me for my decision.

The news that I had stood up in the meeting to become a Christian reached home before I did. "We hear you joined the black legion," said one of my brothers teasingly.

Shyly I nodded, "Yes."

Then he added, "All your fun is over now. That is worse than becoming a nun."

I had no idea what he meant by, "All your fun is over." I hadn't been having that much fun. All I knew was that I now felt clean and strong. They could laugh and refer to the preachers with their black stockings and dark clothes as the black legion but I admired and respected them. To be just a little like them when I grew up seemed an ambitious goal scarcely attainable under my circumstances.

During the next few weeks I felt God's transforming power and love. My pals at school could also see a difference in me. The teenagers of our school were fast developing into a wild crowd, showing little respect for their elders or each other. On our way home from school most of us secretly smoked cigarettes which we had stolen from somebody. If we could not get tailor-mades we rolled our own or made some out of maple leaves. We tried everything that came into our heads, including chewing tobacco and snuff, even smoking cigars. Besides our daring urges to meddle with the forbidden, we carried on a kind of gang rule on the school ground. Anyone who tattled to his teacher or parents was punished by the rest. The older boys and girls imagined themselves to be madly in love and from these flash romances grew jealousies and rivalries.

To this day I am thrilled to remember the effect of the transforming power and love of God on me, following my decision to live for the Lord. No one could have been more destitute of Christian teaching, more ignorant of what it meant to be a follower of Jesus, yet the Lord put a love for Him and His word in my heart.

My whole course of thought and conduct were changed. When I asked my preacher friend how I could know for sure I was a Christian she said, "All you have to do is look at your own life and interests. The Scripture has been fulfilled in you; old things are passed away, behold, all things are become new!" (2 Cor 5:17)

Sure enough, the changes were evident in the ordinary activities of my life, for example, my reading interests. Blood and thunder murder stories, ranch romances and detective stories had been my spare time reading from the time I learned to read. Most mothers see to it that their girls read the right books: perhaps *Joan Fielding at Snow Camp* or *Black Beauty*, but nobody cared what I read. Hungry to read, I eagerly devoured the cheap secondhand novels my brothers bought in bundles at the magazine store, often reading the same book several times. Immediately following my conversion, my brother brought home a large stack of magazines and, anticipating my usual pleasure, said, "These are for you." Something inside of me said "No thank you." I had to tell him that I doubted I would ever read that kind of book again. Puzzled, he asked, "Did somebody tell you not to read these?" "No," I answered, "I just don't think I will ever be reading them again."

On Sunday night my adoptive father and brother decided to go to the theater, an idea which usually had me jumping with joy. Since the theater was not open on Sunday in Canada, we used to drive to the international border and cross over to Sumas in the State of Washington, both for the show and the Sunday beer. But the new Bernice really did not want to go. With great difficulty I tried to explain how I felt, scarcely believing that all this was going on inside me. This time they angrily asked, "Did those preachers tell you not to go to the show?" "No, they didn't say one word about it." Nobody went to the show that night. I retired to my room and by the light of the coal oil lamp read the New Testament the preacher had given me.

Would I be able to continue what I had begun? Could this new life possibly flourish in so alien an environment? My adoption was a failure and worse than a failure. There was no promise for the future in my present situation. My father and brothers took my hymn book and New Testament away and laughingly declared that a thirteen-year-old could not possibly know anything about religion. In desperation, I cried out to God. "Oh God, please help me. You are on my side!" Then, since I was learning fast I corrected myself, "Oh God, please help me. Now, *I* am on *Your* side!"

My preacher friend, Frances Layden, would soon be leaving the district and then who in this world would help me? It occurred to me to run away but common sense told me Leo Gerard would find me somehow and bring me back. Then there would be his rage to face. Troubled and fearful of the future, I confided in Frances Layden what I had so far been too frightened to tell a living soul.

Even now many years later, there are details of my childhood experience I have not verbalized to anyone, nor will I now, though I still have nightmares relating to this stage of my life. It was right after that that God wrought a miracle on my behalf.

5

THE LORD MADE A WAY

The answer to my prayer to God for a way out of this hopeless situation came quickly in a most unexpected way. Within a few days I was saying goodbye to everyone and everything I had ever known.

At the school house we were busy studying, but there was an undercurrent of excitement because that day the teacher would be giving out report cards. At the sound of someone knocking, the teacher opened the door and stepped out into the hall. Curious as we were, we could not see who the visitor was. In a few minutes the teacher stepped back into the room, walked to my desk and said, "The school nurse is here. She wants to speak to you."

In fact, the school nurse had come to take me away. I did not understand what it was all about but I willingly went with her after she assured me I would never again have to go back to live in the same house as my adoptive father.

First she took me to a private home somewhere in the Abbotsford area. I was lonely as could be as I waited day by day for about two weeks for whatever was coming next. But anything was bearable as long as I did not have to go back to Leo Gerard. Frances Laydon, who had alerted the child welfare authorities, came to see me and I was so glad to see her, I fainted.

In due course there was a brief session in court with my adoptive father where it was established that he had failed me in his responsibility as a parent. I had to bear witness against him myself. At the hearing, he asked to see me privately one last time, and all he said was, "How could you do this to me?" I never saw him again; he died some years later when I was traveling in the United States.

After proper legal steps had been taken, I then became a charge of the Department of Child Welfare of the Province of British Columbia. My guardian was to be Isobelle Harvey, Superintendent of Child Welfare.

On the way to Vancouver with Miss Harvey I kept breaking into tears. She did her best to cheer me, assuring me that the best days of my life were yet to come. She also took notice of the report card the teacher had handed me as I left the country school for the last time, and commented that it was good that I had done well at my studies. At one point she asked, "Do you like school?" "Yes," I replied, "I never miss a day if I can help it. School is wonderful."

With an encouraging smile she reached warmly toward me, covering my hand with hers and said, "You are going to have the opportunity to continue in school and get all the education you can absorb." Confused and upset as I was, with so much happening that I did not understand, I could not fail to feel that that was a wonderful promise! I had admired the teacher at our school and thought it would be wonderful to be a teacher — it was the only role model for women I knew. But Leo Gerard had refused to consider sending me to high school.

As we drove along we discussed among other things the fact that I had stood to my feet in the gospel meeting. "Why did you do it?" she asked. I replied, "I wanted to be like the preacher ladies, pure and holy. That is why I gave my life to God."

Every mile of the journey to Vancouver, I kept wondering where she was taking me. When she said finally that she was taking me to the Alexandria Orphanage, I could not believe my ears.

"But I don't want to live in an orphanage," I objected.

Then she explained that I would not be at the orphanage very long, just long enough for her to find a more suitable place for me to live. It occurred to me that she might have it in mind to leave me there permanently and was just not saying so. But nothing could be done about it, and it did seem that all of this was part of the answer to my prayer.

The Alexandria Orphanage was a large rambling building with a small inadequate playground. Contrary to my expectations, I rather took to the place. My bed was in a dormitory along with several other girls my age. There was a set time for rising, cleaning teeth, dressing and making the bed, which someone taught me how to do according to the rules.

Some of the older girls spent their time scheming about how to get outside to meet their boyfriends. Some wanted to run away and get married; others talked wildly of getting out and going on a good drunk. How any kind of a "drunk" could be "good" was beyond *my* power to imagine! When one of the girls climbed out a window and secretly spent the night with her boyfriend, she was punished by solitary confinement. Many of the older ones hated the Orphanage but I had no resentment against the Alexandria. It was heaven compared to what I had heard about such places. Furthermore, my becoming a Christian had resulted in a changed attitude toward everybody and everything.

Shining like a bright star in my dreams was the thought of going out preaching some day, just like Frances Layden was doing. I would go through the country districts preaching in school houses, telling others the same good news she had told me. Meanwhile, I read my New Testament as much as possible.

One day the head matron, whom we all feared, came upon us, a group of teenagers, all talking in our loudest voices. Not one of us had as yet found the tone or volume control on our speaking system. Singling me out as one of the chief offenders, she lectured the lot of us about quieting down and trying to act like ladies. When she was safely out of hearing distance, I turned to the others and said, "Is my voice too loud? That's what she thinks. It is all the better to preach with."

On another occasion when one of the matrons checked me up on a small mistake, I broke into a flood of tears and went crying off into a corner. I heard her say in dismay, "I can't understand that. What is wrong with her?" I did not understand either why I exploded emotionally under such slight provocation. I wanted to make it right with the matron but what could I say? How could she understand that I felt all torn up by the roots. I had a strong need to belong but there was nowhere yet to belong. My stay at the Alexandria lasted just long enough for me to begin to enjoy some new friends at the Kitsilano Junior High. Then my guardian made arrangements for me to go to the Okanagan Valley to live.

Miss Harvey was at the Vancouver railway station to see me off, commending me to the care of the conductor whom she asked to take good care of me. She also saw to it that I was provided with spending money, so that every time the fruit and candy man came by, he had a sale. Twenty-five cents for a pillow seemed quite a bargain to me. Several hours later when his shift was over and he was preparing to get off the train, he asked for the pillow back. I was sure he was cheating me until he explained that I had not purchased the pillow but only rented it.

Mrs. Lott, my new supervisor, was at the Summerland station to meet me. She was a professional social worker employed by Child Welfare, a person with whom I was to get quite well acquainted as she was the liaison between my guardian and me. She kept an eye on me in my new home, worked out problems between me and my foster parents, and made it clear that it was her job to see that Miss Harvey's wishes were carried out. Most important of all, she was a friend and counselor. When everything went wrong with everyone else, I had the feeling that she had my best interest at heart.

Also at the railroad station to greet me were the Motts, my new family. There were four children: Emily, Marjorie, Laura and Preston. Emily, the eldest, was a year younger than I; Preston was just a toddler. In the most loving way possible they welcomed me to their home; taking the cue from their mother and father, the girls spoke about my being their new sister. John Mott had been a minister in the Holiness Movement church but had moved to the sunny Okanagan and a change of occupation when his wife's health failed. Their house was located in West Summerland about half way up Hospital Hill, overlooking beautiful Lake Okanagan. The entire countryside was luxuriant with peach, apricot, pear, cherry and apple orchards. In early childhood I had more than my share of beans and coffee; now I daily enjoyed new-dug potatoes, tomatoes from the vine, freshly picked corn and cucumbers, eggplant and all types of fruit. In their home there was no arguing, no profanity, and no drinking or smoking. The children had never seen a deck of cards nor so much as smelled beer or wine. Daily the family read the Bible and prayed together.

On arrival at their house my heart and mind were in turmoil, my emotions mixed. The new family was nice but, Frances, the person I loved most, was so far away; I might never see her again. I loved Frances Layden most because she had loved me when no one else did. Since the hour of my conversion she had been mother, father, brothers and sisters to me, sustaining me with her letters. Her interest helped me believe in myself. My guardian was kind too but I had seen her only twice.

All mixed up inside and very lonely, I sat at the kitchen table and cried. I knew it was silly to cry but the tears kept coming just the same. Dear Mrs. Mott drew me into conversation, to get at why I was unhappy. That was a hard question to answer because I knew it was not fair for me to walk in, a stranger, and cry at their house. Anyway, I was glad deep down to be there but could not explain why I felt so lost. Then she asked, "Are you saved?"

With all honesty, I said, "No."

"All of our family are saved," she said, "right down to Preston. As young as he is, he knows he loves Jesus too."

Looking at me again more closely this time she asked, "Don't you consider yourself a Christian?"

Without hesitation I replied, "Oh yes, I'm a Christian. I got converted through the meetings in the school house."

It struck me that there was something unusual about this family. The people that first influenced me to accept Jesus as my Lord and Savior belonged to a group known to itself as the Christians and to others as the two-by-twos. They never *ever* used the word "saved" for they thought that nobody could know they were "saved" until they actually got to heaven. They believed themselves to be the only true followers of Jesus in the whole world, and their ideas about what it took to be a real Christian were very definite. For example, they said that the true church could be identified very easily for true Christians followed a number of practices that set them apart from other groups. They did not construct church buildings; their meetings were conducted in rented halls, school houses, and private homes; the preachers did not receive salaries and went out preaching two by two. Nor were any collections taken in the meetings. If the number of believers in a city grew, they formed new groups and met in several different houses.

When Mrs. Mott told me that her family members were each "saved" and that they went to the Baptist church, I felt sorry for them and wished that they belonged to the "true" church. I thought, "If only they could have been in the country with me and heard what I heard, they would be truly converted."

Their regular attendance at the Baptist church was a major problem for me, particularly since they insisted I go with them. When I said I did not want to go to church, they thought my attitude strange indeed for a Christian. It did not seem strange to me because, as far as I knew, the followers of Jesus did not build churches. I for one did not intend to get mixed up with anybody but the "true" Christians.

As the situation grew increasingly uncomfortable, I resolved to settle the question for good so I wrote Frances and asked, "Did you not tell me churches are worldly and wrong? Please tell me, is it wrong for me to go to one?" I assured her, "If you say I shouldn't go, I won't go and they can't drag me. These people are trying to get me to go to the Baptist church." Anxiously I waited for her reply.

When the next letter came there was no mention of church. Much later I found out that my guardian, who read my letters, had told Frances that if she gave me advice contrary to her wishes, she would not be permitted to correspond with me at all. Thoroughly dismayed that I had to go to a place of preaching where they knew so little about the real thing, I went grudgingly to the Baptist church with the Motts. With all good intentions, I fervently wished that all of them could hear what I had heard and be converted like I had been. The only thing I could admit to liking was the fudge the Sunday School teacher gave out each Sunday to those who learned the Bible verses.

At home with the Motts questions of faith came up regularly for discussion. How hard they worked to convince me that my ideas of who is going to heaven were much too narrow! "Heaven will be very small if just you and your friends are going there," Mrs. Mott would say. To which I would reply, "I don't care how small heaven is or how few are there. If there is just Jesus, the preacher and I, I'm going anyway!" It had been made clear to me from the beginning by Frances Layden that the way to heaven was straight and narrow, with just a few people on it, and I for one had no idea how many "few" was. In vain the Motts tried to explain that the true church is made up of believers from many different groups and denominations. Every morning when they had prayer around the family altar, all of the children prayed including the youngest. After some months, Mr. Mott said, "Bernice, wouldn't you like to pray?"

I thought, "God can hear me even if He doesn't hear them." Somewhere earlier on, my two-by-two friends had planted in my mind the idea that in order to get prayers through you had to be a "true" believer. Faltering and uncertain, I prayed my first prayer at a family altar. Cocksure of myself in other ways, I had sense enough to know that my prayer was no masterpiece.

The meetings in the local Baptist church were not as heart-warming and personal as many of the townspeople felt necessary, so some of them regularly attended a Sunday afternoon Bible study and prayer meeting where any believer who cared to could stand and give testimony. Having heard about my peculiarities, the leader said, "Bernice, you have been converted, wouldn't you like to testify?" Perfectly sure that God would be pleased with my testimony but that the rest of them were still outside the door of salvation, I stood up and stuttered out a few sentences. My thought was that what I said might help others — if only they could have been with me in the school house!

Yet before long it became clear to me that these Motts were wonderful Christians, and that I, with so many shortcomings, was only a beginner. Their love and patient understanding was helping a great deal as I adjusted to my new life. It was they and my social worker who encouraged me to take back my birth name, Bernice, to which we added Margaret, and thus get set to enjoy an altogether new life. I had never liked being called Peggy, which the kids at school perverted to Piggy. My old habits of speech had to go also. It was not just the Gerard men that swore; I too could swear like a logger. Even yet there were words in my vocabulary that Mrs. Mott said a Christian should never use. And they had never even heard *some* of the colorful phrases I used.

"Bernice, Bernice!" expostulated Mrs. Mott, "Be careful how you talk! The baby is copying you. He's going about saying, 'Holy smoke!' Everything is 'holy smoke!' "

"But it is not swearing," said I defensively.

"No," she replied, "but it's first cousin to it. Christians are different and don't use slang and worldly talk."

I would try to do better and then — "Oops!" out it came again!

Ashamed, I would ask myself, "Will I ever control my tongue?" Often when I sat down to eat by myself I would be halfway through the meal before I even thought of giving thanks to God. Somewhere I had heard that even pigs give thanks when they eat; they at least look up to heaven and say, "Grunt, grunt." At last, compelled by the growing awareness of my own shortcomings and the contrast between my attitude and that of these loving Christians, I went to Mr. Mott, who was quite a philosopher, and asked, "Do you think I really got converted?"

In a kind, encouraging way he replied, "Bernice, if anybody ever got converted, you did. But it takes time to develop Christian habits and character. You are just a babe in the Lord and have much to learn. As you live for Him and grow in grace you will acquire habits that are becoming to a Christian."

It took several months for the Mott family to convince me that what I had got in the country and what they had were the same. The important thing we had in common was a personal friendship with Jesus as Lord and Savior. Heaven was still relatively small but not as small as I had at first thought. The Holiness Movement people, such as the Motts, would be there and some Baptists. They were just barely "in" when my guardian moved me to Kelowna to live with some Pentecostals.

6

WALKING IN THE LIGHT

Affectionately, I bade the Mott family good-bye. Had I been permitted to choose I would have stayed forever with them but my guardian thought it best for me to live in Kelowna, thirty-five miles up the Okanagan Valley. There I was to receive medical attention, hopefully to be cured of a bad skin condition which caused me much embarrassment. The doctor my guardian chose was a friend from college days.

Through a chain of circumstances that in retrospect seems wonderful, I found myself living in the home of John and Evelyn Lindahl; however, at the time it did not seem wonderful to me. The Lindahls belonged to a small, growing church known as Evangel Tabernacle, which was part of a large fellowship called the Pentecostal Assemblies of Canada, a sister organization to the Assemblies of God in the United States. My bags were no more than set down when Mrs. Lindahl said, "We'll be going to church tomorrow night. Would you like to come with us?"

Tomorrow was Tuesday. I thought, "They could at least have waited until Sunday. Now what do these people have that they are so enthusiastic about?"

Uppermost in my mind was the thought that I was now in Kelowna where the true Christians had several meetings weekly and I would be able to worship with them. It would please Frances greatly to hear that I was attending their meetings regularly. They had rescued me in the country and to their cause my heart was bound with strong ties.

47

In my limited experience as a Christian, with the best of intentions but in far too much of a hurry, I had formed a number of opinions about what was acceptable in religion, and what was to be avoided. Along the way I had been warned against the Pentecostal people who were said to be, of all heretics in the world, the most dangerous. If Hell had one place hotter than another, they would certainly be consigned to it. Not only were they in error but they had a subtle way of snaring others so that they were completely trapped before they even knew it. At once I saw the danger of my position. I was living with Pentecostal people!

Perhaps I had been wrong about the Holiness Movement and some of the Baptists but there could be no mistake about these Pentecostals. At that moment my journey on the straight and narrow road that leads to life seemed even more perilous than I had first envisioned. There was need for prayer. "Please, God, help me stay on the straight and narrow road. I want to follow Jesus. Don't let me be influenced the wrong way."

In the service at Evangel Tabernacle that first Tuesday night my prejudices prevented me from enjoying anything — well, almost anything. When we arrived home from the service Mr. Lindahl said, "Well, Bernice, how did you like it?" My immediate reply was, "I did not like it at all." After all one could not afford to be polite to heretics. In the face of my impudence he had every right to take me down a peg or two but showing no irritation at all, he continued, "Didn't you like anything about the service?" "The orchestra sounded good," I conceded, "but what was all that moaning and groaning about?"

Even though I had not the slightest inclination to be satisfied with any of their explanations, his reply seemed quite satisfactory: "When the preacher says something the people believe the Bible teaches, they say, 'Amen.' That is like saying, 'Preach it, brother! We agree with you when you speak what God says in His Word!' Then too, God loves to hear our praises, so we make no apologies for the praises of the people." Then he asked me to get my Bible and see for myself how the Psalmist David urged the people to be sure to express thanks and praise to God! The passages he pointed out were:

Shout for joy to the Lord, all the earth.
Worship the Lord with gladness; come before him with joyful songs.
Know that the Lord is God. It is he who made us, and we are his; we are
his people, the sheep of his pasture.
Enter his gates with thanksgiving, and his courts with praise; give
thanks to him; and praise his Name.
For the Lord is good and his love endures forever; His faithfulness con-
tinues through all generations. (Psalm 100 NIV)

It was most satisfactory, it was beautiful, and it all sat very well
with my inner inclinations. Nevertheless my prejudices told me the
safest way would be to stay entirely away from their Pentecostal
church so I asked permission of my guardian, through my supervisor, to go to the true church. I believed I was choosing the group with
whom Jesus would have fellowshiped, had He been in town. My
guardian's answer was clear, "You must attend church with the people with whom you live. How can you be part of their family if on
Sunday you gather your righteous robes around you and go marching off to some other church as though you were better than they?"
My counterarguments were of no avail.

The Lindahls' could insist I go to the Pentecostal church but they
couldn't force me to listen. I would be inattentive. Nothing they said
would make any difference to me. Like a duck in the rain, I would
watch the preaching run off. Nothing must soak in. I wished it were
possible to plug my ears with cotton.

It was not easy to be inattentive — the meetings were much too
interesting and my heart too hungry for the Word of God! They
preached, "You must be born again." (John 3:7) Why, that was the
same theme Frances spoke on in the school house! "The wind blows
where it will and you hear the sound of it, but cannot tell from where
it comes, and where it goes, so is everyone that is born of the Spirit."
(verse 8). When the wind blew, nobody could see it, but the effect
could be seen. It had been that way in my own conversion. The miracle could not be explained but the results had been obvious to all.

Week after week the Pentecostal preacher exalted Jesus as Messiah, "He himself bore our sins in his body on the tree, so that we
might die to sins and live for righteousness." (I Peter 2: 24 NIV). My

own understanding of the gospel improved rapidly as week by week they kept on teaching the major themes of the redemption story. Like the boy in Gypsy Smith's song who lay in a gypsy tent dying, I could feel my heart singing, "Tell it again. Salvation's story repeat o'er and o'er." No more than a beginner myself in the Christian way, I was only now learning to rest in the promises of God, experiencing the Scriptural assurance of my position in the family of God, and feeling somewhat relaxed about the "salvation" part of Pentecostal teaching. Then along came evangelist Tom Johnstone who provoked in me a new crisis when he preached for two weeks on the work of the Holy Spirit in the believer's life.

The odd thing about the Pentecostal people was their ability to speak in tongues, and their belief that all Christian believers should do likewise. It was for this that they stuck out like a sore thumb from other evangelicals. Their tongues-speaking was odd to some perhaps, but not to our evangelist who found something about the Holy Spirit everywhere in the Bible, and claimed that as a result of this series of gospel meetings we would all see signs following the preaching of the Word. Did not Jesus promise extraordinary happenings at the very same time as He gave the command, "Go into all the world and preach the gospel"?

At the evangelist's urging I opened my Bible to the final chapter of Mark's gospel, and sure enough there it was:

> Go into all the world, and preach the good news to all creation.
> Whoever believes and is baptized will be saved, but whoever does not believe will be condemned.
> And these signs will accompany those who believe: In my name they will drive out demons; they will speak in new tongues.
> They will pick up snakes with their hands; and when they drink deadly poison, it will not hurt them at all; they will place their hands on sick people and they will get well. (Mark 16: 15-18 NIV)

Interesting, and apparently Biblical as it all was, I was very apprehensive of letting any of these signs work out in me.

Nevertheless, his handling of Scriptures left me with little doubt that Christians of New Testament times experienced these things more or less routinely. He introduced me for the first time to Simon the Sorcerer who, having seen the miracles Philip did, and the Holy Spirit received by the believers when Peter and John laid hands on them, tried to buy the same power so that he too could lay on hands and see people empowered by the Holy Spirit. (Acts 8:5-25) Surely he would not have been interested in purchasing "nothing."

Another story about speaking in tongues involved the Apostle Peter and some non-Jews at Cornelius' house. As far as Peter knew at the time only Jews were included in God's promises. But at Cornelius' Gentile household, while he was telling how Jesus had been crucified, buried and raised again the third day, the Holy Spirit "came on all who heard the message. The circumcised believers who had come with Peter were astonished that the gift of the Holy Spirit had been poured out even on the Gentiles." (Acts 10: 44-45 NIV) How did they know these outsiders had received the gift of the Holy Spirit? What convinced Peter he should risk the anger of his fellow apostles, all of whom were Jews, by baptizing in water the believing Gentiles of Cornelius' house? "For they heard them speaking in tongues, and praising God." (v 46 NIV) If Peter was so convinced by the tongues-speaking, indeed judged it to be a sign of God's working in persons until then considered to be outside God's grace, how could any of us write "tongues" off as nonsense, or on Satan's side?

For those who did not know their Bibles, the evangelist had more surprises: the Apostle Paul also laid hands on people with the result that they spoke in tongues and prophesied. In particular at Ephesus, "When Paul placed his hands upon them, the Holy Spirit came on them, and they spoke in tongues and prophesied." (Acts 19: 6 NIV) Furthermore, Paul has left us his personal testimony, "I thank God that I speak in tongues more than all of you," and solemnly warned, "Do not forbid speaking in tongues." (1 Corinthians 14: 18, 39 NIV) The impression under which I had been laboring that there was not one verse in the whole Bible to support speaking in tongues as a meaningful, Biblical phenomenon was entirely wrong. The Pentecostal people had not made it all up — it was in the Bible.

Heaven was getting larger all the time. It was clear to me now that the praising Pentecostals would not be barred from that wonderful place where the saved of earth will sing in mighty chorus, "Redeemed by the blood of the Lamb."

"Walking in the light" was explained by the Free Methodists in Summerland, whose church the Motts sometimes attended, as a daily challenge, not something to be taken casually. It struck fear in my heart to hear that if you failed to walk in the light of truth received, your light turned to darkness. The Scriptures spoke powerfully, and very clearly:

> God is light; in Him there is no darkness at all.
> If we claim to have fellowship with Him yet walk in darkness, we lie, and do not live by the truth.
> But if we walk in the light, as He is in the light, we have fellowship with one another, and the blood of Jesus, His Son, purifies us from all sin. (1 John 1: 5-7 NIV)

Apparently, some who began well turned aside after a little while but I wanted to be like Abraham who "did not waver through unbelief regarding the promise of God, but was strengthened in his faith and gave glory to God." (Romans 4: 20 NIV) Furthermore, Jesus said that the person who begins following Him, that is, puts his hand to the plow, and then turns back is not worthy of Him.

Green as I was, there was no doubt in my mind that a great deal was at stake as each individual believer decided how to respond as the new light of the gospel dawned. One of the first of Jesus' parables to fall on my ears was about the sower who went out to sow the seed. (Matthew 13) Our preacher at the school house had said we should ask God for understanding and expect to have to take personal action whenever we were dealing with Holy Scripture. Like so many of Jesus' parables, the one about the sower came to my inner being like a message from heaven, even though I had no previous experience with the Bible.

First we listeners could see the man with the seed bag casting forth by hand as evenly as he could. Of course, some fell by the wayside, some on stony places, some among the thorns, and some on good ground. What fell on good ground brought forth fruit, some one hundred fold, some sixty, some thirty. So far, the planting and hopes for reaping were the same as regularly experienced by our farming neighbors. Some of our homesteads were jokingly referred to as "rock and air farms," so inhospitable was the soil. It was Jesus' inter-

pretation of the story that caused me to answer Him back as though
He were present talking with us:

> When anyone hears the message about the Kingdom, and does not un-
> derstand it, the evil one comes and snatches away what was sown in his
> heart. This is the seed sown along the path.
> The one who received the seed that fell on rocky places is the man who
> hears the word and at once receives it with joy.
> But since he has no root, he lasts only a short time. When trouble or
> persecution comes because of the word, he quickly falls away.
> The one who received the seed that fell among the thorns is the man
> who hears the word but the worries of this life, and the deceitfulness of
> wealth choke it, making it unfruitful.
> But the one who received the seed that fell on good soil is the man who
> hears the word and understands it. He produces a crop, yielding a
> hundred, sixty or thirty times what was sown. (Matthew 13: 19-23 NIV)

My immediate spontaneous response to that word from Jesus was
to speak aloud, "Oh God, let my heart be good ground!"

Until now the deceitfulness of riches had been no problem to me,
but it did seem that "trouble and persecution" were about to come to
me because of the Word. How could I dare to tell Frances, the person I loved so much, that I was now at one with the Pentecostals? If I
received the experience the Pentecostals called the infilling of the
Holy Spirit, I would have no choice but to bear witness to what the
Lord had done. Well, no matter what anyone would say, the Lord
must be given first place in my life.

Making up my mind that I was willing to go for all the Lord had
for me, even if it meant I would be a Pentecostal, did not make me
one. Far from it; speaking in tongues, of which some spoke so dis-
paragingly, may have been as easy as falling off a log and half as valu-
able but I could not do it, had no idea what it was like, indeed had no
such inclination.

The tricky part was that the Pentecostals themselves declared
speaking in tongues to be somewhat inconsequential, and yet significant in that it was the initial evidence of the baptism of the Holy
Spirit. Typical expressions of this included "You don't seek to speak
in tongues, but when you are filled with the Holy Spirit, you will
speak in tongues! You do not submit to water baptism to get wet, but

when you are baptized (by immersion) you will get wet!" "The tongue comes along with the shoe." "Big doors swing on small hinges." The hinge in this case consisted in allowing oneself to speak a language of which one's own intellect is in disapproval.

Having declared myself a candidate for the Pentecostal experience I now spent most of the following year seeking — participating whenever possible in "tarry meetings" which were after-service prayer times. There was, of course, no need to persuade the Lord to act, since His willingness to give what He promised had already been demonstrated. Peter summed it up for the crowd in Jerusalem at Pentecost when he said, "Repent, and be baptized, every one of you, in the Name of Jesus Christ for the forgiveness of your sins, and you shall receive the gift of the Holy Spirit. The promise is for you and your children, and for all who are far off — for all whom the Lord our God will call." (Acts 2: 38, 39 NIV)

In addition to intensely personal private prayer, there was the experience of concert prayer with ministering brothers and sisters who intermingled praise, requests to the Lord, and words of advice to the candidate.

"Send the fire." (as at the day of Pentecost)

"Send the rain, Lord." (Zech 10:1)

"Hold on, brother." (in prayer)

"Let go." (of self)

"Fill him, Lord."

In the midst of the symphony of prayer and praise the candidate may also have been praying, "Fill me, Lord." A classic among those old-fashioned praying people was the story of the woman who heard the perpetual backslider praying, "Fill me, Lord." "Don't do it, Lord," she interrupted, "He leaks."

Theoretically, there was no need for "tarrying" as the promise of God had already been given, and the onus was now on the believer to receive; practically, waiting before the Lord was a great idea for a young Christian whose prayer habits and general spirituality were in formation. Every hour of my teen years spent in those old-fashioned prayer meetings seems now to have been golden. Far from having been a misdirection of precious time and energy, I see it now as a period of initiation into the secrets of the way of faith, and intercessory prayer in the power of the Holy Spirit. In practising the presence of God, I learned to pray more effectively, in soul-searching I found personal effort had its limits, and at last by the help of the Spirit I entered more fully into a love relationship with my Lord.

Just when I was wondering if I was one who "could not enter in because of unbelief" (Hebrews 3:19), the church scheduled a series of meetings with evangelist Arthur Slater. Each night he preached the basics of the gospel, expecting the signs of the Spirit to follow: some would believe and be baptized, the sick would be healed, and some would speak with new tongues. (Mark 16:15-18)

For seekers like me, the Word was a light that could show up things that were not supposed to be in one's life, or reveal to one's own self something not fully repented of, or yet unsurrendered. Whenever possible, any wrong between oneself and another had to be made right, a circumstance which found me writing a letter to a man named Rolly Pelon.

Before my eyes, every time I tried to pray, was the one dollar bill I had stolen from Pelon's cabin at his homestead on Pemberton Hill behind the Gerard house. When I was eleven, my school pal Helen and I had stolen his cigarettes, sampled his chewing tobacco, and walked away with two dollars in cash. Nobody had ever figured out who the culprits were. The new word in my vocabulary now was "restitution"; to have truly repented, a person had to be sorry enough to make right what could be made right. Thus, Mr. Pelon must have been surprised to receive my letter asking his forgiveness and returning my share of the stolen money.

Zaccheus, on meeting Jesus, said, "Look, Lord! Here and now I give half of my possessions to the poor, and if I have cheated anybody out of anything, I will pay back four times the amount." (Luke 19: 8 NIV) In my case, I hoped a dollar, not four dollars, would do! But Mr. Pelon's reply was such as to encourage the most dishonest of crooks to go straight. He sent the dollar back and said, "You will never be sorry for deciding to be an honest person."

After quite a period of digging myself up by the roots to see how I was growing, I was led to a new and much fuller appreciation of the grace of God. The questions Paul the Apostle asked his converts were applicable to me: "Did you receive the Spirit by observing the

law, or by believing what you heard? Are you so foolish? After beginning with the Spirit, are you now trying to attain your goal by human
effort?" (Galatians 3: 2, 3 NIV) Regarding salvation, it was clear that
"by grace you have been saved through faith — and this not from
yourselves, it is the gift of God — not by works of which no one can
boast." (Ephesians 2: 8, 9 NIV) To myself I had continually said, "I
am not good enough. How can the Lord fill me with His Holy
Spirit?" But He had begun His work in me by grace, and by grace it
would continue, not by my efforts.

In retrospect, one can compare it to learning to float in the water.
You can see that to float in water is the easiest thing possible — once
you catch on to the secret of trusting yourself to the water! To rest in
the Lord, so that the gift of the Holy Spirit can be manifest, is a somewhat similar experience.

Step by step I had come to see that what my heart cried for was not
an experience for its own sake, and not a ritual, however mysterious,
but a love relationship with God: to meditate on His law, His works,
His person; to love Him with heart, soul and mind. (Matthew 22: 37)
I attained a new dimension of freedom in the Spirit when, casting off
fear, I was able to pray out loud in the prayer room: "Lord Jesus
Christ, Son of the living God, have mercy on me! Thank you Lord
for forgiveness of sins, for loving me. I love you Lord. Jesus, Jesus,
Oh how sweet the Name!" When love overflows the heart, the regular expressions of the lips are too poor. All the words in our English
dictionary are not enough to tell forth His praise. When my own
breakthrough was just minutes away, I was thinking, "Had I ten
thousand tongues I would use them all to sing my great Redeemer's
praise." Some begin forthrightly to speak in a new tongue, others,
like me, begin with stammering lips, and a strange syllable here and
there mingled with praise in one's own language. When the new took
over and the old was temporarily put aside, I was praising God in an
entirely new language. The meaning of each word was unknown, but
my inner self was singing a love song to God. Out of the innermost
being was flowing a river of living water. It was as Jesus said:

> If anyone is thirsty, let him come to me and drink.
>   Whoever believes in me, as the Scripture has said, streams of living

water will flow from within him.
By this he meant the Spirit, whom those who believed in him were later
to receive: up to that time, the Spirit had not been given, since Jesus had
not yet been glorified. (John 7: 37-39 NIV)

My English had first mingled with the new language, and then given
way completely, even as the muddy Fraser, on flowing into the Pacific, at last gives way and is lost in the ocean.

All my life until now, the word "holy" meant nothing, though
many times I had said, "Holy mackerel!", "Holy cow!", "Holy
smoke!" What did "holy" *mean*? Now in my mountain-peak prayer
experience I was being shown, as I experienced what praying Christians call "holy laughter." From my inner being there burst forth a
rollicking joy which cascaded forth in waves of laughter. Was it acceptable to laugh so loudly in the prayer room?, I wondered. What
would people think? Well, they were rejoicing too. We were all rejoicing in God and they were glad to see me rising in victory over past
troubles and tears. I was clean, free, loved by God! I wanted to get on
top of the church's pitched roof and shout to all of Kelowna, "Praise
the Lord! Praise His holy Name!"

Speaking in tongues, holy laughter, and extended periods of deep
prayer together, when the Holy Spirit prayed through the believers,
were commonplace among us in that small-town church. However,
it took years of Bible and university study for me to put it all into a
framework satisfactory to my enquiring intellect.

Nevertheless, sufficient for the time were certain obvious parallels
between events which happened in Bible times and what was happening to us in Kelowna. Of course, there were also teachings in
Scripture which shed light on our pathways. We frequently had to
help people home from prayer meetings because, like those on the
day of Pentecost who were taken for drunken by bystanders (even
though, we are told, it was only nine o'clock in the morning), they
were drunk in the Spirit. (Acts 2; Ephesians 5: 18)

We got carried away as did the woman who washed Jesus' feet
with her tears, wiped them with the hair of her head, kissing His feet
and anointing them with precious ointment. In answer to the criti-
cism of the Pharisee, Jesus simply pointed out that it's the one that

has been forgiven most who loves most. There is no greater cause for rejoicing and gratitude than to know that our sins are cast into the sea of God's forgetfulness. (Jeremiah 31:34)

Many people are ready to write off the preaching of the cross and the Pentecostal experience as foolishness, and from their perspective they are right. What they apparently do not know is that:

God chose the foolish things of the world to shame the wise; God chose the weak things of the world to shame the strong. He chose the lowly things of this world, and the despised things — and things that are not — to nullify the things that are, so that no one may boast before him. (1 Corinthians 1: 27-29 NIV)

But how was I to explain what had happened to me and what I thought the Bible said to my beloved preacher friend, Frances Layden, who had no room in her heart, or theology, for Pentecostals?

For days I worried, afraid she would cast me off as a friend, since I had so soon fallen in with heretics. Of all the people I knew, I loved her most. She had been wonderful to me when I needed a friend. In return I gave her the devotion of my teenage heart. Since she did not believe in the Pentecostal people, it was likely that my decision would mean a breach in our friendship. Furthermore, it seemed the height of ingratitude to turn my back on the ones who had rescued me in the country. But there was no reconciling the two groups as Frances consistently refused to fellowship with anybody who associated with other religious groups.

Apprehensively, I set myself to writing the difficult letter of explanation to my dear evangelist. It went something like this:

Dearest Frances,
I'm sorry to have to write something I know will displease you but I don't know what else to do.
When I first came to Kelowna I rejected the message of the baptism of the Holy Spirit as preached by the Pentecostal people. Then I saw the truth of it in the Bible, and went on to actually receive the experience. You will think that now I have been sidetracked, but I want you to know I love the Lord more now than ever. I must put God first.
— Bernice

Assuring her of my love for her, and my gratitude to God for the message she brought, I signed my name. In that moment of decision, it seemed I could hear the door shut on a wonderful friendship.

The anxiously awaited reply was warm, affectionate, filled with concern: "I understand that these people have been in a position to influence you unduly. I will keep on praying for you that you will come back to the true way." She was later to give years of her life to preaching the gospel in Japan, where I am sure they also loved her very much.

What a day it will be when we all get to heaven! Perhaps one day she and I will meet. Twice she will turn my way to make sure who it is, and then exclaim in surprise, "You here? Why I gave up all hope for you. I thought my labors were in vain."

With joy, I will reply, "Yes, not only am I here but there are millions upon millions more just like me in heaven."

7

MY FIGHT FOR RELIGIOUS FREEDOM

Life Buoy, Lux and Ivory — I tried them all! I even ate yeast cakes and drank carrot juice — still no success! I read all the advertisements on complexion care and carefully followed everybody's advice on home remedies. But in spite of the fact that constant medical care was now available, my bad skin condition failed to improve.

Beyond that my problems were few. Like most teenagers I was a sound sleeper and a slow riser. My social worker averted a major crisis between me and the Lindahls by buying me a Big Ben alarm clock which helped me roll out in the mornings. Even then, for desired results, the alarm clock had to sit on an overturned dishpan in the far corner of the bedroom where turning it off meant getting out of bed.

To Evelyn Lindahl's dismay, at dishwashing time my mind was often far away in a dream world of books. I read whatever was available and a book might even be propped open in front of me as I went through the motions of washing dishes. My Saturday chore of scrubbing the floor was likely to be interrupted as the urge to leap on my bicycle for a quick spin around the block overcame me. But except for such minor irritations as arise in any household when someone is growing up, we all got along famously.

The happiest days of my young life were spent with the Lindahl family, John and Evelyn, and their two little children, Stanley and Vera. John was kind, generous, and willing to get into long discussions with me; I remember him as a good man who loved his wife dearly, showed a lot of affection to his little daughter, and held high hopes for his son.

After the loneliness of my own childhood, even babysitting the Lindahl children was fun. Particularly, Stan would listen by the hour to made-up adventure stories about little kids in dugout canoes on the mighty Fraser, trapping, hunting, fishing, and firing on deer and bear in their own front yard. The heroes never got hurt, and the stories ran in serial form out of my head, never finding an end.

"Pick up your things! Make your bed! Shut the door — quietly," was a good part of the daily conversation as Evelyn Lindahl worked to civilize my behavior in the home. Much of what they were trying to get across about successful family living was news to me. Nobody had ever told me before, for example, that in a setting for a tea table, the cups and saucers should be matched.

Eager as I was to learn to be a part of things, I gladly hurried home from school, set the table and helped serve the ladies whom Evelyn was inviting in for tea. Having never been at a tea before, or handled English china, how was I to know that my version of a tea table, an American Rose cup with Petit–Point saucer, Silver Birch with Black Watch, or Bridal Rose with Wedgewood, looked like a social disaster to everyone present — especially to the hostess who, when the guests were gone, gave me a good scolding. I was sorry she was annoyed with me, but otherwise had a hard time seeing what the fuss was about. In spite of all this, the Lindahls were very supportive, among the first really affirming people I had met.

Nobody knew at the time whether I was to grow up a carpenter, a mechanic or what. I dismantled my bike periodically, with little Stan by my side assisting in our fix-it shop; both of us had grease from ear to ear. Biking adventures were a major source of fun. On one of our side trips when I had been left by John and Evelyn in charge of their children, little Vera, who was straddling the back wheel, in weariness allowed her legs to get caught in the spokes. Terrified lest bones were broken I rushed her to Dr. Reba Willits and was relieved to hear there was no injury, and no bill from the doctor. Dr. Reba usually gave me a gift at Christmas. It felt good to be personal friends with someone as important, good-looking, and nice as she.

It was good to live with the Lindahls, particularly because there was a wholesomeness and naturalness in all they did. We ground our own cereal from a variety of seed and grain, and made our own dill pickles. Under a trap door in the kitchen, down a few rungs of the ladder, the dills and sauerkraut waited in their brine in big crocks for maturity. Understandably, a certain amount of snitching went on. "Who has been in the dills?" someone would call out. I would answer, "Just checking to see if they are ready."

Over the sawdust-burning kitchen range hung wire racks laden with plums that were on their way to becoming prunes, good for stewing, and better than Wrigley's gum for daily chewing. According to the season we were surfeited with enormous cherries, apricots, peaches, pears and apples. From the early Transparents to the late crop of Delicious and McIntosh that kept the packing houses busy through the frosty fall days, there was no limit to what could be enjoyed of sight, sound and taste except one's capacity. An evening of high school homework was in itself an apple festival.

We had Lake Okanagan for swimming, and ferry rides to Westbank for biking adventure excursions. Sometimes a school chum and I would pedal the thirty-five miles to West Summerland for the sheer fun of accomplishing the journey there and back. There were also large family gatherings at Grandpa Flintoft's ranch at Benvoulin for corn boils, tobogganing, and — no special reason at all. For real thrills it was hard to beat the car meet at Winfield where I saw Happy Hooligan of the Hell Drivers go flying through the air and crash through a wall of fire.

A lot that was good and memorable was going on in my life. At the Kelowna High School, my best pal Naida Gibb and I were side by side for first place in our class. Meanwhile, I worked like a beaver at trying to be a good Christian. In line with the other-worldliness of our church family's attitude, I saw myself as in the world but not of it, abstaining from liquor, social dancing, theater-going and the like. Of course, not infrequently, I had a very hard time explaining to people what motivated me.

A certain amount of determination was needed for a person to stand out against the majority. My baptism took place in Lake Okanagan on a very windy day, with a good crowd of high school acquaintances standing on the shore joking and hollering about the fanatics. For me it was all part of a very useful identity crisis; we Pentecostals knew we were not there in the interest of winning a popularity contest.

The baptizing pastor, Horace Catrano, was a humble Christian with few worldly assets. A man of limited education with a foreign accent, he had pioneered the Pentecostal work in Kelowna, beginning services in a rented hall over a Chinese laundry on Water Street. Wryly he would recall, "For the first month I prayed much and preached regular services to the cat. No one else came." In humility, Pastor Catrano spent much time in prayer and taught his people to do the same. Prayer was all we had to go on. Evangel Tabernacle, my home church then, is now a large congregation and a major force in the spiritual life of the city, but in those days I never heard anyone outside our circle prophesy good for us.

In the little church that grew and grew we gathered for prayer after every service, each one on his knees praying aloud. Frequently, from the prayer time I would slip home quietly and into bed so as to preserve the marvelous atmosphere of prayer. Little wonder my dreams were sometimes of myself standing before a crowd of people preaching the gospel. The pastor's wife and others in the church family were sure that one day I would preach the Word, which, of course, was encouraging and complimentary to me personally, as those who preached were highly regarded among us. There was no opposition to women evangelists even in those days, as the Pentecostals, like the early Methodists, held that the gifts of the Spirit are supernatural, and the Spirit moves both in men and in women. John Wesley's mother and Catherine Booth preached revival, after all.

But my dreams in those days were not all sweetness and light. My sleep was all too frequently disturbed with terrifying reruns of my childhood, in which my drunken and abusive adoptive father was stumbling and pawing about. "How come I have such nightmares when my days are now so good?" I asked John Lindahl. I was still experiencing so much upset in my dreams that it was not unusual for me to wake in the morning to find myself out of bed and on the floor. When I lived at Motts', Mrs. Mott used to cover me up with a blanket when this happened. John said, "Ask the Lord to deal with your inner self, the bad memories and all." As I followed his advice, the terror diminished, but the nightmares did not ever go away entirely.

"It's been arranged for you to spend the Christmas vacation in Vancouver. You are to have a complete medical check-up," announced my new social worker, Wini Urquhart. My face lit up with a smile. It would be fun to go to Vancouver on a trip, and wonderful to one day see that all the unsightly blemishes on my skin were gone. Wini was always referred to as my "supervisor." So regularly did she call at our house that she was both friend and counselor, as well as chief contact with my guardian, Isobelle Harvey, the Superintendent of Child Welfare in British Columbia, and I had lots of confidence in her. Wini in later years told me that she was almost afraid to come to our house because of the barrage of questions with which she was greeted. What my guardian thought was all-important to me; the supervisor knew her ideas and plans and passed them on.

On second thought, just one thing bothered me about the Vancouver trip. "Are you sure I'll be back by the time school starts again?" I asked Winnie. In the Lindahl home I was firmly planted and had no desire to be dug up by the roots once more. I had been fortunate in that both of my placements had been with loving Christian families. The Children's Aid Society had evidently assured them that I was not a "delinquent" and we had come to love each other.

In the eyes of my pals at school I was plain lucky. After all who wouldn't like to take a trip to Vancouver during the Christmas vacation? With excitement I discussed my plans with the young people at the church. While in Vancouver I would visit the large churches and find out how they did things so we could put their ideas to work in our group.

In our home on Harvey Avenue we all had a wonderful Christmas, and then on Boxing Day at the Kelowna railroad station I bade the Lindahls good-bye. Before Evelyn and I left the house we had prayer together, and John particularly prayed for the Lord to be with me. Later, they told me that as I walked out the door John said, "I have a strange feeling Bernice is not coming back to live with us." His wife dismissed the thought as a mere notion.

After enjoying life in a home where there was the feeling of belonging, the receiving home in Vancouver was a dreary proposition, even though the woman who ran it was good-natured and well-liked by the children. The Vancouver Children's Aid Society maintained the receiving home and used it as a clearing house for children who were awaiting placement in foster homes. Some of the children had been in and out of the receiving home many times, either because they could not adjust to foster parents, because of their own personality problems, or because they were unfortunate enough to be placed in unsuitable homes. They were everybody's children — and nobody's child. Some of the teenage girls were on the verge of earning for themselves a term in a correction center. For each one, the picture of living was distorted. What we all needed and wanted most was what we lacked — to be loved and wanted by somebody. But I felt good down inside because I knew I was wanted at Lindahls' in Kelowna. The sooner I got back there the better!

The Vancouver visit had been arranged so that I could have special medical care. The tour from one doctor's office to another began immediately, with some surprising results. One doctor said I should wear a different type of shoe, another said that I needed glasses, and still another that I must have my tonsils removed. Nobody had even begun to work on my complexion problem which was of paramount interest to me, when I suddenly had an attack of acute bronchitis.

Impatiently, I lay sick in bed in the receiving home for three weeks. While the foghorns blew incessantly, sounding as lonely as could be, I dreamed every hour of my return to Kelowna. My guardian sent flowers, and my supervisor called regularly, yet the days dragged terribly. I thought of little else but my return home to Lindahls'.

One night after I was well enough to be up and around, the house mother entertained her brother at dinner. The older girls were well acquainted with him since he often visited his sister, and on this occasion he talked freely of his business plans. He had just rented a suite of offices and was making plans to move his business from Eastern Canada.

After dinner they asked me to join them in a game of cards, which I could easily have done, having learned to play bridge, rummy, cribbage and solitaire at Gerards'. I begged to be excused and apologized for holding up the game, explaining that on becoming a Christian I had given up card playing. Until then the conversation had been going along nicely, so some explanation was certainly due them. The house mother was displeased with me and ventured that "the most Christian thing I could do right then was be a sport and make up the foursome." Trying hard to make my intentions and goodwill known I went on to speak of my Christian conversion and dedication to God. The gentleman himself seemed to understand perfectly what I was trying to say and commented kindly, "I have met people who believed this way before, and I admire you for being true to your convictions." In a short while I excused myself, went upstairs to bed and was soon fast asleep.

Late that night, after the card game had been in progress a long time, I was awakened by a dull thud and groans, followed by the cries of the house mother as she called her brother's name. The guest, having felt sick, had come upstairs to the bathroom where he collapsed. By the time the physician arrived, he was dead. The whole house was aroused and in hysteria. Nervous and scared, I lay trembling in bed, entirely miserable until a few lines of Scripture came to me. Over and over I repeated, "The Lord is my shepherd, I shall not want. I will never leave thee nor forsake thee," and then drifted off into a deep sleep. In the morning one of the girls said, "What kind of person are *you*? A man dies in the room right next to you and you turn over and go to sleep. Not one of us slept a wink all night." I shared with her that it was the Bible verses that comforted and put me to sleep.

Every day away from my home in Kelowna seemed an age. As soon as I was well enough, I went expectantly to my guardian's office, sure that there would be no more delays, and that right after the talk with her I would be on the train to Kelowna. It was a great privilege to talk with her; she had great authority over my life and most good things came through her hand. Yet I had seen her only twice before.

She enquired how I was feeling, and asked "How are things at the receiving house?" I thanked her for the flowers she sent. It had been an honor to receive flowers from her, and almost made it worth being sick. The other children had looked on enviously. Then I put the question, "On what day am I going back to Kelowna?"

"You are not going back."

I was aghast. She surely wouldn't move me from Lindahls' now! I dreaded the thought of change, and wanted to stay with what I knew and had come to love. Surprisingly, though I held her in awe, I had the audacity to argue with her, but I had not the sense to know it would do no good.

To leave Kelowna High School was unthinkable, so I began to list off the reasons why. A competition had developed between another girl and me as we vied for first place. The whole school had taken an interest in the friendly competition. "Haven't you heard I am doing very well at school?" I asked her.

Her reply was, "If you do well there, you'll do better here. I want you to go the finest schools where you'll get the best possible education. I'm expecting you to go far. The doctor says your tonsils must come out, so wouldn't it be best for you to stay in Vancouver where the hospitals and medical care are the finest?"

Cleverly, Miss Harvey convinced me, at least for the moment, that I wanted what she wanted me to do. Having gained the point, she then dropped the real bomb. "While you are here in Vancouver I do not want you to go to the Pentecostal church or any church like it!" Her words left me stunned.

Then she asked, "Are you still in touch with that woman who preached in the school house?"

"Yes, we correspond regularly."

"You are not to have anything to do with her either, or go to any of their meetings."

My much respected guardian was taking on a new look. She was bent on tearing me from my religious moorings. In the battle for my mind, one by one she handed out the punches, and each time down I went, though I never failed to come up arguing.

I stammered a protest, "The church means so much to me. If it hadn't been that I stood up to be a follower of Jesus in those meetings in the country, I don't know where I'd be now. The one you refer to as 'that woman who preached' is the best friend I have."

With that my guardian began to ridicule the letter that she had opened, written by Frances to me. She laughed at the affectionate opening and closing. To her it was mere piffle, so trivial and worthless. Defiantly I thought, "It may be twaddle to her but it means everything to me. Why can't she see that Frances believed in me and loved me when no one else could see anything worth bothering about?" Purposefully, my guardian had set about to destroy my dream, tear down my idol, and tamper with my religious convictions.

She continued, "If you defy me, I'll put you in a Roman Catholic convent where you will do what you are told." Whether she really would have, no one knows, but she certainly had the power. She had won every round so far.

I had one more question to ask, "If I am not permitted to go to the Pentecostal church, to what church shall I go?"

She named it. I was to go to a United church.

"Why they don't even believe in the virgin birth of Jesus Christ!" I exclaimed in horror.

With that she lost her temper and commanded me not to criticize other churches. Later I learned that it was her church I had criticized. The interview was brought to an abrupt uncomfortable conclusion.

Everything she told me had caught me by surprise. I now knew that I was not going back to Kelowna, that my guardian thought I was developing into a religious fanatic, and that she thought I was about to ruin my life by sticking to the narrow-minded ideas I got in the country. If I didn't have sense enough to save myself from failure — she was going to do it for me.

8

STANDING ALONE

The imperial edict had been delivered. Perplexed, bewildered and homesick for friends in Kelowna, I still hoped something would happen to make the all-powerful Miss Harvey change her mind. But it was soon evident that she had no intention of relenting, in fact she had a more comprehensive plan in mind than I had previously imagined.

Her plans included cutting me off from old friends including, indeed especially, from Pastor Catrano of Kelowna, whom she referred to haughtily as "that little Italian." On finding himself barred by special order of the Superintendent of Child Welfare from visiting me at the Vancouver General where I was undergoing removal of tonsils, he actually had to call at the Welfare Office to insist he be allowed to see me. Reluctantly she granted him permission to see me for a few minutes only, as though he were a person of unfit moral character.

As could be expected, the pastor interceded for me, the Lindahls and the whole church family: "It is unfair, unkind and no doubt illegal for you as Superintendent of Welfare to cut Bernice off from the friends and church of her choice!"

"It's for her own good!" snapped Superintendent Harvey.

"But you have no right to interfere with her choice of religion," replied the pastor, "and we will press the case in the courts."

Finally, as the pastor reported it, Isobelle Harvey concluded the conversation by saying, "If you take the matter of her religious freedom to court, I will prove on the testimony of our doctors that it was bad for her health to attend a Pentecostal church."

Finally the pastor shared with me by phone that, having discussed the matter with others, including fellow ministers, it was his opinion that I should submit to my guardian's wishes even though we all questioned her judgment. He encouraged me to keep my faith up though I was not happy with the restrictions and new directions imposed upon me, because through it all the Lord was testing me to see if I would stand up for my convictions in the face of opposition.

It was indeed a time of testing. During the next four years I felt the pressure of my guardian's interest in my religious life. Through the people I lived with, she pressed for changes both in my life and in my thinking.

My new home was located on Locarno Crescent at Jericho Beach, one of Vancouver's better residential areas. The rather proud family that lived there were Mr. and Mrs. Clem Hudson and their son Kim, who attended St. George's private school. Five years younger than I, from the first moment of our meeting, Kim was interested in me, and I in him. In the years that followed there developed between us a deep bond of affection.

Lord Byng was the largest high school I had ever seen. On my first day there, it left me feeling "country," swallowed up like Jonah inside a whale.

When I got home that night, Mrs. Hudson asked, "How did you get along at school today?"

"Just wonderful, thank you."

"Did you get to know anyone?"

"Yes," I said, "I met three of the nicest girls I have ever seen."

"Oh, did they ask you anywhere?"

"Yes, they asked me to their house and the mother served us cake and milk."

Mrs. Hudson nodded approvingly, "Did they invite you anywhere else?"

"Yes," I replied, "they invited me to go to the theater tonight."

"And..." said she, "what did you say?"

"I said, It is nice of you to ask me but I don't go to the theater any more since I got converted in the country. Of course, I don't

blame you for going because you probably don't have anything better to do." Mrs. Hudson was wide-eyed with amazement, "You told
them *that*!" I said, "Yes, that's the truth — I did get converted in the
country. If I had not been converted I wouldn't be here now."

Then, in all sincerity she warned me never to talk to anyone that
way again. "That idea may be all right out in the sticks where nobody knows anything but you are now living in one of the most aris-
tocratic sections of this city. Here people have education and culture.
If that is the way you intend to live you are going to be a very lonely
girl!" Coming from her mouth, it was something of a self-fulfilling
prophecy.

When my Pentecostal friends in Kelowna heard that I was living
in a Vancouver household where they were set on talking me out of
my old-time Christianity, they got in touch with friends in Vancouver who in turn were to get in touch with me. I well remember
hearing the phone ring and knowing that friends were phoning and
asking for me. The lady of the house asked, "What is your name,
please? And to what church do you belong?"

"Sixth Avenue Pentecostal Tabernacle."

Bang went the receiver and down went my heart!

She was so right when she said I was going to be lonely, especially
if she succeeded in cutting me off from my religious friends — the
only kind I had.

Many times I heard that Jesus Christ is the answer — but right
now He was my problem! How to stay true to Him and still please
my guardian and the people with whom I lived was a problem impossible of solution. What I believed to be part of Christian consecration, they thought was narrow-minded foolishness. They were apparently well-meaning and sincere, and so was I.

I was having a hard time adjusting to the discipline of the home,
mostly because many of their ideas were new to me. When asked a
question, juniors like me were to respond, "Yes, Mr. Hudson," or
"Yes sir!" On going to bed, shoes were to be set left, right — side by
side. Let anyone come in to sound the wake-up call and find left
where right should be, or girdle and slip helter-skelter, and World
War I broke out all over again. Mr. Hudson had served in the Canadian Army, as a corporal I believe, in World War I, and was dedi-

cated to seeing that none of his training went to waste. Mrs. Hudson, having been "properly brought up" and British-born to boot, was equally clear on what must be written on the empty slate from the country.

Most of what they made such a ruckus over was simple enough once I got the idea. But what touched on religion was much harder to handle. I was learning, but I did not want to learn how to be less than truly faithful to Jesus.

One Saturday during my first few weeks in their home, a crisis arose at the dinner table. The day had gone very well and harmony was filling the house. Mr. Hudson, in a moment of generosity, exclaimed, "Let's all go to the theater tonight." As he looked at his son Kim, he found a ready answer, "Sure Dad, let's go." Then at his wife; no problem there. Knowing I was next in line, and not knowing what I was going to say or even do with my hands, I had reached for my water glass. But my trembling hand was giving me away, so I put down the glass quietly. The clouds were gathering, I would again be in the eye of the storm. Fearful of provoking a furor at the dinner table, and very anxious for acceptance, I nevertheless stood my ground. "I'm sorry sir, but I don't go to the theater."

"You don't go to the theater? (as if he didn't know!) What nonsense! You are no better than we are. We are going and so are you! When I say you are going, you are going!"

It was his will against mine. He knew better. He felt I had no right to say "No, thank you." Scared stiff, I prayed, "Lord, what do I do now?" Almost immediately the answer came. Mrs. H., seeing my distress, turned to her husband and said, "We have discussed this long enough. Leave her alone." They went to the theater without me. Kim reported to me the next morning, "It was a great show, Bernice. You should have come with us."

Through my years in that home, the major themes never changed, neither theirs nor mine. My teenage piety rubbed rough against the wisdom of the household. In the verbal battles that broke out, the rules were established that it was the juniors' lot to answer "Yes, sir" and "No, sir," and to give longer statements only when called upon. There was nevertheless a saving custom: when she felt like lecturing me on religion, he would say, "All right, Dearie, leave her alone."

When he was hot on my trail, she would let him go just so far and then say, "Now let's drop the subject."

Both my first and last days during high school, senior matriculation, and normal school (teacher training) in Vancouver, were spent in the Hudsons' home. When Mr. Hudson left Woodwards to become a buyer for another company, they sold their home and took a break to travel abroad. By the time they settled again in a new home at the University Gates, where Kim persuaded them to have me live with them once again, I had lived with two other families during the War years.

The first of these families had three little girls who each wore a different, newly starched fancy dress every day. Their chief reason for having me in their home was that they needed a baby-sitter, vegetable peeler, dishwasher and general housekeeper's assistant. Ironing those twenty-one dresses each week and doing a fair share of the general housework kept me very busy. When, finally, one of my teachers at Lord Byng complained to my guardian that her usually excellent student was lagging because of lack of study time, my guardian had me moved.

Again I was surprised to be moving, even though my life was lived on the fringe of the family's concerns as if I were any hired maid. I remember vowing that if I ever was the mother of a household I would see to it that everyone at the dinner table was welcome to a fair share of whatever food was there. I remember that liver, of all things, was special and reserved for the family. The mother would say, "You don't mind, do you?" Yes, I did mind, and I also minded that only family had real toothpaste while I, the welfare kid, had to use salt or baking soda on my toothbrush. Silly to remember it after all these years? Yes, but to this day any children visiting *our* house can share our toothpaste and help themselves to whatever we are having for dinner, and enjoy the feeling of family.

In that home, as well as the one in which I lived next, I sometimes gained permission from the mother of the family to attend a young people's service or some special gathering with Christian friends of my choice. Nevertheless, my guardian's orders remained the same. I regularly attended St. Philip's Anglican, Mrs. Hudson's church, and now, after some discussion, my guardian's choice.

In this church of her choice I taught a Sunday School class of twelve-year-old boys, most of whom attended private schools. It was not unusual for one to come back to the class after an absence of several weeks and explain that he had been away with his family in Europe. I thought they were wonderful boys and could not fail to notice how polite they were, even on a class picnic, when the menu had on it only hot dogs, mustard and sand. When asked to teach the Sunday School class, I had wondered if my services would be acceptable since I was Pentecostal. But the vicar of the parish had told Mrs. Hudson, "That's all right, there are some good people among those Pentecostals."

Probably my guardian felt that attendance at such a church would wean me away from my radical views. Quite the contrary — every time I sat through the services, though I enjoyed most of it, I knew even more certainly what I really wanted. For example, when the Sunday School Superintendent commented on temperance, I was shocked. His views and what I believed my boys should be told were entirely opposite. He said, "It is all right to drink wine but don't drink too much. To be temperate means to refrain from doing too much of anything," which, of course, was true. Then he made an honest confession as he pointed to the sore on his lip and said, "I got this from smoking my pipe too much. Don't do as I do." To me his temperance lesson was a flop. To myself I said, "The Moslems do better." Total abstinence from alcohol is commanded in Islam. As for me, I have since remembered with fondness Geoffrey Chaucer's Good Priest:

> Christ's lore and His apostles twelve
> He taught but followed first himself.

For a long time I knew only one girl at Lord Byng who believed as I did. It troubled me greatly that born-again believers should be so much in the minority at my school. Certain events in my high school experience served to emphasize the loneliness of the way I had chosen, and caused me to ponder whether or not I was doing the best for myself, or for the Lord.

One year, when I was president of the public speaking club at

Lord Byng, we decided that it would be great to finish off the year with a party. After the general discussion I said, "It seems that everyone is in favor of having a dance. We'll have to appoint someone to take care of the arrangements — the president won't be there."
"What is wrong with the president? Why won't she be there?"

My answer was, "As most of you know, when I was thirteen years old and living in the country I became a born-again Christian. Since then I have not gone to dances, but that need not hinder your dance. You can certainly have it without me."

Someone spoke up and said that after such a wonderful year together it seemed ridiculous to have the main event without the president. I said, "I'm sorry, kids. I don't mean to spoil your fun but I honestly cannot attend the dance." By way of compromise, they arranged a banquet, to be followed by a dance. I agreed to attend the banquet.

On the night of the event, by the time the banquet was drawing to a close, my mind was on my exit. I did not want to get into any embarrassing situations, as some well-meaning person tried to save me from myself, and prevail on me to stay for the dance. I wanted to be true to God and to my convictions, and staying for the dance was not part of it. The club was made up of wonderful, clean-cut young people, most of them church members. I liked everyone and certainly did not feel superior to any of them. To stay for sociability's sake would have been a pleasure but I knew what I had to do.

The crowd, knowing what was in my mind, made an effort to persuade me to stay, in good spirit. Maybe they even arranged for one of the nicest boys in the group to come forward and ask me to dance with him.
"Thank you, Dave, but I just can't do it. I don't even know how to dance."
"Well, that's no problem," said he, "I'll teach you."

By this time there was quite a group gathered round, everyone in a gay mood, plotting together to draw me into the fun. Soon there was a line-up of good-looking boys, all of them volunteers to help teach me to dance. To slight their invitation and to appear a wet blanket was the last thing I wanted. But I could not pretend I was someone else. Much as I longed for acceptance by my school friends, I could not go back on what I had received.

On the streetcar home I felt lonely and uncertain. Most of the girls and boys I had just left were from good families. Their dress was better than mine; there was no question about their background. They and their folks had good reputations and most of them, if asked, would have said, "Yes, I am a Christian."

Could it be that I was mistaken? Was I making life harder for myself by tenaciously clinging to strange, narrow-minded ideas? Did I really get converted in the country? Was I the girl for whom old things had passed away and all things had become new as a result of my decision to serve God? Now it all seemed like a dream.

Home at last in my own room, with tears I earnestly sought the Lord. There was really no one else to talk it over with so I could find out once and for all what was required of me, and what was neither here nor there. I confessed once again my faith in the Lord Jesus Christ, thanked God for forgiveness of sins, and pleaded for His guidance. I was weak and miserable but He was strong and merciful. In the days that followed I learned more and more of His grace and keeping power.

9

HERE I STAND

What every child needs most, wants and thrives best on, is to have a mother and father who love him and also love one another. I did well in school but hated special days when parents were invited. Other girls proudly walked the school halls with their mothers, while I wished I were somewhere else.

Once, in conversation with Chris, one of Mrs. Hudson's friends, I remarked that Mrs. Hudson never commented approvingly or seemed to notice that I did well in school. Chris replied, "She may not say it to you but she has mentioned it at the bridge club. She seemed quite proud of your school record." To know that she noticed and approved even a little pleased me greatly. In my eyes she was a quality person for whom I felt both admiration and affection. But it seemed my country conversion was like a rock of offense between us, bringing nothing but vexation of spirit.

At the time there was no way for me to see what design the good Lord had in placing me with that particular family to be a thorn in the flesh. Years later during the early Sixties after I had come back from the U.S. and enrolled at UBC, as he lay dying in Shaughnessy Hospital, Mr. Hudson himself filled me in on the details. In our early years together, all I knew was that in every discussion of my faith and how to live it, I was bound to come out the loser.

Now he told me that I was constantly a reminder of a way of thinking and living that he had decided to forget for he had once been converted himself. For example, even my saying grace at meals turned into an event to be remembered. Kim had regularly said grace at his father's request, which consisted of rattling off in Latin what he had learned at St. George's. Then his father would demand that it be repeated in English, then repeated again more slowly, until finally not only God but all of us knew that our gratitude had been properly expressed.

The first time I was asked to give thanks for the food, I repeated what we always said at Motts' and Lindahls'. It was not so much a set grace as a prayer, and in it was, "Bless this food to the nourishing of our bodies and us to Thy service." In amazement Mr. Hudson looked at me, "Why you say it just like my old man used to say it!" From what he said about his father I gradually formed a picture of him in my mind as a Bible-believing, God-fearing man. In his life-time he gave generously to the church and in his old age he had little of this world's goods. His son felt that his father's religion had been a liability, and did not intend to so burden himself.

They were so sure I was ruining my life with religion. They were certain that evangelical pulpits were filled by racketeers and that the pews were populated with people who had failed in love or business, or had lost their health. When I turned down an invitation to a Scout dance and consistently refused to attend all school dances, Mrs. Hudson prophesied forcefully that I would be an old maid. Not just an old maid — an unhappy old maid! Furthermore, she declared that it was impossible for me to be even a good school teacher as long as I held to my old-fashioned ideas.

By the time I had finished one year of university and was in teacher training at the normal school, other girls of my age from our neighborhood were developing into social belles. "Why can't you be like Adelle next door?" Mrs. Hudson asked me, "She takes a cocktail and is learning to move in society." So the girl next door drew forth the praise of her parents and even the admiration of the neighbors, by being able to drink an impressive number of cocktails at a party, and still conduct herself as a lady. Bully for her, I thought. When drinking records were compared, I was a failure. Nevertheless, I was a better student than she and the fighter on the inside of me said, "Don't lie down and play dead just for them. Be yourself!"

"Are you afraid that you have a weak background, and through social drinking might turn into a drunkard? Do you think perhaps your real father was a drunkard?" probed Mrs. Hudson. Any mention of family background was a touchy subject with me because for all I knew I could have been hatched in a cabbage patch. "Did Gerard get fresh with you?" I was asked pointedly. What weaknesses were mine that made me want to live differently? "Have you ever seen anyone in this house drunk?" asked Mr. Hudson insistently, defensively.

"No."

"Liquor is used here in this home as it ought to be — in moderation," he explained, trying to be patient. What an affront to his moderation was my silent abstinence! Having lived by now with extremes of both kinds, my choice was, "No alcohol! Somebody else can drink mine. Why don't they just help themselves, and leave me in peace?"

At one of their formal dress parties when men came in tuxedos and ladies in long dresses, my favorite of all their family friends came, glass in hand to the den where I was doing my homework, and said, "Have a sip. It is just a harmless cocktail. There is hardly any alcohol in it." To say yes was easiest, because I needed her warmth and friendship, but the no! came out clearly nonetheless, because I had seen enough alcohol at Gerards' to last me a lifetime. Some time later, at a wedding, I enjoyed generous helpings of ice cream and freely imbibed the punch. Later Mr. Hudson laughed heartily at some of the wedding guests who, as he saw it, considered themselves too holy to drink liquor but had enjoyed the punch — he had spiked the punch!

Comments about my looks made me as uncomfortable as references to my background. Even so, I would not use make-up. "Anyone as homely as you are should do everything possible to help herself," Mrs. Hudson would remark impatiently. I couldn't argue for my own good looks. She had the facts of the case before her. But my idea of placing emphasis on inward beauty and not on outward adornment was actually a principle taught in Scripture. If only I had known and could have quoted to her:

Some folks in looks take so much pride
They don't think much of what's inside.
Well, as for me, I know my face
Can ne'er be made a thing of grace,
And so I rather think I'll see
How I can fix th' inside of me
So folks'll say, "He looks like sin,
But ain't he beautiful within!"

These somewhat rustic lines would have comforted me then as there is, after all, some truth in them. But later a better understanding of the value of a good self-image was to come my way. How different was John Mott's counsel: "You will be a fine-looking woman someday. Anyway, don't worry about good looks. Beauty is in the eye of the beholder. Finally, character will come shining through, and will be a treasure forever." Dear John Mott and his loving Emily bless my life still with the remembrance of the love and daily kindness they showed me.

Years later, nearing the end of her life, Emily, who had suffered cobalt and other treatments in the facial area, had a fragrance and peace about her very presence such as to suggest "angels in the room." "Bernice, I want to go home," said she. "You know where I mean when I say home, I mean heaven." And John, frail in body and suffering lapses of memory, patted her lovingly and said, "But I would miss her so." And then I remembered saying years earlier to Mrs Lott, my Summerland social worker, "I want to grow up to be like Mrs. Mott." "You will! But you are going much further in education," was her reply.

As I look back on it all, I see that in my immaturity I was too certain of the do's and don'ts of Christian living. What exactly was gained or lost, to this day I cannot say with surety, but at the time I was sure that if I gave in on one point and then another, the testimony of a separated Christian life would be lost, and maybe I would be lost too.

In the battle for my mind and will, no holds were barred. One morning a woman down the way from the Hudsons murdered her sleeping husband with a hatchet. The whole city was horrified. As I came by the scene of the murder on my way home from school, I saw a large crowd gathered around the building. Later, as I was busying myself with regular after-school chores, Mrs. Hudson asked, "Did you hear what happened down the street?"

"Yes,wasn't that terrible?I suppose she was temporarily insane."

"Yes," replied Mrs. Hudson "She was insane, and it was religion that put her off. A lot of people who end up at Essondale Psychiatric Hospital were religious fanatics to begin with. If you keep going on this religious tangent, that's likely where you'll end up." That was my object lesson in religion for the day.

They saw to it that I read *Elmer Gantry*, Sinclair Lewis' book, challenging me to read with an open mind and see for myself what a lot of racketeers evangelists were. My knowledge of evangelists was very limited but I could not accept that they were all the blackguards my friends painted them. The discussions were regular and always upsetting to me. No matter what I said or thought, mine were merely the arguments of a teenager against those of experience. But I had one powerful point in my favor — I had been converted in the country! Suppose *all* the evangelists were wrong: God was not wrong, and He had done a good work in me. I had been saved by grace through faith in Jesus Christ. (Ephesians 2:8)

They were remarkably tenacious, and come to think of it, so was I. The argument over my Christian faith and how I should live it dragged on over five years through the War with the final crisis catching me completely by surprise. The constant drip that wears the stone was making an impression on me. The unfavorable atmosphere and separation from fellow believers was taking its toll on my spiritual life. There was no inward vigor even though I was sticking in cold principle to what I believed. Daily I read a brief portion of Scripture, quickly offered a silent prayer for God's help and direction, and hurried off to school.

My dream of preaching the Gospel in country school houses had given place to a dazzling picture of a young career woman with an excellent position and a good salary. My appetite for education which was keener than ever was whetted by the girls' counselor at Lord Byng High School who had taken an interest in me. Not only did she talk to me about life at the university, but she encouraged me to believe I could receive bursaries and scholarships.

The University of British Columbia was where I wanted to be, and the sooner the better. Little wonder my disappointment was great, when for reasons unknown, Miss Harvey ordered that I continue at Byng in the senior matriculation program. Though she had promised me "all the education I could absorb," she was now even in the face of the counselor's plea, requiring that I do my first year university at high school where the course selection was very limited. Bitterly I noted that Henry from next door, though a mediocre student, was off to the University of British Columbia "because he has his own folks and they have money."

The "welfare" stigma was giving me a complex as well. I hated lining up for books at Children's Aid, and being handed around from one worker to another. I disliked many of their rules, such as that the last supervisor should not keep in touch with me, because it might be difficult for the new one to get and keep my confidence. But good for Wini Urquhart! Rules or no rules, she did not leave me in Vancouver to rot but called on me every chance she got.

In spite of my negative attitude, my fifth year at Lord Byng went off quite well. Then, with UBC still in my thoughts, I received a bursary to cover my tuition for teacher training in the grey stone structure at Twelfth and Cambie, across from City Hall. Some students there already had university degrees and were adding teacher training.

We student teachers were put through our paces, actually doing lessons we were soon to be sent out to teach. The school was fun; I always seemed to be finished ahead of time, and hungry for good company. On campus, under the leadership of Mary Beaton, a student at UBC, was the Inter-School Christian Fellowship, of which I was an active member. Off campus, not far away at 18th and Main, was the Holiness Movement Church where Reverend Willis Stonehouse was pastor. The pastor's home was a hospitality center for a great many young people who were in Vancouver, either studying or in the armed forces. I was not permitted to attend this church on Sundays, but I went on Saturdays and during Grade Twelve and following, my social life revolved around it.

At a loss to know what to do with my spare time, I found the parsonage a real haven, and the pastor's assistant, Joyce Free, a good friend. It soon became a habit with us to take Saturday afternoons for short excursions to Capilano Canyon, Lynn Valley, Grouse Mountain, Stanley Park or some other nearby beauty spot. Vancouver, one of the world's magnificent harbors, has a ninety-mile waterfront, and is the gateway to the Orient for all of Canada. The Lions, mighty twin crags that rise to more than six thousand feet above the harbor, are its majestic guardians.

We did not plot to upset the *status quo*. The rules against my attending evangelical services were still in effect, though, as water always finds its level, I too gravitated toward people of faith whenever possible. Scarcely considering what could come of it, we fell into a pattern of rounding out our Saturday outings with a stop in downtown Vancouver at the open air meeting conducted by Joyce's church. The pastor and several others from the church would stand in a circle around a little folding organ, sing gospel songs and give brief messages from the Bible to passers-by. Most of the listeners were in no hurry. Some were too much under the influence of liquor to hurry; others, being very poor, had no place to hurry to.

At first I stood on the sidewalk over against the building, looking on while the Christians presented the gospel. But something inside me said, "This is all wrong. Have I not become a Christian? Well then, my place is in the circle." I knew my guardian was against my participation in such meetings but now that I was at the street service it did not help matters very much for me to stand simply as an onlooker. I might as well participate and show whose side I was on.

Without our deliberately planning ahead, it worked out that faithfully every Saturday Joyce played the organ, and I sang lustily in the circle, and also gave my testimony. Soon Pastor Stonehouse was urging me to study Scripture so I would not be repeating myself week by week but would have something fresh to give. It all came as naturally to me as breathing. After all, I had been converted in the country. One Saturday evening close friends of the Hudsons on their way to a formal dress affair at the Hotel Vancouver chanced to pass our corner and exclaim, "Is that Bernice Gerard? Do Muriel and Clem Hudson know she comes down here?"

A couple of weeks later Miss Harvey, my guardian, called me to her office. I excitedly tried to guess why she wanted to see me. Perhaps she was going to give me money for new clothes, commend me for doing well in school, or reprimand me for doing something that displeased her.

She wasted no time in getting to the point. I was scarcely in the door of her office in the Vancouver Court House, when she addressed a question to me. "What is this I hear about you, down there on the street corner spouting like a soap box orator? Do you think you need a university education to go down and talk to the drunks? Is that what you think I am educating you for?" She made what we did sound low and vulgar. I appeared to be the most ungrateful wretch alive.

Superintendent Harvey continued, "You have had wonderful opportunities and I have seen to it that you have had everything you needed. I promised you all the education you could absorb and now I find you using it down on the street corner with people who could not care less. With all I have done for you, I asked in return only one thing of you, and that one thing you would not do! I did not ask you to give up religion. I only asked that you follow a faith that would be more in keeping with intelligence and culture!"

She continued, "I hear that you do well in your studies of psychology. I suggest you try a little introspection. Look into your own mind and examine your emotional and mental processes. Find out what makes you think and act as you do. When your academic record is excellent and your social adjustments are good, why do you spoil it all by insisting on going to some mission hall? Why can't you worship God in a mighty church where, as the organ peals out its anthem, you walk down the carpeted aisle, kneel and pray, and then arise quietly and go? Nobody knows you came and nobody knows you went. But you have worshipped your God. (She made it sound so dignified and wonderful.) But you have to go to a little church where they pump your hand at the door and say, 'God bless you, we are so glad to have you. Will you sing a solo today?' Is it because you have to be the big toad in the puddle?" There was a sting in her remarks.

Once more I tried to explain that I was not ungrateful, and had not intended to be uncooperative. I had been converted in the country and could not go back on my experience. If it had not been for my decision to become a Christian, I would have had no opportunities at all. With this my guardian did not agree: "You have the wrong perspective. Your religion was a help to you in the beginning but should now be used as a stepping stone to better things. It helped you then but now it is hindering you."

But I knew in my heart that there were no better things.

Then she made her final pronouncement, "You are through! I have done all I am going to do. You can get out and earn your own living at the first opportunity."

With all sincerity I expressed my thanks for all she had done for me and told her I was sorry I had not pleased her. Feeling very much the orphan girl of my country days, I turned and left her office. Step by step I made my way down the great stone stairway of the Vancouver Court House, praying fervently and urgently as I went, "Please Lord, shall I go back and apologize? Shall I tell my guardian I am sorry and that I will try and be more broadminded? Maybe I could take the occasional cigarette and the occasional cocktail and go to the good shows once in a while. Please, God, if I am just being stubborn and narrow-minded, let me know. I'll go back and tell her I am sorry." If ever I needed an answer, I needed it then.

I was down the stairs and well on my way to the streetcar stop. God had not given me a direct answer. I heard no voice and felt no unusual impression. But I did remember a young people's service where I stood with my hand raised singing, "Take the whole world but give me Jesus. I'll not turn back. I'll not turn back."

I had my answer! Now my step was more firm. To myself I said, "All right, Gerard, you sang it, go ahead and prove that you meant it."

10

NO LONGER A LONELY ORPHAN

All the way on the streetcar ride home my guardian's words kept ringing in my ears. In an effort to reappraise the situation, step by step I thought back to the gospel meetings in the Jubilee school house, and then back from there to my own origins. Inevitably, I stood between two unhappy alternatives: either to displease the Lord or to displease my guardian. Having displeased my guardian, I was overwhelmed with a sense of failure.

Now sooner or later Mrs. Hudson would have to hear the details of Miss Harvey's pronouncement, but I hoped it would be later. To my surprise and dismay Mrs. Hudson met me at the door with tears in her eyes. Evidently, she already knew. Only once before had I seen her weep and that was when England was in the blitz and her Mother was in the bombed zone in London. Mrs. Hudson, of course, was disappointed in me.

Accusingly, she said, "You lived in one of the finest homes in Vancouver. I treated you as my own daughter. Now I hear that you spend your spare time with the drunks in the down-and-out section of the city."

I tried to explain that we were not there because we preferred their society but we were there to preach the gospel and help them to be better people.

Scornful of my youthful zeal, she said sarcastically, "Oh, yes, leave it to the teenagers! You think you are going to convert them, do you? They could tell you more about life in five minutes than you have learned in your whole lifetime." The next day at the normal school I took a couple of Christian pals into my confidence, hoping they might come up with some new insight: "My guardian has given me my walking papers because she thinks I am a failure, Mrs. Hudson thinks I am a failure, and I certainly feel like one." The students thought that likely I had done the best thing even though my guardian could not see it. In an effort to cheer me, they quoted Romans 8:28. "And we know that all things work together for good to them that love God, to them who are called according to His purpose" and reminded me that nobody ever made a sacrifice for the Lord but that He generously repaid them.

We student teachers knew that because the teacher shortage was acute during the War, some of us were to be sent out early at Easter. The authorities had decided that a select group of students be chosen before graduation to fill teaching positions where the need was pressing. These students would spend the last two months of their normal school year teaching for pay, instead of doing practice teaching under supervision.

None of us knew which students would be sent out early, but it was rumored that they would be the top students in the school. As it turned out, of the ten or more sent out early that year, I was the first.

Mrs. Hudson was now lecturing me regularly, going over and over the ground we had already covered. She felt that owing to my pitiful stubbornness I had lost a great opportunity to get a university education through my guardian. One morning after breakfast, as her son Kim and I left for school at exactly the same time, he reached over the bicycle rack, sympathetically put his arm on my shoulder and said, "Mother is really riding you these days, isn't she? Don't mind her, she lectures me too — mostly don'ts." Then he gave me a vertebrae-shaking pat on the back and added, "But I sure would like to see you smoke a cigarette," and was on his bike and away.

Little wonder I was so overjoyed when the principal of the normal school met me in the hall and informed me that he had a teaching position for me, available immediately. In his hand was a telegram from the School Board in Rossland, B.C., stating that an elementary teacher with twenty-five years experience at MacLean School was leaving her job two months before the term's end. The principal said,

"If you want the job, send the School Board a telegram." For years in British Columbia, more often than not, young teachers had to start in the remote areas of the province in small one-room schools, and only later had opportunity to graduate to the staff of a city school. The job was a good choice, under any circumstances, and an excellent choice in mine. It did not take me five minutes to decide to say, "Yes."

On my arrival in Rossland, the principal, Ed Perkins, met me at the bus station and took me to a boarding house. The landlady, who had a rich Scottish accent, welcomed me graciously and showed me to my room. As soon as my bags were in the room, I turned to my hostess, "What churches do you have in this town?" Starting with what sounded like dry and formal churches, she began to name them. No doubt she believed she was starting at the top of the list and going down, but *I* felt she was starting at the bottom and going up! A churchwoman herself, she was doing very well, but even when she had finished the list I had not yet heard the name of the kind of church I was hoping for.

"Aren't there any more?"

"Yes," she said, "there is the Tabernacle. The Tabernacle was founded by two young women who came here as evangelists. In their meetings in the Orange Hall and in a tent there were so many people converted that they were asked to stay and establish a church. There had not been anyone converted in the town for eight years." The Scottish way she rolled that word "converted" did me good — I had been converted! But there was more to be said about the Tabernacle.

My new friend continued, "You can hear these two young women on CJAT, the Trail radio station, every Sunday morning. It is rather interesting you know; the people at the Tabernacle believe in tithing." Then, assuming my ignorance of the meaning, she explained, "When you tithe, you give one-tenth of your income to the church. Since most of the men work at the Canadian Mining and Smelting Company at Trail where they get big wages, and they all tithe at that church, you can imagine how much money those girl pastors take in!"

About then, I felt it was time for me to say something because, as far as I knew, they would soon be taking in my tithe also. So I said,

"That's the church I will be going to." She tried unsuccessfully to conceal her surprise.

The next day was Sunday, so I made my way to the Tabernacle to Sunday School. When the teacher of the Bible class, Pastor Jean McColl, noticed the new pupil she asked, "May I put your name on our roll? We would love to have you with us every Sunday."

"Yes, you may put my name down as I'll be here every Sunday. My name is Bernice Gerard. I am the new teacher at MacLean School." Jean seemed a little surprised at my enthusiasm.

Monday, after my very first day of teaching, I put the daily plan book in the drawer, tidied my desk, and went home for supper, fully aware that something entirely new was now to unfold in my life. Lonely in the new town, I went for an evening walk and I was drawn toward the Tabernacle where Jean and Velma McColl were out digging in their flower garden, giving special attention to the gladiolas.

In due time they invited me into their apartment for tea. The conversation never lagged, not even for a moment. Quite understandably there was an immediate bond of comradeship between the McColl sisters and me. In fact, we got on so well together, that by the second month of my short-lived teaching career, my landlady felt that a financial adjustment was necessary. When I handed over my board money on pay day, she counted it and said, "This is too much." "It is the amount we agreed on, is it not?"

"Yes," said she, "but this month you lived more with the McColl sisters than you did with me." Whereupon she gave me a five dollar refund.

It was during my first two months of teaching that my old guardian, the Superintendent of Child Welfare, Isobelle Harvey, dropped in at MacLean School while she was on a tour of the province. I was glad to see her, and took the opportunity to say again how much I appreciated what she had done for me. I sensed that she felt good about my new position. My class was on the playground doing gymnastics, so there was not much time to talk.

It was she who broached the subject that had been on my mind for a long time although I had never asked her about it. "Are you still interested in finding your own parents?"

"Yes, very much so."

"Do you have any idea who they were?"

"The adoption papers in the basket in the little dark room off Gerard's kitchen said my name was Nielsen. A girl who once lived in Fort St. John said she had known a family of that name, some of whose children had been adopted out, but I have been afraid to check and see if it's true, for fear of what I may find," I replied.

"You have been bitter about your adoption, haven't you?"

I admitted that was true.

Then she said, "I want to assure you that you have no reason to feel bitter or inferior. I am sure your parents were of good stock. It was likely a tragedy that separated you from them. Why don't you try to get in touch with them? Do you remember where the adoption papers were drawn up?" she asked.

"Yes, the papers were drawn up in New Westminster by a lawyer named Sullivan."

By the end of our conversation, I had made up my mind to take action without delay. She encouraged me to follow up any clues that might lead me to my family, in particular to write the lawyer, telling him the adoption was a failure, and asking his help in finding my natural parents.

On leaving Vancouver, I had firmly resolved to keep on studying and return as soon as possible to attend UBC — partly out of ambition, and partly out of defiance. The "guardians" of my life and thought had prophesied that my strange religious outlook would likely prevent me from being a good teacher, and had taken the view that I was not worth educating further because I wouldn't put the brains I had to proper use. My response was, "Wait and see! I'll make it on my own."

However, it was not going to be too easy to follow through immediately on my plan. In only two months I had gotten so involved with the McColl sisters in gospel radio broadcasts and out-of-town rallies that my leaving for summer school would have been a great inconvenience to them. So I took a job instead, looking after a country store at Beaver Falls, while the owner and his wife went off on a long holiday. One night when I was alone in the living quarters at the store, I wrote to Mr. Sullivan, the lawyer, and to a girl named Joyce who, I had reason to believe, could be my sister.

The information about the girl who might be my sister had been given to me during my last days at Lord Byng High School. A friend, Irene, had invited me to her home for Christmas dinner, but I was not able to accept the invitation. When my name was mentioned in the conversation at the table Irene said, "I'm sorry Bernice can't be here. She is a Christian but is having a lonely time of it." She and her boyfriend dug into my background and came up with a startling thought: He knew a family in the north of British Columbia whose name was Nielsen; in fact he used to go out with one of the girls — Joyce. She had mentioned to him that when they lost their mother, some of the children were given in adoption. She and her sister and brother often wondered how the absent ones were getting along, but their father would not discuss the question with them. After further discussion, they even decided that I looked like the Nielsen family.

When Irene told me about Joyce, I was quite excited, but I felt it would be wiser to leave enquiries until I was independent. It seemed that now was the time to write the letter. So I wrote:

Dear Joyce,
    If you are my sister, you will understand this letter. If not please for-give my intrusion...

After explaining the entire situation to Joyce, I knelt in the kitchen where I was writing, held the letter to her and the one to Sullivan in my hand and prayed, "Oh God, if you want me to know my own people, please guide these letters. If finding them would only mean heartache and bring no good to anyone, I am satisfied to leave things as they are. I thank You for all You have already done for me."

In October as the leaves had turned to gold and Mt. Roberts was once again becoming a big white candy mountain, I was back teaching, happy with my Grade Four class, and living with the McColl sisters. Now at the end of every month I paid them my tithes and my board; sometimes I had to borrow a little from them to tide me over. On my payday we always had steak by way of celebration.

One particular payday will never be forgotten! With a troupe of children on each arm, I made my way home from school at the noon hour. The smell of frying steak was in the air; my plate was served, and beside it were several letters. I was attracted by an unusual curiosity to the letters and by an unusual hunger to the steak. The letters won.

"Dear Sister Bernice," began the first one. The postmark was unfamiliar, the handwriting strange. Absent-mindedly I murmured, "One of my religious friends, I guess."

The letter was from Joyce, to whom I had written. She confirmed that we were sisters; she was about to get married in Victoria and wanted me to come and be a bridesmaid. My heart burst with pleasure.

"Imagine anyone writing me like that! Family, eh? Sight unseen she is willing for me to be a bridesmaid!" My joy was unbounded, although I was unable to attend the wedding.

In that mail there were two more letters from my family. One from my brother Fred who was in the Canadian Air Force, and one from my sister Violet, who, it turned out, was a young widow who had lived with her son not many blocks from me in Vancouver. Later I received a telegram from my father. "Welcome back to the family. Hope we can make up for lost time. Love, Dad."

Each member of the family wrote, telling about themselves and their experiences. In my letters to them I rejoiced over my good fortune in finding them and told them as much as I could about myself. I could not omit the most important part of my life's experience: I had heard the good news of the gospel and said yes to the Lord, and from then on many blessings had come my way because of the goodness of the Lord. But to know my father, brothers and sisters was the fulfillment of a wonderful dream. I could not wait to see them all face to face and learn more about our family, especially more about my mother.

11

TAKING THE DREAM ON THE ROAD

But before I could get very involved with my family, my life took another turn. During my second summer in Rossland, Pastors Jean and Velma, and I, still a teacher at that time, ventured east to conduct evangelism crusades in Saskatchewan and New Brunswick. We had by now developed a considerable repertoire of Western-style gospel music, vocal trios, duets and solos which were a regular feature of The Gospel Half Hour on Radio CJAT Trail. The McColl sisters had a good reputation and plenty of ministry contacts. I was thrilled to wear their black and white preaching garb as we launched out for a summer of evangelism.

In Saint John, New Brunswick, in the old theater where Susie and Caro Davis had pioneered Pentecostal ministry and seen many hundreds come to God, I was wide-eyed, and eager to learn. Frequently, the entire congregation of several hundred would "dance before the Lord." Sister Susie literally spun like a top on stage with such grace and speed that she seemed inspired from above. In a Saturday night prayer meeting, we heard a brother praying, evidently for us, "Make them dance, Lord!" My heart was dancing, but my feet were full of lead. The Davis sisters, formerly from Macon, Georgia, were women of charm and dignity, shining examples of what the Lord can do with consecrated women. Prayer and more prayer, wonderful meetings including miracles of healing, and baked beans every Saturday night is what I remember best about our time under their roof.

My part in the meetings was to sing, pray and share my testimony: how, when and where I found faith, and what it took for me to keep it. The Davis sisters, whose main concern in life was God's harvest field, were sure I should go into the full-time ministry of evangelism. "The call of the Lord is on your life," they said confidently. But I was far from sure, notwithstanding that they knew Aimee Semple McPherson personally, and had experience in discerning directions for people's lives.

Back in Rossland, after one more year of teaching, the three of us launched into special services in Victoria, B.C., during the summer vacation. The plan included my going to classes at the Summer School for teachers, and of course, keeping up with my responsibilities each night in the services, plus the church social life that was also time-consuming.

While we were still in Victoria, I awakened Jean and Velma one morning at two o'clock with an announcement, "I am not going to summer school tomorrow."

Sleepily they scrutinized me, "And why not?"

"I am going to give up teaching and give myself to the full-time ministry." They knew I had been wrestling with the problem for months and expressed approval that I had decided to dedicate myself to God's work, with one qualification. "But please remember, we have not talked you into it. It is your decision, and it's between you and the Lord."

In a few months, we were packed for a long journey, ready to live and work in the United States for an indefinite period. The Evangel Temple in Miami, Florida, was to be our first place of ministry because, when the Neeces, who were pastors there, came to Kelowna as evangelists, I had become friendly with Mrs. Neece. Rev. Charles Neece invited us to minister there and underwrote guarantees to the United States government for our alien resident status.

We left Saskatchewan on a cold November day in 1945. En route to Florida in our Ford V-8, we enthusiastically accepted most challenges as presented. "Stop! All the orange juice you can drink, only ten cents!" Coconuts, watermelons, grapefruit, oranges, dates and pecans were for sale along the way, not to mention pralines and key lime pie. Everyone said, "Y'all come back!" which we first took to be a question requiring a yes or no answer from us.

Before we got to Miami Beach our handbags were snatched from the car at a Florida service station. We really had launched forth into a cold wicked world! And so unaware were we of the harsh realities of southern segregation practices that we stopped in the black section in Atlanta and asked the black operator of a motel if he had space for us. Somewhat shocked at our ignorance, he said, "Y'all cain't stay here, you is white folks." Since darkness was setting in, we hurried on to find something reasonable, something for naive Canadians like us.

In Miami at last, we settled in a rented bungalow with coconut palms in the front and grapefruit trees in the back, and began our first evangelism crusade in the United States of America. We did not know that we had fourteen years "on the road" ahead of us, as well as testings and trials which were severe enough to have sent us home in defeat. By this world's standards we were not asking much. We did not even think of health insurance, pension or stated regular salary. We were committed to living by faith — which meant trusting for shelter, food and clothes and for enough through the love offering, the collection for the evangelists on the last night, to get us to the next place. We lived in makeshift quarters in church basements, in motels and hotels, and at last, when only Velma and I made up the team, we lived in a thirty-two-foot Airstream trailer. Life got more comfortable as the years went on but the effect of our early consecration was that we learned to be content in whatever state we found ourselves.

We had an honest commitment to servanthood. When asked, "What remuneration do you expect?" we would reply, "We put no price on our ministry." Clem Hudson, back in Vancouver, had said everything possible to discourage my launching out as an itinerant evangelist, implying that it was about the same as choosing to stand on a corner, tin cup in hand, begging for one's daily bread. Jean, Velma and I held quite the opposite view: instead of losing dignity, one gained, insofar as one sincerely lived the life of faith. Paul had made it abundantly clear that those who preach the gospel are to live by means of the gospel.

Don't you know that those who serve at the altar share in what is offered on the altar? In the same way, the Lord has commanded that
those who preach the gospel should receive their living from the gospel.
(1 Cor. 9: 13, 14 NIV)

A few months after we arrived in Florida, we met with road-
blocks. After being well received, and well recommended by pastors
in Sanford and Jacksonville, we became the subject of negative gos-
sip. The McColl sisters had come out of the Apostolic Mission in
Regina, Saskatchewan, which was not a member of the Assemblies
of God denomination. A Sanford pastor, drawing his own conclusions, decided we were off-brand Pentecostals and probably dangerous to the unity of the churches, and therefore should not be allowed
to minister. At the request of Miami pastor Charles Neece, the District Superintendent (Bishop) of the Florida Assemblies wrote to his
counterpart in British Columbia to ask about the three of us. The
Rev. P.S. Jones replied, "The McColl sisters are good girls, and did a
good work in Rossland, B.C." All this came to our ears by hearsay.
"Could we have a hearing with the Superintendent?" we asked hopefully. The answer was, "No." We were virtually "on the street" except for our aging Ford car, and two or three friends in Jacksonville.

In Tampa, we preached in a Pentecostal Holiness church, and
lived in an improvised apartment, more or less victorious over resident cockroaches. In Deland we rented a school auditorium; in Day-
tona we were with a small pioneer church. When the Assemblies
churches were closed to us, the Pentecostal Holiness Church invited
us to request their credentials instead, and become their state evangelists. We appreciated their kindness, but could not get the peace to
say yes. We had only one small invitation in the northern United
States, in Ocean Park, New Jersey. We began to think that perhaps
we should go north, back to Canada where people knew us, and get
our credentials straight. Velma, Jean and I prayed together. I cried,
asking the Lord, "Did I leave teaching school for this?" It hurt to be
judged unfairly, and falsely accused, with no opportunity for a
defense.

Once we decided to go north, we received the help we needed. A
Tampa mechanic put a new motor in the Ford with no charge for
labor. Our Jacksonville friends gave as many dollars as they could

muster. We knew there had to be better days ahead, and we were right. The new motor had to be broken in, which required one thousand miles or so of slow travel, preferably at night. In Ocean Park, we were warmly received and recommended to Pastor and Mrs. Robert Boyle of West New York, New Jersey. It was not clear then, but in due time, we would see the pattern of our ministry developing.

From West New York, where we again had good meetings, we went to Zion Bible Institute, Sister Gibson's Bible School in Providence, Rhode Island, just in time for their annual graduation ceremonies and conference. Everyone there was living by faith — no fancy meals, and no fixed charge. If you could pay, you did; if not, the meals and lodging were free. By the time we were to say thank you and good-bye to Sister Gibson, she was recommending us to Rev. E.L. Lassegues, founder of the French Pentecostal Church and Bible School in Montreal, who happened to be at his alma mater for the occasion. Pressing several bills into Jean's hand, Sister Gibson, the president and founder of the school, said, "The Lord has impressed me to give you this. I believe He is going to open new doors, and bless your ministries richly."

New doors were certainly opened! First of all, with Brother Bouchard we had weeks and weeks of meetings in the French Pentecostal Assembly in downtown Montreal. We sang, and preached through an interpreter the plain, powerful word of God. Non-believers confessed Jesus Christ as Savior, the demon-possessed were exorcised, and believers empowered. The meetings often ended well after midnight.

Then the Bouchards, having heard our story of troubles in Florida, suggested that we should go with them to the Cobourg and Braeside Camp meetings in Ontario, where they would introduce and recommend us to the leaders so as to get proper credentials. At Cobourg, Rev. Willis McPherson immediately invited us to participate. His wife remonstrated, "But, dear, you haven't heard them *sing*." The Rev. J.H. Blair, at Braeside in Paris, Ontario, was equally hospitable, even eager to use us in the large public services and youth leadership.

It was at the Cobourg Camp meeting under the inspiring preaching of Wesley Steelberg of Springfield that I received an unexpected answer to an important prayer. At age thirteen, when I was living at the Motts', my eyesight was damaged, possibly by measles, and I began to wear glasses. Now, in my very early twenties, I was having headaches and some difficulty reading fine print. So I began to pray, "Lord, I need new glasses." Since the three of us shared equally the financial support that came in, it meant we needed three times the price of my eyeglasses before I could afford them.

Then came the unexpected answer. While Steelberg told of marvelous healings in his own family, my faith began to rise. His father had a piece of steel in his eye, which came out in answer to prayer. Wesley, as a boy, disobediently played with an axe in his parents' absence and cut off the end of one of his fingers. Then, knowing God healed people, he asked the Lord to attach it again. Frightened and worn out with anxiety he fell asleep with one hand firmly over the other, holding the severed finger in its proper place. When his parents found him, his hand was perfectly whole. Besides sharing his personal experience, the Rev. Wesley Steelberg was hammering us with Biblical promises.

Before I reached the altar so that Wesley Steelberg could minister in prayer, I knew that I was healed. That night, without glasses, I could read the small typewritten words of the song book on the music stand across the vibra harp. I was healed, and was glad to share my good news with the hundreds in the audience.

A couple of days later, on a pathway between our cottage and the tabernacle, I met Jean, wearing my coat. "Are you really healed?" she queried. "Yes, haven't you heard me tell about it?" "Well, yes, but I just want to make sure. You are certain, are you?" I was getting exasperated. "Jean, you doubting Thomas! Of *course* I am healed!" She reached into the coat pocket, pushed my glasses towards me and said, "Good — I just sat on your glasses!" Fortunately, the healing lasted a good twenty years. Though I wear glasses now, my eyes are in good condition; it's my age that makes the difference.

J.H. Blair, pastor of Central Gospel Tabernacle in Hamilton, was to be a very special person in our lives. His encouragement and recommendations provided the link with Rev. A.A. Wilson of the First Assembly in Kansas City, who, on one occasion, personally booked one full year of engagements for us, mainly, though not entirely, in large American churches. He knew, and so did we, that we should not confine our interest to large churches only. To be in God's will was most important.

It was Pastor J.H., as we affectionately called him, who helped us get settled in the Missouri District in the United States. We had learned much from our previous experience about the need for well-established credentials. I also determined never to hastily reject a person or ministry simply because they belonged to a different denominational group. As the Bible says, "Keep on loving each other as brothers. Do not forget to entertain strangers, for by so doing some people have entertained angels without knowing it." (Hebrews 13: 1, 2 NIV) Not that we were angels — but we *had* experienced rejection as strangers.

The Assembly in West New York, New Jersey, was to become for us a frequent point of rendezvous with Robert and Louise Boyle who gave such a welcome as to soothe our wounded spirits, so that we returned again and again. For fourteen years we travelled as evangelists in North, Central, and South America, in the West Indies, Europe and the Near East. Evangelists, in general, have received rather bad press. The truth is that it takes a lot of dedication and courage to get launched and keep afloat on such uncharted waters.

"Why do churches have evangelists?" some ask. Evangelists are called by pastors and their churches to help local believers to get new people to visit the church and come to faith. Success-oriented pastors, especially in the American churches, put pressure on the visiting ministry to perform, that is, "be well received" and attract a good crowd of new people; to help get at least some new families into the church. It sounds simple, and sometimes it was. We generally gave ourselves to extended times of prayer and fasting and called the people to do the same; we worked through advertising, radio and television, and door-to-door visitation to shake the bushes for possible fruit. We all knew that the work was the Lord's, and He only could give the increase; nevertheless we worked as though everything depended on us.

Gospel or no gospel, life as an evangelist was not always one grand sweet song. At Bethel Temple in Sacramento, for example, the first time around we had three weeks of excitement with good

crowds and good results: dozens coming to faith and over sixty baptized in the Holy Spirit. Pastor Nelson Hinman exclaimed, "This
takes us back to the early days of blessing in this church." But on our
second visit, we followed the city-wide Oral Roberts Crusade. The
people were weary; our meetings were poorly attended, and Pastor
Clyde Henson, evidently very disappointed that his plans to capture
a large share of the results from the Roberts meeting were not working out, made no attempt to encourage us in any way. In times like
these, we simply had to encourage ourselves in the Lord, as King
David did. (1 Samuel 30: 6) Furthermore, we were encouraged by
the knowledge that the Lord did not require us to be a scintillating
success; rather He was mindful of our faithfulness in service.

But in Stockton, California, we saw the Spirit at work in the life of
a woman named Etta Hoffschneider. Etta had previously gone to an
Oral Roberts meeting to stand proxy in the healing line for her sister
who suffered severely with arthritis. She came away a believer in
Jesus Christ. Now in our nightly meetings she was learning the way
of prayer. We would pray with her for the release of the Holy Spirit,
expecting her to begin to praise God in a heavenly language. Because
she was then a cocktail waitress in a bar, she would hurry off to her
work, to earn money to buy medicines for her suffering sister. "Do
you drink, Etta?" we asked. "Oh, no, *I* don't drink. When a customer buys for me, the bartender puts orange juice in my glass, and
credits my account with the price of the liquor the customer requested for me."

We discussed Etta's work with her several times, enough times to
know that she saw no conflict of interest between seeking the Lord in
nightly prayer meetings, and then going off to one of the worst joints
in town to serve liquor. We wanted to see how the Lord would handle this one. She was so well loved and respected by all who knew
her, that it was as though she had been a "closet" believer all the
time, although she said that at the Roberts meeting God caught her
by surprise. On Thanksgiving evening, black-haired, brown-eyed
Etta could scarcely wait for the prayer session. It was her night of
special joy and love. She was praising God with all her heart, when
she burst forth in a language she had never learned. She was high in
the Spirit, and overflowing with God's love.

Suddenly, she looked down at her watch, and exclaimed, "I must hurry or I'll be late for work." Then, as if caught by surprise, she said, "Oh Lord, You are so wonderful and Your presence so powerful here. I can't go to that Club tonight!" Then on second thought she added, "But I must go. The boss is counting on me. I'm his head waitress; I must give him notice, and an explanation." The new Etta had new values and therefore an emerging new life style, but the change did not come about as a result of our admonitions. It was thrilling to see the supernatural work of the Holy Spirit in her.

Pastor Leland Keys of San Francisco's Glad Tidings Temple, one of the historic Pentecostal powerhouses, received us well. Pastor C.M. Ward of the "C" Street Assembly of God in Bakersfield also encouraged us in our labors, and again, quite a number of people responded in life-changing ways. An itinerant evangelist, especially in the Forties and Fifties, could well be attached to a congregation for weeks at a time, with meetings every night, sometimes excepting Monday. Once the refreshing waves of blessing began to roll in, the things of God took priority with pastor, people and guest preachers.

Once in Galveston, Texas, a pastor with "deer hunting fever" actually closed an extraordinarily good meeting, because his fifty dollar hunting permit was about to expire. His piety was spilling out all over as he attempted a "religious" explanation for shutting down what the Texans called "a real good revival meeting." We, the evangelists, were disappointed, and out of a job, at least temporarily. After a rainy week in his tent in the woods, he caught nothing but a cold and arrived home somewhat chastened, his fever cured until next hunting season.

There was a shared belief among us that nothing should be allowed to interfere with the King's business, and the King's business required haste. Rescuing souls was of such urgency as to call for whatever personal sacrifices the Lord required. In Kansas City, Missouri, where we conducted a number of meetings extending from three to six weeks, we were midway in a series, when word came that Dad McColl was seriously ill in Regina, Saskatchewan. The McColl Sisters decided that they would stay with the meeting, and trust the Lord to take care of their father. Of course they placed comforting phone calls home to mother. Pastor A. A. Wilson, who was a typical plowboy-to-the-pulpit Pentecostal from the early days, approved heartily. He simply said, "Trust God for your father. You do God's work and He will do His." Wilson cited cases of front-line preachers who chose to stay and preach an important meeting already announced, rather than rush to a dying mother's bedside. In our case, fortunately, Dad McColl was spared. It was the Christian version of "the show must go on," only we had even more reasons for going on for it was not just entertainment!

In Kansas City, a young rebel named Ruth, who worked in recreation, came regularly to the meetings. "I have been coming against my own best judgment," said she. "I just can't stay away." In a private conversation she shared with me a story of booze and sex orgies such as I had never imagined, never mind actually heard of. "Can I change?" was her question. Still somewhat stunned, I told Pastor Wilson about the girl who was so deep in bondage. His reply has stuck with me all these years, "If the blood of Jesus Christ is not sufficient for her total cleansing and forgiveness, then we are all lost, and our case hopeless!"

Ruth's mother, who was behind the scenes, hoping we would influence her daughter for good, invited all of us for dinner. This was a special event in Ruth's eyes, for which she must be on good behavior. Alas, the very day of the dinner date, Ruth came to our apartment thoroughly drunk. Not one of us three knew anything about hastily restoring sobriety. Nevertheless, a plunge in a cold bath, coffee and still more coffee, and Ruth was fit for her Momma's table, Momma none the wiser as to how her only daughter had fallen off the wagon.

A few nights later in the final minutes of the "altar call" Ruth and a friend came to the front to meet the Lord. She threw herself on her knees, and called on God with all her heart. To my surprise and fascination, she in that one prayer session went from her decision for Jesus Christ to a mighty baptism of fire. We heard her "speak with tongues and magnify God," and were convinced, as was Peter regarding the Gentiles at Cornelius' house, that she had received the Holy Spirit as well as we. (Acts 10: 47)

As I said earlier, we were continuously on the road for fourteen years except for those all-too-rare annual visits to the McColl home in Regina. The real reward is our spiritual children. "They are a hope, and joy, a crown of rejoicing." (1 Thess 2: 19) The joy is already felt; the supreme moment will be when those we "have begotten through the gospel" (1 Cor 4: 15), and we are together "in the presence of our Lord Jesus Christ at His coming." (1 Thess 2: 19) It is an avenue of blessing and promise of reward to every single believer: "He that wins souls is wise." (Proverbs 11: 30)

Life was full of colorful new places and faces, as well as opportunities to work with dedicated, loving people, most of whom were interesting and entertaining personalities by anyone's standards. In the main, we worked with the pioneers of the Pentecostal movement and their immediate successors, many of whom had been phenomenally successful: for example, there was Bond Bowman of Brightmore Tabernacle in Detroit where, in six weeks of red hot meetings, I, as a beginning evangelist, learned what it is like to be ministering when the Holy Spirit is moving in power; Wallace Bragg at Highway Tabernacle in Philadelphia; Leland Keys of historic Glad Tidings in San Francisco; Raymond T. Richie of Evangelistic Tabernacle, Houston; Leroy and Angel Sanders in Cincinnati; Cyril and Ruth Homer in Terre Haute, Indiana; Lester Sumrall in South Bend; Emil Balliet of Central Assembly, Springfield, Missouri, where at the time many of the national executives and department heads of the Assemblies of God attended; and a host of others in churches great and small. The customs and attitudes of the time called for extended efforts, not just a night or two, but, if the response merited it, up to sixteen weeks of gospel meetings. These pastors were dedicated servants, and in a large measure the unsung heroes of the fastest growing movement in twentieth-century American Christianity.

Our subsequent years of sawdust trail evangelism in our own Tent Cathedral began with a surprise donation. When Mom Boyle of the West New York Assembly was making her will, she told her daughter Alice that she was going to include the McColl-Gerard Trio in her bequests. Alice replied, "Why not help them now; they are eager to buy a tent for summer crusades." We got the tent and by May, our first month of tent meetings on the Bergenline, West New York, New Jersey, was in full swing. If most of the population had no inclination to come to the church, then our church would come to them. Under the brand new canvas we had rough but comfortable seating for one thousand people. We three women had to learn how to erect the tent, so that we could instruct the volunteers in each new location. But the first time, the city men from the West New York congregation travelled with us to Scranton, Pennsylvania, to show the folks there how to get the "big top" up, and keep it there. They returned home chuckling, "Did you see those miners swing those huge sledge hammers!" Through the hot humid summer, most afternoons there would be rains, thunder and lightning and gusting winds; and the tent was not insured. But the tent crusade went on four weeks anyway, and was a roaring success.

"Nothing like it since the days of Billy Sunday," said the old timers. Elaborate Italian dinners were common hospitality. Course after course would arrive from the kitchen and then, when the guests began to lose their appetites, the hostess in feigned offence would say, "What? You no lika my spaghetti?" The after-service prayer times, and counseling sessions were heavy with the smell of garlic. We evangelists joked about beginning to eat garlic in self-defense.

Our acquisition of the Tent Cathedral, led inevitably to a church planting ministry. David Wilkerson of *Cross and Switchblade* fame helped the little Pennsylvania town of Phillipsburg to become much more widely known, for when he was pastor there, he travelled to New York to reach gang members with the gospel. But it was Handy Christopher and the McColl-Gerard Trio who founded the church Wilkerson was later to pastor. When we were there, Jean, Velma and I lived in a rustic dwelling on an abandoned mining site, and travelled the few miles into Phillipsburg to our tent meetings in town. "They are emptying the churches!" "Have you heard those girls? Why, they swear like truckers!" Such a furor was created by idle tongues, and the lies they told that fortunately most of the residents of the town and surrounding area came to see for themselves.

Christopher, who had pioneered eleven churches, was asking in his prayers for a big fish or two, that is, for conversions of those with influence in the community. Soon, a mine owner, his wife and family went under the waters of baptism, and she received healing for a serious spinal injury. Christopher's wife cooperated not at all in the ministry; she took a job washing dishes in a local cafe rather than involve herself in entertaining the evangelists. But he took it like a lamb.

Another successful church planting took place in Jersey Shore, Pennsylvania, initiated and supported by the Assembly of God in Williamsport. We went door to door, inviting people to the services. Of the few families interested in the project initially, all were apprehensive as to whether any others would put their foot in the tent. Opening night we arrived to find our few initial supporters sitting in their cars waiting to see who else came before they committed themselves. Fortunately for us optimists, some seventy-five decisions were made and a good healthy church planted.

In London, Ontario, we planted a church, beginning with plenty of wind and bluster. "Big steel poles and bleachers tumbled violently around a dozen members of the London Gospel Temple Saturday evening when rain squalls gusting up to fifty m.p.h. toppled the giant tent on Clarke side road," reported London's daily newspaper, the *London Free Press*. We had just erected the tent, and I was saying to the pastor and a dozen volunteers as we stood inside, "I think we should tighten up the canvas because it seems a wind is rising," when a sudden mighty gust caught the tent as though it were a giant umbrella, and dropped it into the next field.

Immediately, the CBC television crew was on hand and Pastor Don Emmons was on camera assuring everyone, "We're down but not defeated." We were up and running very soon, with the crowds coming as planned. Royalview Pentecostal church was the direct result of that summer outreach.

Once before we had seen the Tent Cathedral go down, under a seventy m.p.h. hurricane force wind, no sudden gust, but a solid relentless push against the side walls of the tent. It was 2:00 a.m. when one of the main bolts which held the high-up central ring to the front center pole let loose so that, section by section, the roof fell down and the entire canvas was battered and torn.

"Your God must not think much of those evangelists. He let their tent blow down. Couldn't He have stopped that wind?" were the taunts of many of the townspeople to our supporters. But many were very sympathetic to the three young women, enough to help us replace the two damaged sections and get back into action. Aimee Semple MacPherson's autobiographical film documentary tells how she too sewed torn canvas and prayed as she sewed. In America the opportunity was there for the taking — anything to win a few more for the Lord Jesus Christ.

In Verona, Ontario, we conducted the opening crusade for founding pastors Hope Smith and Laurie Price. Years later, on their invitation, we pitched the tent in Belleville. Gordon and Hazel McElhoes pioneered Frankford, Ontario, where we saw sixty or seventy decisions in the meetings following the dedication of the attractive new church. On our return a year later, all the people who had made decisions were safely in the flock. One hardy farmer confessed his continuing shortcoming: when the horses were hard to handle, he still tended to curse them out in his former vocabulary. In Smiths Falls, the meetings were blessed and we ourselves so busy with daily radio shows and outreach that Velma sighed, "They will write on our gravestones, 'They Took Advantage Of Every Opportunity And Left No Stone Unturned.'" It was a little joke on ourselves and our holy zeal to do the King's business.

In Pembroke, Ontario, in a rented tent under the pastoral leadership of Guy Holmes, dozens made decisions, and seventy-five persons received the Pentecostal experience. Since the tent was only accessible by foot bridge, all our equipment had to be carried in and out for each service. Each evening after the public meeting and the after-service prayer time, we three would arrive at the house of a woman named Leah Johnson for tea and toast, when the conversation would inevitably center on prayer and Scripture. Pastor Holmes was not impressed. "The Johnsons are simply crazy about the evangelists, when you are gone, they'll be gone also." To which I replied, "But Brother Holmes, we could be going out each night with the boys!" As it happened, the results of the meeting were lasting, and the friendships too. Five or six of the young men were fired up to go into the full-time ministry, among them Robert Johnson and his brother Wally; Leah's only daughter Shirley was to fulfill her call to ministry as the wife of Robert Taitinger who became General Superintendent of the Pentecostal Assemblies of Canada.

As the years passed, we were led, step by step, into ever-expanding fields of ministry. Our first overseas venture included a plan to spend two months in England and continental Europe. While some, like Rev. J.H. Blair, encouraged us, there was never a lack of "impossibility thinkers" standing by, offering negative comments, such as, "The British will never receive women," and "The Brits are very conservative; they won't like your music." No wonder that it was with some hesitation that we set out for England and the Continent, where we hoped to attend the World Pentecostal Conference in Paris. Whatever fears we had concerning our reception by conservative English congregations disappeared early in our tour. From London onward, our American-style gospel music and all-girl preaching team proved a genuine asset rather than a liability.

We were invited to sing almost every night at the Paris Conference where evenings were devoted to worship and preaching, and music played an inspiring part. The highly separatist groups of Pentecostals were gathered together at a World Conference for only the second time in their history. Among them, some envisioned increased cooperation and fellowship between Pentecostals. Others, who clashed with them, feared a loss of individuality or perhaps involvement in serious compromise, in which man would be pleased, but not God. As for me, my youth and inexperience were the only possible defense for the fact that I was oblivious to the ecumenical dimensions of that gathering, little dreaming that years later I would come to know as a personal friend, and actually work with "Mr. Pentecost," David du Plessis, the prime mover for the conference, who saw the need and had the courage to eventually bring the factious Pentecostals together.

Through the nightly contact with the delegates and visitors from thirty-five countries, we were deluged with invitations. We could not get everywhere we were invited but we did preach in Belgium, Germany, Denmark, Italy, Switzerland and Sweden.

Two years later in 1952 we were on our way again to foreign pulpits. This time we spent several weeks in Mexico where we were assisted by missionary evangelist Wayne Meyers and were introduced to the leadership of the Latin American Orphanage in Acapulco. We were getting to know their work so that we could represent them in the U.S.A. and back home in Canada in order to raise funds to help

Mexico's homeless. After Mexico we flew south, preaching in Gua-
temala, Costa Rica, Honduras, Nicaragua and Panama. From there
we continued south of the equator to Lima, Peru, where we launched
a crusade with the cooperation of ten Assemblies of God churches.

The last country on our southern journey was Bolivia, not because
we had heard a voice from on high saying, "Bolivia and no further,"
but because that was as far as we could go with the money we had.
Our *modus operandi* at this time was to do evangelism in Canada and
the United States, sell our gospel music records, save every dollar we
could, and then give ourselves to missionary evangelism for as long
as possible. Our inclination was to decline any missionary gifts from
the poor people of places like Peru and Bolivia, but the missionary
pioneers had a different view: "Please, don't give back the love offering! We are teaching the people to give according to Biblical principles, and to expect God's blessing in return. Please do not undo all
that we have done in putting the people on a good foundation." The
phenomenal growth of the movement in South America in recent
years is evidence of the wisdom of their words.

We arrived in Bolivia at a time when the missionaries were perplexed by a peculiarly Pentecostal problem. They had won many for
the Lord, and trained in the Bible School some sixteen or twenty
workers as pastors. But now when, according to education and ministry experience, these should be ordained, they could not proceed
until God did a miracle. A prerequisite for ordination with the Assemblies of God, U.S.A., is that the ministerial candidate has had the
Pentecostal experience, with the initial evidence of speaking in
tongues; the missionaries earnestly desired the same for the Bolivian
disciples.

Up to that time no one in the Assemblies in Bolivia had received
the Pentecostal experience, so in the nightly meetings we began to
encourage the people to expect an outpouring of the Holy Spirit. The
worship atmosphere was highly formal, at least until the fire fell.
Night by night almost all the students and a number of the regular
members were baptized in the Holy Spirit. Most of the baptisms of
fire took place in the prayer room after the main service. The formerly quiet, reserved Bolivians then broke into spontaneous praises.
The landlord who lived upstairs registered his objections by thump-

ing the floor with a large heavy object.

One student, who was usually of a stoical countenance, was so overcome with joy that his fellow classmates nicknamed him "Gozo" (joy). He told them, "I am from high in the Andes. Before I came to the Bible School I could not speak Spanish. Now I am baptized with the Holy Spirit and I have praised God in an unknown tongue also! Gloria á Dios. Gracias Jesus!"

When the day of our departure came, the entire student body requested permission to leave school, and see "the sisters" off at the airport. Later, when we were back preaching in North America, we received word that the outpouring of the Spirit had spread across Bolivia as far as Lake Titacaca. Missionary Everett Hale and his wife felt that God had led us to Bolivia to aid them in the spiritual warfare. For us, the demonstration of God's supernatural power in the meeting at Cochabamba was more thrilling than flying the Andes or any of the other wonders of the journey.

A year and a half after our return from South America, we again went to Europe. This time we took with us the Oral Roberts film, *Venture into Faith*. In conversation with Oral Roberts in Sacramento, California, we stated our objectives: ours was to be a soul-winning effort in every detail. The film would be shown one-third of the time, and we would conduct our own services the rest of the time. When the *S.S. United States* set sail from New York, everything we needed for the British tour was stowed away in the hold: the movie projector, several hundred of our own gospel recordings, gospel literature and our Pontiac which was to carry us to over forty British cities and continental Europe.

The four months in England were one of the most fruitful periods in our ministry. Everywhere the auditoriums and churches overflowed. We saw hundreds of people take their stand for Christ at the altars.

From England we crossed the channel to Cherbourg and then drove in our own automobile to southern Italy. In the two months that followed, we were to preach in Egypt, Lebanon and Trans-Jordan, and visit the new State of Israel.

In Beirut, Lebanon, five different missionary groups cooperated in the meetings. Once again we saw an outpouring of the Holy Spirit.

In forty years of Pentecostal preaching in Lebanon, no one had previously been baptized in the Holy Spirit in a public service. After visiting Damascus, we journeyed south to Jerusalem and from there to many places of Biblical significance in the Holy Land. Our viewing of the land and people proved so faith-inspiring that on return I wrote *The Holy Land Guide To Faith* which we published ourselves.

But the real scandal of a divided Christian church, and the vision of our Christian responsibility for the survival of Israel had not yet become real to me.

"Take a pew . . . while I invoke the wisdom of the mayor and Alderman Gerard . . . "

A cartoon from the Vancouver *Sun* lampoons Bernice's career as an alderman. (August 16, 1977).

Silent walk on the beach at West Spanish Banks.

Bernice Gerard preaching at the Seoul Full Gospel Church with Pastor Yonggi Cho interpreting. INSET: Bernice Gerard with Pastor Yonggi Cho.

Malcolm and Kitty Muggeridge (centre) join Heather Morris, President of the Alliance for Life of Canada (left of Malcolm) and Doug Roche, M.P. (extreme left) at the Walk for Life on Parliament Hill, November 3, 1973. Bernice is behind and to the left of Heather Morris.

Bernice Gerard urges Vancouverites to remember Canada's goodwill to Israel.

12

WINDS OF CHANGE

When I first began traveling with Jean and Velma, one of their close friends said to me, "Confidentially, it will never work. You'll always be the odd one out. After all, they are sisters." Then, as the years rolled by and it seemed our traveling evangelism would go on forever, the same friends said, "It will never stop!" Robert Louis Stevenson noticed the same thing when the steam locomotive was invented. "It will never go," said the critics. Then as it began to roar and puff, they cried, "It will never stop! It will never stop!"

First of all, Jean, our main preacher, left us to settle with her lay preacher husband, Clyde Roberts, in Mobile, Alabama, but not before casting her preaching mantle on me. Then, at the World Pentecostal Conference in Hamilton, Ontario, Dick Chapman, a Vancouver businessman, let Velma know he wanted to marry her.

As we were taking Dick to his hotel, sitting three abreast in the front of our automobile, he leaned a little toward me in the driver's seat to say, "I am going to be taking Velma away to be my wife. I know you have worked closely together for many years, and you will miss her. You will always be welcome in our home." Without a moment's warning a flood of tears literally gushed from my eyes and down my cheeks. "May God's will be done," said I, trying hard to contain my emotions. Velma dug her elbow into my side, "I haven't said yes yet!" she whispered. Through the years Velma had received a good many proposals. What would she do with this one?

After Jean's wedding in Regina, in the privacy of my own heart and prayers, I rededicated myself to Christian ministry. This included remaining single, if it was God's will for my life. My desire for further education was yet unfulfilled, but I did not see how I could leave the team to go for education. My prayer had no more than been offered, when every word of it was tested.

I wanted to get married myself. I was head over heels in love with a man, and he with me — before I knew he was divorced. My head said, "He's been single six years. He's a new Christian. Surely, the church can't ask him to stay single the rest of his life. What about people who live common-law; some have even had more than one partner? Such persons can come into the church and very quickly, if they have shown evidence of the new birth, go on to marry the pastor's daughter, or the loveliest girl in church. But people who get properly and legally wedded have that marriage certificate to haunt them. Is the church entirely consistent with Scripture in all this?"

I knew my head was not holding its own in the argument with my heart; nevertheless the debate between myself and the Lord continued relentlessly. "Perhaps I am not meant to continue in the ministry of preaching." I knew full well my denominational fellowship would lose no time in lifting my Missouri District credentials, if I married a divorced man. "There are many different ways of serving God" said the other voice.

There seemed no end to my capacity for rationalization, that is, thinking up good reasons for bad deeds, in this case for choosing a marriage which was out of bounds for me over continuing a blessed preaching ministry. The object of my passion was in my opinion very attractive; the chemistry was right, and I thanked God he was sincerely living a Christian life. Somebody would be his wife, and given the way we felt about each other, why shouldn't it be me? Intermittently, I envied the worldlings I knew who seemed to simply do as they wanted, and suffer no pangs of conscience.

His red roses, phone calls and love letters kept coming! I was wearing his ring and was in the mood for marriage. But I also knew that I was not thinking straight. In an attempt to save myself from the error of my own ways I prayed every day, very sincerely, "Lord, help me. Your will be done!" Looking back I can now see with clarity that the Lord gives the very best to those who leave the choice with Him.

We broke off the engagement by mutual consent, and the wedding did not take place. I cried, but not for long.

When Velma and I finally began our journey west to Vancouver, we and our tent crusade equipment made quite a caravan. Our final meeting in Ontario was in Windsor where Pastor William Fitch and his congregation helped us buy a large used flatbed truck, on which to load the big tent, metal seat ends, Hammond organ, piano and public address system. A railroad man, Eli Suza, took his vacation period to drive the truck west. Velma and I drove the Olds '88, with our Airstream trailing behind us; she was on her way to her wedding in Vancouver, and I was beginning to get very excited about going to the University of British Columbia.

"You won't make it through university, if you insist on keeping up a preaching schedule on weekends. They spring exams in class on Monday, and when they do, you'll be sunk," was Kim Hudson's advice. His commerce degree made him the voice of experience, at least in my eyes.

"You are all booked up for two years — California, Missouri, Texas, etc. How can you leave that kind of a calling to go sit in a university to listen to unbelieving professors?" some of my other friends asked. At first that question troubled me also. So I wrote to each of the places on our proposed schedule, explaining that now Velma was getting married, I was traveling alone, and I asked, "Do you still want me to come?" To my surprise, every single pastor replied, "Yes, we are glad to have you." I was not going to get out of it by getting them to drop me. In the end, after much prayer, I felt the quiet peace of heavenly permission, not a command which said "you must," but a nod, "It is good for you to go to university."

When I was a child living in the Fraser Valley, the University of British Columbia might as well have been on the planet Mars instead of a mere seventy miles distant, so great was the psychological space between me with my adoptive father and that institution. "Will I go to high school in Mission City, Daddy, or Abbotsford or where?" was the question I put to Leo Gerard when I was in Grade Eight, after our teacher told me she thought it would be sad if I could not go. He muttered something in response about there being no way he would be wasting money on educating a girl. "You'll only be running off with some no-good fellow anyway."

Now, after spending fourteen years on the road as an evangelist, I found myself standing in a long line of students, about to register for second-year Arts. Then I was interviewed by Dr. Malcolm MacGregor, head of the Classics department and personality-about-campus, who was helping me choose my courses: "When did you do your first year?" "Sixteen years ago." "Have you had any philosophy or psychology?" "Not much." "What have you been doing since you left school?" "I have been an evangelist." "You have been an evangelist! Heavens above, you *do* need help. Here, I'll see you get into Professor Rowan's class. He'll help you sort things out."

MacGregor loved throwing out the challenge. He would talk to freshmen like a corporal laying down the law to newly enlisted men. With an air of condescension, as if most of them could barely read and write, he would say to the fresh-faced beginners at the university, "We aim to make you literate." As he looked at me, wishing me well, I sensed that he felt a certain pleasure in knowing that I was going to be given a good shaking up at UBC.

During freshman orientation sessions, guidelines new to me were put forward. The idea of a life of constant intellectual exploration where everything is subject to critical evaluation and nothing held sacred was a concept that fired my imagination. It had taken years to get here and now, come what may, I wanted to play the game. In due course, however, I learned that, while the academic community prides itself on its objectivity, it often worships some highly questionable idols: the gods of success, scientific materialism, mere intellectualism and the spirit of this age.

In Professor Rowan's Philosophy 100 class, God was laughed off the campus. The number of freshmen and second year preseminary students who lost whatever faith they had before they even got to seminary was very high. The professor was a good teacher and very funny. The class was often in a state of roaring laughter, the butt of the joke being the virgin birth of Jesus, or the multiplication of the loaves and fishes, the Children of Israel crossing the Red Sea, or some other Biblical account of the miraculous.

As I had no idea of my own level of performance in the course, I determined to say nothing in class until I knew I was doing well.

Weeks went by with no challenging questions from the class to the professor. He had it all together; how could anyone contend with him and come away without disgrace? Then an inspiration was given me: I obviously was not capable of defeating the professor in an argument on philosophic grounds, but I could, indeed I must, bear witness to the reality of the gospel.

His class was known to be an open forum. The rule was, You may ask questions at any time; just don't interrupt me when I'm 'hot.' On my feet, and shaking a bit, I put my objections to him and the class, "Professor, you are not as rational in your arguments as you say we should be. You insist that Jesus is a good man, and His disciples honorable men, yet you at the same time refuse to accept the New Testament account of the works that Jesus did. You say Jesus did not multiply the loaves and fishes, rather He hypnotized His followers into thinking the crumb they got was a miracle fragment. You say Jesus could not have walked on the water, nor turned water into wine. Yet His disciples believed in Him, and committed their lives and all they had to Him; they were ready to die for Him."

> Jesus Himself said, "I am the bread of life. He who comes to me will never go hungry." (John 6: 35 NIV) "I am the light of the world, Whoever follows me will never walk in darkness, but will have the light of life." (John 8: 12 NIV) Jesus also said, "I am the way, and the truth, and the life. No one comes to the Father except through me." (John 14: 6 NIV)

The class was listening intently as I, Bible in hand, blundered on with my protest. "Sir, you say Jesus was a good man, and yet, according to the principles of rational discussion, He cannot be both good and bad, true and false, at one and the same time. He is either what He and His faithful disciples say He is, or He is deceived, or a madman, or a liar!"

With that the professor exploded, "I would never say those things about that Man! Would you like to debate with me?" "No sir, I do not feel competent, but I simply had to point out that you are not being fair to the Christian witness."

"Class dismissed" said he, even though we had a quarter hour yet to go. Not far from the classroom door, a group of Christians gathered around me. We had not realized that there were so many of us in the class, and that we had all been feeling the same way.

Philosophy 100 was not the only course in which God was laughed off the campus. In general, scientific materialism was taken to be the best of all faiths, and multitudes of students were in the process of being thoroughly persuaded against even the possibility of God, let alone faith in a risen Savior. All this in the face of the fact that the students themselves, for the most part, were open, idealistic, and ready to honestly examine the claims of Jesus Christ, as well as those of other belief systems.

Coming as I did from a religious milieu, it occurred to me that even for me, with so many years logged in Christian service, the university could be a risky place. Suppose someone presented me with proof that God did not exist, what would I do then? At that point I had no clear idea what would be required for such a proof, or if anyone had come up with evidence that would satisfy the demands of rational argument.

Once I settled in as a student, having learned how to handle footnotes and survive in my new world, my attention turned to the special needs of Pentecostal Christian students. From high school days I had been a member of the Inter-School Christian Fellowship, and now fell easily in step with the Varsity Christian Fellowship. So did most Pentecostals, but the Pentecostals were not getting as much encouragement from their pastors and home congregations as they needed: there was too much apprehension as to what could go wrong when they set out for higher education. Pentecostal students, I observed, were a minority group suffering a persecution complex. They learned to get along with other Christians by keeping quiet about what they truly believed.

At that time, the Plymouth Brethren dominated Inter-Varsity; they disapproved of tongues-speaking, healing, exorcism, and women preachers. Application forms for staff positions with Campus Crusade included the question, "Do you speak in tongues?" If the answer was yes, even though the applicant did so only in private prayers, the applicant was rejected. In the Sixties at UBC, many young Pentecostals were doing well in leadership, winning honors in both the academic field and student affairs. I asked a particularly bright, promising student who was in the forefront of Varsity Fellowship, "How does it feel to be a Pentecostal among the Plymouth Brethren, the Bible Presbyterians and others?"

"Fine, I get along just fine."

"You have been a leader for four years. Have you ever shared what it means for you to have had the Pentecostal experience?"

"No."

"Not even once? Nobody asked you anything, and you did not feel you needed to honor God by explaining what the infilling of the Spirit meant in your life?"

"No."

On my recommendation, the Pentecostal Assemblies decided to appoint an official chaplain, and, to my surprise, they selected me. The Anglican chaplain, Alan Jackson, made me welcome in his office, and the Assemblies paid my expenses. At the time UBC had almost fifteen thousand students, ninety of whom were active Pentecostals. I was eager to see Christian students pull out all the stops and go for all the university experience had to offer, but not to the detriment of their walk with God. We had to be ready to take up the cross of agonizing over intellectual difficulties. In the midst of uncertainties, when in all honesty we see our own resources to be far from adequate, we must be willing to share what we know to be true. A clearly reasoned presentation of the gospel is important, not as a rational substitute for faith, but as a *ground* for faith.

Many Christian freshmen come on campus in a fog. They do not know what of theirs to be proud of, or what, if anything, to apologize for. It is some time before they see the campus as it really is. How to do an honest job as a student and at the same time develop one's own potential (spirit, soul and body) is something they need to consider. Some neglect their studies as they busy themselves in religious activities; some study hard and are glad to hide in the stacks because they fear they will lose their souls if they dare to face university life square on.

It's too bad that it is not possible during the freshman orientation programs for each student to get clued in on the meaning of such glorious phrases as "intellectual integrity," "objective thinking," and "academic freedom." It would not be long until most would be able to discern between the dream and the reality. The dream one must pursue at all costs, but the reality will confront one soon enough. The campus is in fact an example of radical secularization — and, as such, is a good place in which to study the mythological aspects of an almost complete commitment to scientific materialism.

There is something distinctly "mythological" in our society's commitment to scientific materialism with its total disregard of a supernatural dimension, which human senses are not capable of comprehending in detail, or capable of proving by natural means of testing.

My full-time traveling evangelism had given way to summer crusades in an attractive new 60 × 120 foot air auditorium made of nylon, covered with vinyl plastic. The truck that came west with us, and all the equipment, was now handled by Hugh Bradford, a businessman from Victoria who, with his wife Vera and their four children, spent their summers with us in God's service. At the Capri Shopping Center in Kelowna, in the park at Prince George, at Warfield in the Trail area, on the highway at Maple Ridge, on Kingsway in Vancouver, at Duncan on Vancouver Island, at Whalley on the King George, on the the Army base at Vernon and in many other places people saw Jesus Balloon (as the children called it) take shape before their eyes, and stay standing for a month or more.

While I was still a student, albeit a graduate student working on a master's degree, I preached in various churches on weekends, and in the Cloud Cathedral in summer. I also taught English and Church History part-time at Western Pentecostal Bible College in North Vancouver. Then we heard about a church building on Vancouver's south slope, a former Christian and Missionary Alliance church, ready for occupancy and up for sale. The pastor and board at Broadway Tabernacle wondered if perhaps Velma and I would be interested in opening a new church on the south slope. Only intending to stay for a few months, we began services September 20, 1964, as the founding pastors of the Fraserview Assembly.

But our church was born just in time for the charismatic renewal. We were also to see two buildings erected on that same site: first of all in about seven years a five-hundred-seat sanctuary, and, by 1980 a sanctuary to accommodate eleven hundred persons. Our pastoral responsibility ended in 1985, after twenty-one good years.

Back in the Sixties, we were seeing social change, and even revolution. The University of B.C. now had over 25,000 students, and Simon Fraser University about 5,500. At these two universities, where I was serving as chaplain, we actually saw the revolutionists bring the business of the university to a standstill. At Simon Fraser, radical students seized the administration building. At the University of British Columbia, a group of protesters urged on by Jerry Rubin occupied the faculty club and there let loose a pig. Later, a Vancouver newspaper cartoonist showed an aging sow sitting in the mud of her sty surrounded by her large brood of piglets. One of them was saying, "Mother, tell us again how you led the student revolt at UBC."

When the god-is-dead theology hit the campus, several events occurred which made some of us Christians think that "for such an hour as this we have been called to the campus." The Anglican chaplain at UBC burst into print in *The Ubyssey*, our student newspaper, as a god-is-dead theologian. He was in due course transferred by his bishop to an up-country parish but the sheer frustration of hearing official campus clergy speak to undermine instead of build faith helped the Christian students decide to get into action. In answer to prayer, the Lord gave me the idea of having students buy pages in the radical, frequently vulgar *Ubyssey* in order to give their testimony and arguments for the faith. By now, our students were angry and eager to be all-out Christians, bearing full witness to the supernatural; over the next couple of years we put out our supplement, called *The Wayfarer*, two or three times a year.

Shortly after "god-is-dead" came a new wave of intellectual despair, followed by a reaction against the sterility of mere intellectualism; also, students for the most part seemed to feel that scientific materialism, the religion of the majority, had been found wanting. A nation's physically well-fed but metaphysically starving youth began reaching out for beatific visions in the only way they knew — with a five-dollar bill and a few grains of LSD. There was a new openness for religious experience, but this need was not being met by the churches, many of which were liberal and essentially unbelieving. They were involved in ecumenism — some called it ecumania — and believed that their situation would be improved if they all got together. But they still could not communicate with searching students.

Our student prayers as campus Christians always bore a major theme, "Lord, help us to be effective witnesses and to lead others to faith in Jesus Christ." But there were so many diverse elements among those interested in any cause: campus liberals professed Christianity but were interested mostly in social action and the ecumenical movement; hard-line evangelical fundamentalists only grudgingly conceded that Pentecostals are Christians at all; there were campus communists, cultists, acid mystics; and, of course, the seemingly non-religious majority. The frustrations in the situation forced me to consider a new approach.

When in quiet desperation our inexperienced student group began to sponsor guest speakers, films and testimonials which emphasized the supernatural today, we created an acute embarrassment for many of our fellow evangelicals. After the showing of *Teen Revolt*, one of David Wilkerson's first films, they were demanding an apology from us. At one point, just as we had seen hundreds of students jostling one another in the hallways of a big-city high school, David Wilkerson asks one of the students, a new Christian, "What are they doing at your high school?" "They are all in the washrooms shooting drugs," he answers. We the viewers could just imagine *all* those students in the washrooms and, just when the mood should have been sober, the students broke into loud roars of laughter. The film was very low-budget, and poorly produced; the message of lives transformed, nonetheless powerful. In any case, the campus scene was becoming more and more unpredictable.

Winds of change were blowing and we were all to be influenced one way or another. Already in full communication with leaders in the ecumenical movement, "Mr. Pentecost," David du Plessis, arrived at the University of B.C. by invitation of the affiliated seminaries. They were willing to hear him out, but no Pentecostal had been interested in discussing Christian unity with them before. David was interested in dialogue because, in a prophetic word from Smith Wigglesworth, he had been instructed by the Holy Spirit to witness to liberals and Roman Catholics. So little understood was he among Pentecostals that his ministerial credentials with the Assemblies of

God, U.S.A., had been lifted, not to be returned until many years later when the true nature of his unusual ministry had become clear to almost everyone.

While "Mr. Pentecost" was at UBC, Dr. Werner Cohen, a professor teaching the sociology of religion, invited him into his class to discuss the phenomena which were allegedly being manifested among Christians of many groups. As the class time drew near its close, the professor asked, "Would you be willing to speak in tongues so we can hear for ourselves?" Of course, the last thing David wanted to single out for special emphasis was "speaking in tongues"; however, he said, "Yes, I will speak in praise and prayer to God in tongues, if you will all consent to bow your heads while I pray."

As a guest in the class, I looked carefully to observe that all heads were bowed. When there was no interpretation provided to give meaning to the unknown language in which David spoke, I was uneasy, but really, the matter was not in my hands. Months later, a student informed me that David du Plessis had spoken in an oriental language known to the student, but unknown to David. The student, sensing the supernatural work of the Holy Spirit, had come to faith. As David had discerned, his unknown words turned out to be in praise of God.

My invitation to John Giminez and his seven Singing Addicts created possibly the greatest interest among non-Christian students. Each member of the group had been involved with drugs, crime and gang wars in the ghettos of New York. Now they were saying that it was the power of God through the Name of Jesus and His precious blood that set them free. The supernatural baptism of fire, the Pentecostal experience, was an essential aspect of their deliverance. (Luke 3: 16) They who had been thieves, extortioners, jailbirds, men of violence and drug addicts received a generous, good-hearted reception from the crowd packed into the lecture theater. "I had my first stick of marijuana when I was eleven years old." "My best friend gave it to me at school in New York." "I had my first shot of heroin when I was fifteen." "I was a dope addict for sixteen years — in and out of jail, a criminal record, the works — until I found a way out." Said Johnny, "I was kicked out of school in Grade Three for trying to burn down the place." The students responded to Giminez with a roar of approval.

The addicts, who now saw themselves as having "addicted themselves to the ministry of the saints" (1 Cor. 16: 15), received a great deal of publicity in Vancouver, partly because they were subject to a deportation order because of previous criminal convictions at the time they attempted to enter Canada. Our Associated Full Gospel Students Society helped the group appeal, and Canadian Immigration Minister Jean Marchand reversed the order, so the singers were able to present their dramatized version of the horrors of drug addiction.

Shortly after they left Vancouver, I heard that the Addicts had gone back to shooting it up. "No, it can't be! Surely, not," was my first response. Then, in exaggerated disappointment I cried, "Drive me to the nearest pier and let me jump off."

The truth is that Johnny and his friends did have serious difficulties: some of them went back to drugs, but later on found solid footing again. Twenty years later John's miracle is still good: he and his wife Ann are pastors of the large Rock Church in Virginia Beach, and he is head of the Rock Satellite Network and chairman of the huge Washington for Jesus rallies.

The changes at UBC involved us in the charismatic renewal, without our having a clue as to the breadth and significance of the neo-pentecostal movement elsewhere. For, in many churches, the Holy Spirit was still a subject no one wanted to talk much about. For example, I heard a young fellow tell Rev. Derek Prince, a Pentecostal Cambridge scholar who was doing a noon-hour lecture series on the theology of the Holy Spirit, "I've got a problem. I've received the Holy Spirit but nobody in my church wants to talk about it." Later Harvey told his own story in the noon-hour session while Prince was still with us.

At Christmas time, his girl friend had told him that for her, the best gift of all was the gift of the Holy Spirit. Since Harvey belonged to an active church which claims some eight hundred members, he made his first attempt at conversation about this baptism in the Spirit with a man who had been a candidate for the deacons' board. Surely *he* would know about these things. However, the man simply replied, "You've been talking to those Pentecostals!" After asking his Sunday School teacher and his pastor, without receiving any help, he decided to investigate "the subject no one wants to talk about" for himself in his own Bible. As a result, he received the baptism of the Holy Spirit in bed in the early hours of the morning. His words to those already baptized were "Be sure to talk about it. Many others would receive, if only they knew God's promises."

Soon these hidden things would be in the open for many of the hungry ones. I remember what student leader Ken Gaglardi told me later as we were walking with Rev. Bernie Warren, a United Church minister, who was openly rejoicing in God as we crossed the campus, "We Pentecostals were really quite respectable until these charismatics came along."

13

SOMETHING NEW IS HAPPENING

"Can you believe it, now some of the old line denominational clergy are speaking in tongues, and praising God like Pentecostals do?" enthused Charles Harris, administrator for Oral Roberts Ministries in Canada, and an old friend of mine. "Really? That's unbelievable! Who, for example?" I asked in astonishment. "There's Dennis Bennett, an Episcopal clergyman in Van Nuys, California, and Tommy Tyson, among the first of Southern Methodist clergy to have the charismatic experience," replied Charles. To which I replied, "Do you think they will ever come here for ministry? I would love to invite them for a series at UBC and in the city." Charles was confident that Tommy Tyson would be glad to come; in fact Charles would arrange the contact without delay.

Thus, my first encounter with the charismatic renewal came through Rev. Tommy Tyson, a Methodist who had been appointed by his bishop to be chaplain at Oral Roberts University. Tommy's noon hour lecture series on the renewal, sponsored by our student group, promised to contribute a great deal toward our understanding of what people were calling the current tongues-speaking movement in the Episcopal, Lutheran, Methodist and Presbyterian churches. Dr. John Ross, though not involved with us, allowed the use of St. Andrew's Presbyterian Chapel on campus for prayer sessions. In the very first series of its kind, some fifteen students received the release of the Spirit.

It was all very exciting now that some people in the old-line de-

nominations had begun acting like Pentecostals. Tommy Tyson, the
Methodist, arrived at the airport in company with a Roman Catholic
priest, Jerry Schindler. Stunned, I thought, "Woe is me, what will
our people think, when they hear I am working with a Roman Catholic?" The student gathering was at my home, the Chapman residence in Oakridge, with around sixty in attendance. Tommy prayed
with people upstairs and down; we were not just hearing about renewal; we were experiencing it.

The Pentecostal Assemblies of British Columbia had been the pri-
mary sponsor of our Pentecostal chaplaincy; however the ministry
had never been narrowly denominational. But now Pastor Reg Lay-
zell of the independent Glad Tidings church asked me, "What are
you doing? Our students tell me you had a Roman Catholic priest at
the student gathering, and you were all praying together!" "He
wasn't there by my invitation, Pastor; to my surprise he arrived at
the airport with Tommy Tyson; it was a kind of package deal. When
I heard he was born again and filled with the Holy Spirit, I received
him as a brother."

Meanwhile, the priest was having his own problems about working with a Pentecostal woman minister. Tommy told me Jerry resolved his difficulties in prayer after reading my first autobiography,
Converted in the Country. "She's like the Apostle Paul, only a
woman," was his conclusion. Tommy Tyson came back as one of
our "visiting firemen" several times. "Visiting fireman" is what June
Lythgoe called our group's constant flow of guest speakers. Tommy
thought I would do well assisting him in chaplaincy at Oral Roberts
University. The offer included an attractive salary, and the opportunity to work on a Ph.D at Oklahoma State. For three days I
walked around in a state of excitement, asking God for direction.
But in the end I declined the invitation, choosing interaction in a secular university, and the media, above the more cloistered environment of the Christian university.

June Lythgoe, a master's candidate at UBC in the Department of
Anthropology and Sociology, was a leader in the Student Christian
Movement. Along with others in chaplaincy circles, she followed
with interest the activities of the new breed of Christian activists. She
said to me on one occasion, "There ought to be one chaplain like you

on every campus." One, she meant, was needed, two would be too many!

It was I who provided her with five charismatics and five classical Pentecostals from the campus community as subjects for research. The aim was to examine the role of the baptism of the Holy Spirit as a transforming experience in the life of the participant. On my part there was some uneasiness: what if the ten should be led as lambs to the slaughter? Sociologists researching religious matters have been known to come forward with outlandish conclusions, some of which have drawn a great deal of publicity. On seeing the published thesis, I sighed with relief. June had been both honest and fair. As summed up in the abstract, "The experience was seen by the participants as a 'healing' experience in that it offered an answer to their problems and dissatisfactions. The meaning of the baptism of the Holy Spirit was found to differ between those who had a continuous association with the Pentecostal church and those who had not. For the latter group the experience constituted a radical moral transformation whereas in the case of the former, the experience was a step in a continuing religious career." [1]

Furthermore, and surprising to me "of little faith," Lythgoe's thesis, though presented at a secular university, remains as an informative and highly accurate commentary on Christian renewal movements at several universities in the Sixties. As to our local movement, she comments, "The movement is stimulated by the able leaderships and personalities of several individuals whose concerns and convictions are persuasive. Mention must be made of untiring efforts by a local Pentecostal minister. She is supported in her efforts by both charismatic colleagues of other denominations and by the congregation she serves. Although this particular congregation adheres to the organized Pentecostal Assemblies, it is unique in composition. 'Hidden' Pentecostals stream through the church and it is a rare occasion when the indigenous congregation is not sprinkled with ecumenical representation. It must be remembered however, that the movement is 'Spirit centered' rather than organizationally based and so the focus of the movement is not to be defined. Consequently when seeking to locate the movement one must look toward individuals rather than institutions." [2]

It was exciting to see age-old barriers crashing down, and a new free flow of love and caring developing. The impact was the same whether in the Christian university community, or at the local church. David du Plessis described the new day of cooperation as follows: it was as if the farmers along the river bank fenced off their ducks from the neighbors', but when the flood came, the ducks, glad to be done with fences, swam happily together unhindered by the old constraints. Likewise, Christians were happy to worship together and enjoy, even briefly, a foretaste of heaven where there will be no fences. Bob McDougall, the Jesuit priest who worked for several years with David Mainse of 100 Huntley Street, Canada's major daily television ministry, agreed with me publicly in a meeting in Vancouver that the experience of the early charismatic renewal had been wonderful, just like a honeymoon. Everyone loved everyone else. Then immediately we were both caught up short with the thought, "And look who is talking. It's the only honeymoon *we'll* ever have!"

In the years we traveled, especially in the Deep South, Texas and California, we always had access to radio and frequently to television. Now I had a hankering to break into radio in Vancouver. Wilf Ray, director of religious broadcasting at CJOR 600, said that they could possibly find three minutes for me. What would I like to call it? I replied, "For sure *not* 'Moments of Meditation'; maybe 'Pentecostal Viewpoint.' " Wilf was surprised and said, "The Pentecostals are not a very popular group!" He probably thought I was creating an obstacle for myself. My view was different: "Pentecostals are thinking, mainstream Christians. We need to let people know." The injustice and unfairness of a lot of the prejudices floating in the Christian community was something I wanted to fight. My ministry soon enlarged beyond the limited "Viewpoint" to a live interview open-line radio program in 1967, as every Sunday we sought Christian perspectives on topics of current interest.

Thus, what is now known in the Pacific Northwest as the Sunday Line Radio and Television Communications Ministries began just as the charismatic renewal was breaking out in Seattle and Vancouver. Kevin Ranaghan, a young Roman Catholic theologian, was my first guest on the radio open line.

Curiously, it was on the UBC campus that the charismatic renewal in Vancouver began. After Tommy Tyson, who ministered on campus and at the Hotel Vancouver, came Ed Gregory and the Inter-Church Team. In each of the campus ministry outreaches there was a concurrent series in the city of Vancouver. The news of renewal in old-line churches was spreading fast. For me, a woman and a Pentecostal, it would not have been easy to be effective as a chaplain, except that Cathy Nicol, a campus worker with Varsity Christian Fellowship, had already shown that women were more than adequate for an excellent campus ministry. I was praying for creative ways to do Christian ministry when Ed Gregory's letter arrived. Their team had just concluded a successful outreach in Louisville, Kentucky, and felt led to come to UBC. They had read about us in *The Wayfarer*, our own Christian publication within the larger student newspaper, *The Ubyssey*. On Gregory's first visit I established contact with Rev. Robert Birch, pastor of St. Margaret's Reformed Episcopal, a man who had chaired the Billy Graham Crusade in Vancouver, and was generally respected in the community.

In the fall of 1967, a local committee under the chairmanship of Robert Birch, came together at the Chapman-Gerard residence in Oakridge to plan and pray for the Inter-Church Team and its ministry to the greater Vancouver area. The ministry was to be dedicated to Christian renewal, exalting the Lord Jesus Christ and honoring the Holy Spirit today.

Pastor John Watts of Broadway Tabernacle, Rev. Les Prichard of the Evangelistic Tabernacle, and Rev. John Holland of Kingsway Foursquare served on the committee, urging their people to support generously, pray fervently, and work quietly for the intended outreach. The Pentecostals played no public part; the Western Pentecostal Bible College students served tables at the dinner, did the clean-up and prayed as they worked.

Kevin Ranaghan, instructor in theology at St. Mary's College, South Bend, and doctoral candidate at Notre Dame University in Indiana, arrived in Vancouver with other members of the Inter-Church Team Ministries precisely on the day students, clergy and lay people in his area of Indiana were gathering at Notre Dame University to celebrate the anniversary of the outpouring of the Holy Spirit upon Roman Catholics one year before. Ranaghan was able in four days in Vancouver to tell most of the story of the Pentecostal movement among Roman Catholics. He explained, "The move is essentially one of trying to get back to the basics of Christianity and clear away all the nonsense, all the pomp and circumstance, all the medieval, baroque and imperial accretions — an attempt to get back to the pure gospel." He reported that in his area about five hundred Roman Catholic students, clergy and lay persons had received the Pentecostal baptism, including speaking in tongues.

The charismatic prayer gatherings at Notre Dame to which Ranaghan was giving leadership numbered about two hundred persons. The movement in the eastern university communities can be traced to the time when two Roman Catholic laymen, both members of the faculty of Duquesne University in Pittsburgh, were drawn together in a period of deep prayer and discussion about the vitality of the faith.

Ranaghan's role was indeed dramatic, and no less so was that of the other members of the team who represented various church backgrounds. The panel included Dr. George Pattison, formerly rector of St. Andrew's Anglican Cathedral in Prince Rupert, B.C.; Rev. Ed Gregory, formerly staff person with Varsity Christian Fellowship at Purdue University; and Rev. Mel Boring, a Princeton Theological Seminary graduate. Together they made a formidable team.

In Vancouver over four hundred clergy and lay leaders were guests at the seminar dinner at the Peretz Auditorium in Oakridge in 1967; among these were university and theological college professors, prominent ministers from various denominations, a few Roman Catholic priests and about eighteen nuns. One visitor commented that the gathering, which had strong representation from the liberal Protestant, Roman Catholic and fundamentalist leaders was such as had never happened before. He could have added, "and may never happen here again."

The Rev. Dennis Bennett and his wife Rita, of St. Luke's Episcopal, ministered in the same auditorium even more powerfully the following year under sponsorship of our local Inter-Church Fellowship. Hundreds of persons were receiving the charismatic experience, many to their own amazement.

Alice Klein, wife of Pastor Corstian Klein, minister of Hope Reformed Church in Vancouver, remembers that her husband at first declined the invitation to a free dinner. But she said, "Why not? Why don't we just go?" It was Kevin Ranaghan, the young Roman Catholic with the New Testament in his shirt pocket, talking about Jesus, that first caught her attention.

Their church had been in conflict over the charismatic question. Some of their leading laymen had taken measures to suppress the charismatics. They had ruled that no charismatic should be a Sunday School teacher, youth leader or hold other important positions in the church. Corstian remembers that the Hope Reformed congregation had experienced struggle over the renewal since 1964. "I was fighting for the unity of the church. Unfortunately, not all our people were motivated to get a better understanding. When I was first there you couldn't touch me with 'charismatic' anything."

"So I went to the dinner intent on approaching the whole question from a strictly theological point of view. As it happened, I opened up to the Holy Spirit in private. As soon as I changed positions, I informed our board and congregation that I would not be making a hobby of the renewal. My intention was to give the Word of God precedence. As a pastor I hoped to lead the congregation to a more nonjudgmental attitude, and I did."

Subsequently, Corstian Klein had a dramatic healing from a disabling heart condition in the Kathryn Kuhlman miracle service in Seattle. I myself heard Kuhlman identify a person "with a serious heart condition who is sitting in the left of the lower auditorium, back rows." I saw Corstian go to the platform at Kuhlman's request, and immediately following, ascend the balcony steps to test his healing. His doctor bore witness that the healing was genuine. Now a resident of Lynden, Washington, Rev. Corstian Klein says gratefully, "Thanks to God's healing power, I had some fantastic years immediately following that healing." Years later, open heart surgery for another problem revealed that the right artery which originally had been identified by the specialists as totally ineffective, was still perfectly healthy.

On Kevin and Dorothy Ranaghan's invitation, I attended the Roman Catholic Pentecostal Conference at Notre Dame, Indiana, a university founded by the Holy Cross Fathers in 1840. At first, the impressive baroque domes and abundance of decorative crosses somewhat unnerved me. I said to myself, "I am not going to feel at home here. They won't like it that I have come." Instead of feeling confident, even joyous, I was depressed by the beautiful campus and the sight of priests and nuns greeting one another with the kiss of peace. I felt myself in an alien culture.

Alone in my room at the Morris Inn, I knelt to pray and take account of what was going on in my own soul: I was here at Notre Dame to learn. Every day in recent months I had been challenged with evidence as to different ways in which God's mercy was being shown. He was upsetting some of my old ideas, but I wanted to move with His direction. Beside that, the Notre Dame adventure could be an interesting fact-finding tour. If the Heavenly Father is doing something new with the Roman Catholics, we too ought to know about it. My meditation finished with a prayer of commitment: "Lord, you know why I am here. If I am to go quietly about the campus and say nothing all weekend, I'll do it. If you want me to minister to someone, I'll do it. If you want someone to minister to me, I'll receive it. Please guide me, Lord."

After dinner at 7:00 o'clock, I was still chiding myself, "I should never have come to a place like this all by myself. Darkness is setting in; if this campus is as safe as the one back home, I should *not* be wandering around alone looking for the Holy Cross Gym." Doubts notwithstanding, my prayer was about to be answered. In the hotel lobby, I found it easy to ask four men who seemed part of the conference if I could go along with them to the meeting.

One of them put out his hand, "My name is Bill Truesdell." It turned out that he was a Jesuit priest, who, together with the other three, was researching the Pentecostal movement. Conveniently, these four men from Bellarmine School of Theology at Loyola University had a big academic umbrella under which they were carrying out a private pilgrimage. In the same group were two Sisters of Mercy. "Mercy is just what I need," thought I gratefully, "How perfectly appropriate." They took me into their circle so I did not end up lacking friends at Notre Dame.

They knew nothing of the Pentecostal movement, Roman Ca-

tholic or otherwise. In fact, I knew more about the Catholic Pentecostals than they did. But they were eager to help me understand the
Roman Catholic side of things and I was excited to get into the 9:00
o'clock sharing meeting to see how the Catholics carried on. The
chairs were arranged in a circular way; the Notre Dame and other
leadership sat in the center with a guitar or two.

In the openness of the sharing meeting, with my heart bursting
with joy and gratitude for the beauty of song and praise flowing from
hundreds of university young people and clergy, I stood up to identify myself: "I am a chaplain at the University of British Columbia
and Simon Fraser University. I rejoice in what I see." At that moment Abbot Father Columban Hawkins of the Trappist Monastery
in Lafayette, Oregon, got up out of his seat, came toward me in the
aisle, and gave me the kiss of peace. As it happened, I had had the
enormous privilege of participating in a retreat about a year earlier
in Portland, Oregon, and was part of the prayer team when the
Abbot received an overflowing anointing of the Holy Spirit. On that
occasion he had given me his blessing, and now this time it was as
though my passport to complete freedom in this Roman Catholic
conference had been firmly validated. The conference, on hearing a
few words from the Abbot, gave me a tremendous clap of welcome
so that the lonely insecure Pentecostal had reason to be ashamed for
having doubted the leading of the Lord in providing the Notre Dame
visit.

The researching Jesuits were each one responding to God's own
challenge to them. Father Bill Truesdell went on to be a leader in the
Chicago charismatic community. One of the Sisters of Mercy was an
administrator of a large hospital in Chicago, and one a social
worker. The more we discussed the work of the Holy Spirit and the
fresh vision of Jesus God was giving hungry people everywhere, the
more eager they were to participate.

"Anyway," said I, "my strength is not in the theory, but in the
practice. You can talk about these things and read about them but
what you really need is to get down to the personal application
through prayer." Eventually, one of the Sisters asked me, "May we
have that prayer?"

"First of all," said I, "Let's make sure our lives are settled in Jesus

Christ." I knew, of course, from previous conversation that she was a sincere believing Christian. Her own prayer poured forth first of all as a set prayer according to the Catholic liturgy. A major theme seemed to be "Lord have mercy upon us." She was among the first of the nuns I prayed with, so I listened with great interest. Then she began to sing in somewhat of a chant, and from there as effortlessly as the song birds, went into a song of praise in an unknown language.

In a matter of minutes she put her arm around me, squeezing tight and said, "Glory to God, isn't He wonderful!" That afternoon, in the general sharing meeting I happened to sit next to Graham Pulkingham and his wife, who belonged to an Episcopal community in Texas, and heard them singing loudly and clearly in the Spirit. After the meeting I asked my nun friend, "How were you doing?" She said, "I was singing in the Spirit, doing my part."

As it happened, Father Columban Hawkins was planning to be on the West Coast in a few days. With very short notice, our small core group in Vancouver called Roman Catholics together at a UBC professor's home, among them Mary Kelly of the Burns Hanley book store. Mary reported later that she had not realized that non-Catholics prayed with the same fervor and sincerity as did Roman Catholics.

The Abbot was a scholarly, dedicated believer, who had sought as a boy in Ireland to respond to the most difficult missionary task the Church could assign him. According to the Abbot, his labors of love and dedication, his scholarly pursuits had been satisfying in a measure, but he felt himself to have been standing passively on one side of a great wall, believing many of God's promised blessings were just beyond. On receiving the Spirit's special anointing, he now experienced personally what he had for so long affirmed intellectually but failed to actually receive.

In Vancouver the meetings with Fr. Columban Hawkins were the first evidence of a spreading, uniquely Roman Catholic, charismatic renewal. The Sisters of the Precious Blood in the Shaughnessy district of Vancouver longed to see the Abbot. He had very little time to spend there but requested me to go with him and Father Don Wilson, a local priest. To the Sisters, Father Columban said, "This is

Sister Bernice. You may ask her and Father Don for help. They will discuss and pray with you."

The entire group was a joy and delight to know. Before long the group was on fire for God in a new way, with just a few holdouts in their number. In silence as a cloistered order, they had pursued a life of devotion to God; now the new wine was bursting the old wine-skins, and the ministry of praise was added to their ministry of prayerful silence. The Superior explained, "Now instead of simply making the sign of the cross, on entering rooms, or at special moments, we say 'Praise the Lord!'"

Wayne Meyers, a missionary statesman with a vision for the nations, who had spent decades ministering Jesus Christ to needy Mexicans, had seen endless conflict in the course of his ministry with the Roman Catholic Church. On being introduced to the meetings at the Monastery, he instantly recognized the mighty work God was doing in all our hearts.

After a while, the Monastery in Shaughnessy was no longer open to "sharing meetings," whether by the Order's decision, or by the local bishop's decision, I do not know. Similarly, the Sisters of the Good Shepherd at St. Euphrasia just north of the U.S. border, opened their facilities and hearts to prayer with other Christians, and then withdrew from outside contact, but not before several of the Sisters, including the Superior, experienced the baptism of fire.

There was, of course, considerable exchange between Vancouver and Seattle. The senior priest of the large Church of the Blessed Sacrament in Seattle, Father Joseph Fulton, came several times to Vancouver for Inter-Church meetings, and even to preach at the fledgling Fraserview Assembly where Velma Chapman and I were pastors. Through his involvement in the renewal by the Holy Spirit, he experienced several attitudinal changes. Now he loved us all, though he had formerly disdained hippies, and felt he had little in common with non-Roman Catholics such as we. Now he loved to speak simply of Jesus, and tell what the Lord had done in his life through the release of the Spirit.

By the time I visited the Notre Dame Campus for the Fifth International Conference on the Charismatic Renewal in the Catholic Church, June 18-20, 1971, I had been involved for some time in a primarily Roman Catholic weekly prayer meeting in Sunshine Hills, a few miles from Vancouver. Bill and Lorraine Baldwin called me one day at the Simon Fraser chaplain's office. They had been in some of the Inter-Church meetings in which I was involved, which were by this time chaired by Pastor Robert Birch. "Would you consider coming to our home for prayer meetings, if we call in our friends and neighbors?" My answer was yes. I had no way of knowing that for me the series of prayer meetings would last for eight years, until the time I entered city politics.

The room was full of cigarette smoke. The singing was good, and the gospel ministry the same as anywhere. I prayed in the closing moments for a man to receive the anointing of the Spirit. He seemed tired after all his praying, and maybe a little discouraged, so he lit up a cigarette. I thought, "Thank God our church can't see me now. They'd wonder what we're doing, trying to minister God's Word in this cloud of smoke. Soon the praying, smoking believers ruled among themselves, "No smoking during the meeting." Then, "No smoking except in the coffee corner," and finally the majority gave up smoking altogether.

Hundreds of people poured through the weekly prayer meeting: nuns, priests, some sharing the ministry; hippies, ex-convicts, university people, neighbors, friends, anyone, everyone — people who were seekers. Wonderful things were done in the Name of Jesus.

At the Fifth International Conference at Notre Dame, when the Bishop's list of persons authorized to say mass and hear confessions was read out, David du Plessis laughed heartily when he heard "Father B. M. Gerard" listed among them. The Sunshine Hills prayer group had listed B. M. Gerard as their spiritual advisor. David joked, "Keep up the good work, Bernice, you may get to be a Monsignor someday!"

Winds of change were blowing, as sooner or later we would all come to see. Certainly I myself was changing, I hope for the better. One of my early exchanges with Alan Jackson, my fellow chaplain, is even now a memory I hold uncomfortably. When he invited me to his home for dinner, I knew that he regularly entertained literally hundreds of campus people, from the president of the university, professors and chaplaincy colleagues to hundreds of students, some for coffee and some for a relaxed, delicious dinner. It was lovely to be included.

He was his own butler, receiving me most graciously at the door. "Will you have a glass of wine? No? Not even sherry?" "No, thank-you." "You don't drink alcoholic beverages at all? Well, how about ginger ale?" "Yes, thank-you," I replied. He wanted to know, was I a prohibitionist or a teetotaler? The first is concerned to see that other people do not drink, the latter personally chooses not to. My abstemiousness was in good part related to my childhood when I saw people abusing others because they had drunk enough liquor to dull their minds, vulgarize their speech, and brutalize their conduct. I had other reasons as well, but this was no time to share them. It would not have been polite.

My host Alan Jackson, the Anglican chaplain, had not been long at UBC so I knew very little about him. Five minutes in his living room was enough to convince me that his wife must be one classy lady. The silver and crystal ware gleamed against the white linen tablecloth, the smell of delicious food in preparation promised a gourmet meal; good music was playing softly, and prints of great art adorned the walls.

With neither haste nor delay, I had been shown to the table; a standing grace was said, and my host seated me, all in one gracious gesture. Now after the appetizer and soup came, the main course was deftly served. I was thinking, "Where is his wife? I suppose she is weary of his much entertaining. It could be a bore to get caught in rounds of entertaining centering on his ministry." I heard later that he entertained two hundred for dinner and twelve hundred for coffee that year. I too, at Chapman's residence, saw dozens and dozens of students in our home for meals and fellowship. Then the following gauche remark literally fell out of my mouth, no brain power whatever behind it: "Have you any children?" "No," he replied, "I have never been married. I am a celibate priest." Too late I remembered that the Anglicans have them too. Horrors, thought I, "How did I get on to that subject? I could have asked first if he had a wife."

He may have enjoyed my embarrassment just a little. Certainly I had opened my mouth and put my entire foot in it. On another subject I did little better, nor was I aware in this instance of my own serious shortcomings in understanding. At that particular time, campus ministry people like Alan Jackson and his United Church of Canada counterpart, Jack Shaver, were warmly enthusiastic about the ecumenical movement. The thought that Christian churches were awakening to the need for more togetherness cheered them no end. The subject of the ecumenical movement inevitably found its way sooner or later into campus Christian conversations.

At that time the movement for change in the Roman Catholic Church was especially significant, although I was not sympathetically aware of it. "The whole world expects a step forward," said John XXIII as he opened the Second Vatican Council in October 1962. When in 1965 Pope Paul VI formally closed the Council, he heralded it as "among the greatest events of the Church." Significantly, more than twenty-four hundred patriarchs, cardinals, bishops and religious superiors who took part in the Council's deliberations on behalf of five hundred and sixty million members, declared that the Roman Catholic Church desired closer contact with all people, religious or not. A decree on ecumenism, committing Catholicism to work for Christian unity, for the first time acknowledged Protestant bodies as churches that share God's grace and favor.[3] To some this announcement was good news, to others an omen of evil to come. The General Presbytery of the Assemblies of God, U.S.A., unanimously passed a motion which put them on record "as opposed to ecumenicity based on organic and organizational unity, and the combinations of many denominations into a World Super Church, which probably will culminate in the Scarlet Woman or Religious Babylon of *Revelation*."[4] In addition, they recommended "that none of the Assemblies of God ministers or churches participate in such manner as to promote the ecumenical movement in any of the modern ecumenical organizations of this order on a local, national, or international level." Finally, they cautioned, "This is not to be interpreted to mean a limitation be imposed on any of our Assemblies of God ministers regarding his Pentecostal witness or participation on a local level with interdenominational activities."[5]

Besides providing a warning to the faithful, the elected leaders of the Assemblies were taking action regarding David du Plessis, one of their own prophetic figures. He was given a whole year in which to withdraw from the fellowship; failing this, his relationship with the Assemblies of God as an ordained minister would be terminated.

David's reply to his denomination (August 4, 1962) denied any misconduct on his part, and requested his brethren "to have a little more patience" with him. "Brethren, I have not joined anything in the line of organizations. I have simply obeyed the Spirit and set out to witness to ecclesiastical leaders in all confessions and movements, along the more excellent way. If my brethren feel I have sinned against them, or the kingdom of God, I am now completely convinced that the only action that will be fair to all concerned would be a trial as prescribed in the by-laws of the General Council of the Assemblies of God."[6]

There was no trial. His credentials were lifted in 1962, to be restored by the voluntary action of the Assemblies of God nearly two decades later. To be fair to all, the viewpoint that identified the Roman Catholic Church with the apostate church drunk on the blood of the martyrs (Rev. 17: 6) was and still is commonly held by many fundamentalist Protestant Christians. My own prejudices were also fueled by first-hand knowledge of severe persecution of Pentecostals in Italy, Mexico and Latin America carried out by Roman Catholic clergy. Pentecostals in Italy were denied the right of Christian burial in Roman Catholic-controlled cemeteries. It took the intervention of the World Council of Churches to get them freedom of religion in Italy. On my shoulders was the burden of a considerable weight of anti-Catholicism which revealed itself when the Anglican chaplain and I turned to ecumenical affairs. "What do you think of Pope John XXIII?" he asked, "Isn't he a marvelous person?" "I really don't think of him at all," said I, "I know many people are enthused about big changes with the Roman Catholics, but most Bible-believing Protestants have grave misgivings about these maneuverings." He continued to press me, "Are you at all interested in unity of the church universal?" "Yes, but not in some huge merger. We understand the unity to be in the invisible universal church. Visibly there is diversity, and that is healthy. The more diversity the better!" Later, I was convicted by the Holy Spirit for the flippancy of my response. It was almost as if I, and many like me who loved God and honored His word, rejoiced in schism and divisions.

At that level of understanding, I remember no grief in my heart over severe schisms that had rent the body of Christ, and no desire to see healing. On the interpersonal level things were different. People of all colors, creeds and convictions were to me endlessly fascinating. All kinds of friendships were possible and enjoyable. Simply having to look a person in the eye, and relate to them realistically does a lot to help us unload the burdens of bigotry.

Having arrived on campus with the idea that I would call no man "Father," I was soon compelled by common courtesy to give each individual his title according to the custom within his tradition. Some were "Rabbi," some "Doctor" (medicine, philosophy, education, or theology), some Protestants preferred "Pastor," others "The Reverend," or with most evangelicals, simply "Reverend." True, Jesus did say to His disciples;

> But you are not to be called "Rabbi," for you have only one Master and you are all brothers. And do not call anyone on earth "father," for you have one Father, and he is in heaven. Nor are you to be called "teacher," for you have one Teacher, the Christ. The greatest among you will be your servant. For whoever exalts himself will be humbled, and whoever humbles himself will be exalted. (Matthew 23: 8-12 NIV)

The teaching of Jesus was against those who do their works to be seen of men (v 5), and love the uppermost places at feasts, and the chief seats in synagogues (v 6). In any case, if we were to fulfill the letter of the text in a legalistic way, we ought to leave off using the term "Mister" which is a weakened form of "master." The custom of all friendly exchange in the campus community, in any case, was to use first names, never mind the titles.

In my voyage of understanding on the sea of ecumenical relationships, I had embarked as a teenager in the country believing the true family of God to be very small indeed. As time went on, the school of hard knocks and the experience of being on the receiving end of bigotry made me want to be as broad in sympathies as possible — but not to the point of being broader than Jesus. The major turning point for me was the experience of prayer and worship with people of other communions through the renewal. The fresh winds of the Spirit were influencing us to new applications of old familiar Scripture passages.

"Ecumenical," meaning universal, embracing the entire inhabited world, was, and still is for many professing Christians, a pejorative term. But there is a Biblical ecumenism which ought to receive our attention. In His high priestly prayer recorded in John 17, Jesus first of all identifies those who belong to the true church:

> For you granted his authority over all people: that he might give eternal life to all those you have given him. (v 2 NIV)
> "Now this is eternal life: that they may know you, the only true God and Jesus Christ, whom you have sent. (v 3 NIV)
> "I pray for them; I am not praying for the world, but for those you have given me, for they are yours. (v 9 NIV)

He makes the definite distinction between those who are of the world and therefore alien to the church, and those who are in the faith. The dramatic impact of knowing that Jesus prayed not only for His immediate followers but also "for them also who shall believe on Him through their word," which includes modern-day believers, is tremendous. His prayer will be answered! His heart's desire for His people is that they also may be one, even as He and the Father are one. The effect of this unity and love between Christian believers will be that the world may believe the Father sent the Son to be the Savior of the world. (John 17: 21)

It is not good enough to slough off responsibility for demonstrating love and unity with others who proclaim the lordship of Jesus, by referring, as I once did, to the vision of the invisible church. The world does not see the invisible, it sees *us*.

Malcolm Muggeridge mocks the concept, so popular among liberals, that a mere merger will provide great surges of new strength. He sees unbelieving but professing Christendom in its various groupings staggering like drunks at a bar attempting to hold one another up. Weakness added to weakness equals weakness, but believers joining hands and faith with believers are a glory to God and an attractive persuasive force.

Notes

1 Mariann June Lythgoe, *The Baptism of the Holy Spirit: A Study of the Meaning of Religious Experience*, Master's Thesis, University of British Columbia, 1969, abstract.
2 *Ibid.*, 33.
3 *Time Canada*, Toronto, October 5, 1983, 84.
4 See Revelation 17.
5 Official correspondence to David du Plessis, signed by Barrett Peterson, General Secretary, General Council of the Assemblies of God, September 14, 1962, P.T.O.
6 I have a copy of David du Plessis's reply, August 4, 1962.

14

JUST BEING A WOMAN

The question of women in ministry is not a simple one, nor one I can avoid any longer as I tell my own story. My first impulse has been to ignore this complex issue and write as the majority of ministers would write, that is, as a man would write. One finds no explanations, no justifications, no apologies for "being mere men" in the ministry. However, for many years I have done what some say is a "man's job only". In some cases they mean, "It's a man's job, so get out of the pulpit!" In others, they are attempting a compliment, as in "You preach like a man." Just as, in another context, they might say "You drive real good, just like a man."

It is no secret that women have had to struggle for recognition of their full personhood; what is surprising is that the church with all its respectability is in so many areas the last bastion for male chauvinism.

On October 18, 1929, Mrs. Emily Murphy, 61, of Edmonton, was declared by the Privy Council of the House of Lords in London to be ... a person. The magnitude of that event must be appreciated within the framework of Emily's time. This was no mere legal quibble. Until our present century, women in Canada had few opportunities to enter any of the professions except teaching. They could not vote, sit on a jury, hold public office, choose their domicile or citizenship or be treated equally under the law. The prevailing attitude was summed up by the Premier of Manitoba who said in 1914, "When I come home at night, I don't want a hyena in petticoats talking politics, but a sweet gentle creature to bring me slippers."

It was Emily Murphy who initiated an appeal to the Supreme Court of Canada for a ruling on the interpretation of the word "person" as it appeared in the British North America Act which was, at that time, our Constitution. Five Alberta women signed a very simple petition to the Supreme Court of Canada asking, "Does the word 'person' in Section 24 of the BNA Act include female persons?"

After a long wait, these women — and indeed all of Canada — received word that women (along with criminals and idiots) were not legal persons within the terms of the BNA Act and therefore not eligible to sit in the Senate.

Canadian women were deeply disappointed in the ruling. The Honourable Mary Ellen Smith, the Liberal MLA for Nanaimo who became the first woman member of cabinet in the British Empire, wrote to Emily Murphy from BC. "The iron dropped into the souls of women in Canada when we heard that it took a man to decree that his mother was not a person."

The Alberta Five appealed the decision to the Privy Council of the House of Lords in England, which at that time was Canada's final court of appeal. The proceedings in London took four days and once again judgment was reserved. Days grew into weeks, weeks dragged into months. Finally, on October 18, 1929, before a crowded court, the Lord Chancellor of Great Britain, Lord Sankey, delivered the decision. Although women were still not admitted in their own right to the House of Lords, their lordships had generously determined that women were indeed persons, adding, "...and to those who ask why the word should include females, the obvious answer is, why should it not?"[1]

In 1973 a Canadian stamp of 8¢ value was issued in belated tribute to Nellie McClung who had stumped across the Canadian prairies at the turn of the century securing the vote for women; she was also one of the Alberta Five. She applied her insights and intuitions regarding women in the secular and public arena, but the foundation of her thought was Christian. "The time will come ... when women will be economically free, and mentally and spiritually independent," foretold Nellie. A McClung quote that came directly out of her church life is, "Women may lift the mortgages, or build churches, or any other light work, but the real heavy work of church, such as moving resolutions in the general conferences ... must be done by strong, hardy men."[2]

Please understand me, I am not belligerent on this subject. I am bored, bored as a black person is bored with discussing what's wrong with apartheid. Nevertheless, for friend and foe, I force myself to collect my thoughts, and share how I, as a woman, pastored the same church for twenty-one beautiful years, preached twice on Sundays and midweek, ministered the communion, baptized believers, performed wedding ceremonies, counseled the living, buried the dead, acted as chairman of the board and chief administrative officer, and then, with a peaceful heart, chose to shift gears and go full time into writing and radio and television ministry.

For those who have conscientious objections to a woman's leadership in a church, such as Elizabeth Elliot, I have no bad feelings. When a fellow pastor said, "I am booking Elizabeth Elliot's schedule; would you like to have her for your televised Sunday evening service?" I was immediately enthusiastic. What a blessing her visit would be to our people!

Then came her letter saying that she was willing to come if I was willing to have her as a guest speaker despite the fact that she did not believe in women pastors. She would come only on the condition that we put a man in charge of the service that evening. "Certainly. No problem. Of course!" was my first internal response. Then the absurdity of it hit me. This rearrangement of the hierarchy was for one night only, presumably to make our guest feel comfortable because now, God was presumably pleased with the way we were doing things. But the Holy Spirit, who really *is* in charge, knows all things, including who is who and why. Not only was I in charge of the television service, I was the only one in sight who had the know-how for the production. Regrettably, we lost the benefit of Elizabeth Elliot's excellent ministry.

The fact that Elizabeth Elliot was willing to come at all at the invitation of a woman pastor indicates to me her good spirit, for these questions of ministry *are* legitimately matters of conscience. As one of Canada's leading pastors said on a conference floor in St. John's, when the ordination of women was being discussed, "If women insist on being pastors, it is on their conscience." But the message conveyed by this influential male pastor sounded as though for a woman to preach and minister the gospel as one called by God is the equivalent of her stealing or living promiscuously. In his view, she ought to have trouble with her conscience, because she is going against God's will.

I have no time for debate with those who raise the subject of womens' ministries with the intent to silence or harass women. There is a lot of meanness in people that finds ready expression in targeting persecuted minorities. Let *them* follow *their* conscience. Like Nehemiah of old, my reply to their attack is, "I am carrying on a great project and cannot go down. Why should the work stop, while I leave it and go down to you?" (Nehemiah 6:3 NIV) "Four times," says Nehemiah, "they sent me the same message and each time I gave them the same answer." (v 4) As for me in Vancouver, exposed to public opinion through thousands of callers on television and open line radio, I have been endlessly challenged, questioned, cajoled, condemned, and alternately complimented and commended. Among those who think we women pastors should explain why we feel no guilt over serving God in pulpit ministry are all too many who see themselves as good Christians. One pastor in my own denomination, which is generally open to women's ministries and even to women's ordination, said to me in surprise, "You are not chairman of the board, are you?" He had, in a moment of folly, silenced the women of his congregation, on the grounds that in the spontaneous utterances of prophecy which came from the general congregation, more men should be heard from. Maybe so, but what has that to do with the role of women in the church family and why must their gifts be suppressed? As to the chairing of board meetings, if being a pastor is a labor of love and servanthood, there is nothing in servanthood that cannot be allowed to a woman. Most good pastors, men and women, serve, and lead by consensus of the mature leaders in the team.

Some encountered our ministry and were changed. A Christian leader who lived next door to a recently bereaved couple had an experience with them and me which caused him to modify his position on women pastors considerably. In sorrow, Joan and Norman, who had lost their beloved small son through cancer, would go out for a drive on a Sunday night and listen to me on radio CJOR. The first time I saw them was when they came down the aisle of the church hand in hand to give their lives to God. Their late night listening had brought them both to a decision. "We need the kind of faith Bernice has."

Next day they jubilantly told their neighbor about their newfound faith, expecting him, a church leader, to be as happy as they were, especially since he had sometimes invited them to attend his evangelical church. Happy he was not. "Aren't you glad we made the decision?" they asked with the innocence of newborn babes. "Well, er ... yes, but it's a shame you had to do it there! The church has women pastors," said he with a gloomy countenance.

Joan and Norman reported to us later that their neighbor's response upset them terribly, almost to the point of causing them to turn away from their earlier decision. It was all too confusing. In bed at night they tossed and turned, struggling for the correct answer. Was God really against women teaching and preaching? Both of them prayed, "Oh God, we need help!" "Then," said Joan "a Scripture came just like a little telegram from somewhere in the air. She knew hardly any Bible verses, so this was special. "It shall come to pass in the last days," says God, "I will pour out my Spirit and your sons and your daughters shall prophesy." (Joel 2:28) With Scripture came a question, "Who has been the greatest help to you as, in your grief, you have been seeking after the Lord?" "Kathryn Kuhlman and Bernice Gerard," came the answer, immediately and clearly. As Norman and Joan discussed the matter they both had peace. Later their neighbor stood in the entrance to our new building and said, "I have always thought women ought not to take leadership, but when I see the soul-winning that goes on here, I say to myself, 'Who am I to judge?' To you I say, God bless you. I'm sorry I was negative with Joan and Norman."

My experience as a pastor has been good. Despite the negative examples just presented, my co-worker Velma Chapman and I enjoyed the best possible relationships with our congregation, men and women, boys and girls. The truth is, people forget that the minister is a woman! "Do you find it tough having to relate to a 'skirt' in the pulpit?" asked a visiting preacher of one of our none-too-spiritual young married men, "It must be hard to have a woman for a pastor." To which our young man responded, "Oh? I hadn't noticed." In Egypt, as guest speakers, we women were ushered to the platform, out of the women's section, *and* out of the men's section, into what we called jokingly "no man's land." But we were given the liberty of the pulpit to proclaim the Word and glorify God. Spiritually speaking, when in the place of worship we all relate to God and one another in the Holy Spirit, male or female is not an issue. Humanly speaking people naturally will have their preferences. How many times have I heard the remark, "He (or she) doesn't *like* women preachers," to which I respond, "So what's new? Many people do not like any kind of preacher!"

In this brief account of what is presently foundational in my own understanding, I simply share what I believe to be true, and find liberating to me as a person. Liberation for a Christian woman is not a movement or an organization but "a state of mind in which a woman comes to view herself as Jesus Christ sees her — as a person created in God's image whom he wants to make free to be whole, to grow, to learn, to utilize fully the talents and gifts God has given her as a unique individual."[3] My own thinking has been influenced by authors both secular and Christian; I would urge the reader who is interested in studying these issues to check out my footnotes for recommended reading.

Who Said Women Can't Teach, recently authored by Charles Trombley, hits the hard questions square on, and, I believe, will be immeasurably helpful to women who feel a call to service but are concerned to do it God's way. Charles was in the beginning stages of his book about women when he chose to minister on the subject at our church. I was not annoyed but was faintly uncomfortable since it put me and the congregation in a fish bowl. It was as if a white person had gone into an all-black church and said assuringly, "It is okay to be black, don't worry." On the other hand, I knew we needed men to speak up in favor of women ministers. Heaven knows, enough of them have written to silence women. Charles has written in my copy, "Here is the book for which you gave me a trophy," recalling that I'd promised him some kind of an award if he wrote it. He deserves our everlasting gratitude because, however much I may want to ignore the subject, it will not go away.

It is a blight on our Christian testimony worldwide that women are obliged to defend themselves for being women. Even at Christ for the Nations in Dallas, a school with seventeen hundred students and a world outreach that puts most groups of similar size to shame, students kept asking me "Do women have a right to lead and preach? I'm not used to hearing women really *preach* like you do." They certainly did not get their bias from observing the ministry of Freda Lindsay, the gifted administrator, teacher, leader and co-founder with her husband of the CFNI Ministries. My question is, "From where does all this junk about women come? Who supplies the disinformation and the emotional bias?" It is a deep spiritual question which has its origin in the Garden of Eden.

The ministry of women is the same ministry as engages the energy, gifts and life commitment of men. As Catherine Booth of the Salvation Army said, "Why should a woman be confined exclusively to the kitchen and distaff [a staff on which flax or wool is wound for use in spinning], any more than a man to the field and workshop? Did not God, and has not nature assigned to man his sphere of labor to till the ground and dress it? And if exemption is claimed from this kind of toil for a portion of the male sex, on the ground of their possessing ability for intellectual and moral pursuits, we must be allowed to claim the same privilege for women."[4]

In studying Genesis, I have observed that the Lord God did not plan for men and women to be in conflict or competition, but instead to be partners both in family life and doing God's will on earth. The subordination of women described in Genesis 3: 15-16 is clearly the result of sin. The Lord God curses the serpent and the ground, and predicts enmity unlimited between Satan and the woman. The degradation of women observable today in our so-called enlightened world, is ample proof that women are still in a special way Satan's target, with the intent to destroy the human family. Women sold into prostitution in India, Thailand, Hong Kong, Canada and the United States; a multi-billion-dollar trade in pornography, printed and video, in which women chiefly are the objects of sadistic or humiliating practices; these and more are evidence in our time that putting women down is a notable aspect of Satan's present task. Crudely, people joke, "Women are okay in their place. Barefoot, pregnant and at the kitchen sink!"

The modern thrust for women to think well of themselves is not in itself ungodly. Some go to ungodly extremes as in the pitting of the rights of the woman to have control of her own body over against the very life of the innocent unborn child. But the Edenic vision for woman is sublime indeed. Trombley in his chapter "Male and Female Made He Them" puts woman in God's intended context: "God made woman, not for man to rule, control, or make decisions for, but to be an equal partner who would rule with him and care for the garden with him. Who gave the orders? Who made the decisions? God! (Genesis 1:26,28; 2:15). Sin had not yet corrupted mankind; strife, aggressiveness, domineering attitudes, and the struggle for preeminence were unknown. Mankind bore the image and likeness of God himself. They acted like God, talked like God, and accepted each other as God. Paul said in I Corinthians 13:5: 'love does not seek its own.' Where there's the God-kind of love, there isn't any desire to take charge of another person. Whenever I hear 'Who is in charge?' I hear the voice of sinful man striving for dominance."[5]

When the Lord God spelled out to Satan, Eve and Adam the dire consequences of rebellion, Eve heard him say "In sorrow you shall bring forth children; and your desire will be for your husband, and he will rule over you." (Gen. 3: 16 NIV) Ever since the Fall, some have assumed that the Lord himself is pleased when women are oppressed, and think when they see women in subjection, "Good! That is the way it must be." Their interpretation is a grief to women and a discredit to God Almighty. As I see it, and as Trombley sees it, "Rather than God's 'cursing' them, He warned them prophetically, telling them how it would be. He knew Adam's fallen nature would make him a tyrant. He knew he would abuse and use the woman, eventually reducing her to the position of common property. It wasn't God's desire; it was the terrible result of sin. Not a curse, but a consequence.

Had the imperative form been used, the meaning would be a direct command and man would have to dominate the woman in order to fulfill the command. The more carnal and violent the man, the more perfectly he would fulfill this order, but thank God that wasn't the situation at all. The verb is in the simple imperfect form, warning them what would happen. Did God curse the woman? Absolutely not. Did he curse the man? Absolutely not.[6]

To the man the Lord God said, "Cursed is the ground because of you; through painful toil you will eat of it all the days of your life. It will produce thorns and thistles for you. ... By the sweat of your brow you will eat your food until you return to the ground ... for dust you are, and to dust you will return." (Genesis 3: 17-19 NIV) The history of the human family reveals that men have fought to put down thorns and thistles, have employed every possible means to perspire as little as possible, and with all that is in them, fought to delay the day of death.

The true reversal of the consequences of the Fall is brought to us by Jesus Christ. "For since death came through a man, the resurrection of the dead comes also through a man." (1 Cor. 15: 21 NIV) "Dear friends, now we are children of God, and what we will be has not yet been made known. But we know that when he appears, we shall be like him, for we shall see him as he is." (1 John 3: 2 NIV).

One's appreciation of that gift of God, equality of personhood with every other member of the human family, is heightened by Scriptures that present great redemptive themes. The price of redemption is exactly the same for every man, woman, boy or girl regardless of color or creed. Each of us is redeemed "not with corruptible things like silver or gold ... but with the precious blood of Christ, as of a lamb without blemish and without spot..." (1 Peter 1: 18,19). The redeeming power of Christ makes it possible to go back to the ideals of Paradise. He came to make the crooked straight.

During my time in chaplaincy at Simon Fraser University and the University of British Columbia, women's issues were in the foreground of discussion. Students who came to campus from stable Christian families were drawn into conflict over the churches' historic record on women's rights, and whether women today can expect fair and equal treatment from the established church.

At the time my own interests led me to the works of radical secular feminists, as well as those of Bible-believing evangelical scholars, male and female. To them and to the students whose sincere questioning demanded on behalf of the church an answer that represents Jesus more adequately than in the past, I owe the development of many insights.

I believe that Christian women everywhere should burst into a litany of praise, because Jesus promoted the dignity and equality of women in a male-dominated society. Every Christian woman should see herself as a liberated woman, set free by a Man nearly two thousand years ago. "Jesus was in favour of, and promoted the equality of women with men. He advocated and practised treating women primarily as human persons (as men are so treated) and was willing to contravene social custom to be true to the principle of equality of personhood." [7]

The status of women in Palestine during the time of Jesus was very decidedly inferior. Despite the fact that heroines of faith were recorded in the Scriptures, according to most rabbinic customs of Jesus' time — and long after — women were not allowed to study the Scriptures (Torah). One first-century rabbi, Eliezer, put the point sharply: "Rather should the words of Torah be burned than entrusted to a woman. ... Whoever teaches his daughter the Torah is like one who teaches her lasciviousness." [8]

In the vital area of prayer, women were so little thought of as not to be given obligations of the same seriousness as men. For example, women, along with children and slaves, were not obliged to recite the Shema, the morning prayer, nor pray at meals. In fact the Talmud states, "Let a curse come upon the man who (must needs have) his wife or children say grace for him." Moreover in the daily prayers of Jews there was a threefold thanksgiving: "Praised be God that he has not created me a Gentile; praised be God that he has not created me a woman; praised be God that he has not created me an ignorant man."

In the great temple at Jerusalem women were limited to one outer portion, the women's court, which was five steps below the court for men. In the synagogues the women were separated from men. In public life, as well as religious life, women suffered greatly from discrimination. A rabbi regarded it as beneath his dignity to speak to a

woman in public; except in rare instances women were not accepted
as valid witnesses in a court of law. In marriage, the role of women
was seen exclusively in terms of child-bearing and child-rearing. Di-
vorces were easily obtainable by men. Women in Palestine, on the
other hand, were not allowed to divorce their husbands. In short, the
status of women was exceedingly low. They were inferior, unequal
and completely subordinate. Into such a society came Jesus.

Jesus taught women the gospel, the meaning of the Scriptures and
religious truths in general. He talked to women in public. The Samaritan woman at the well said to him, "How is it that you being a
Jew, ask a drink of me, who am a woman of Samaria? For Jews have
no dealings with the Samaritans." (John 4:9) The disciples, on returning, ignore the fact that Jesus was speaking to a Samaritan and
emphasize the fact that he was speaking to a woman, as John re-
ports. "His disciples returned and were surprised to find him speaking to a woman though none of them asked, 'What do you want
from her?' or, 'Why are you talking to her?'" (John 4: 27) The over-
whelmingly negative attitude of the rabbis toward women is entirely
missing in Jesus. He and the woman discussed the most profound
spiritual truths. To her Jesus said, "God is a Spirit; and they that
worship him must worship him in spirit and in truth." (John 4: 24)
Finally, he revealed himself as Messiah, and received ready acceptance from the woman.

Women who became disciples of Jesus not only learned from him
("learner" was the original meaning of the word), but also went with
Him in His travels and ministered to Him. In Luke 8: 1-3, several
married and unmarried women are mentioned along with the
Twelve: "After this, Jesus traveled about from one town and village
to another, proclaiming the good news of the Kingdom of God. The
Twelve were with him, and also some women who had been cured of
evil spirits and diseases. Mary (called Magdalene) from whom seven
demons had come out; Joanna wife of Chuza, the manager of
Herod's household; Susanna; and many others. These women were
helping to support them out of their own means." (NIV) There was
also a considerable number of women who walked with Jesus all the
way to Calvary's mountain. Mark 15: 40, 41: "Some women were
watching from a distance. Among them were Mary Magdalene,

Mary, the mother of James the younger and of Joses, and Salome. In Galilee these women had followed him, and cared for his needs. Many other women who had come up with him to Jerusalem were also there." (NIV)

Jesus quite deliberately broke with another custom. It could not have been anything but deliberate that Jesus' first appearance after his resurrection was to a woman who was then commissioned by him to bear witness to the good news of the risen Jesus to the eleven (John 20: 11 ff; Matt. 28: 9 ff; Mark 16: 9 ff) In typical male Palestinian style, the eleven refused to believe the woman, since according to Judaic law, women and children were not considered competent to bear witness.

Another example which highlights the good news of the gospel is that of the love and understanding Jesus showed toward the woman of ill repute at the Pharisee's house. When she began washing Jesus' feet with her tears, wiping them with her hair, and even kissing his feet as she anointed them with precious ointment, the skeptical Pharisee saw her as an evil sexual creature. (Luke 7: 36 ff) "The Pharisee ... said to himself, If this man were a prophet, he would know who this woman is who is touching him, for she is a sinner." Jesus deliberately refused to view the woman as a sex object; instead he rebuked the Pharisee and ministered to her as a person. Jesus then addressed her, even though it was not proper to speak to women in public, especially women of poor reputation: "Your sins are forgiven. ... Your faith has saved you; go in peace." (v 50)

Similarly moving is the account of the woman who had a hemorrhage of blood for twelve years because it touches on the taboos that have made life difficult for women. (Matt. 9: 20) In her reluctance to come to public attention, she said to herself, "If I just touch his clothes, I will be healed." Mark records "Immediately her bleeding stopped and she felt in her body that she was freed from her suffering." (5: 29, 30 NIV) Wonderful! But why did Jesus, knowing immediately in himself that power had gone out of him, turn to the crowd and say "Who touched me?" Her shyness was not because she came from the poor, lower classes, for Mark pointed out that over twelve years she had been to many physicians and ended up with no healing and no money. It was probably because for twelve years, as a woman with a flow of blood, she was constantly ritually unclean. (Luke 15: 19 ff). This not only made her incapable of participating in any temple worship, it made her in some way "displeasing to God," and rendered anyone and anything she touched (or anyone who touched what she touched!) similarly unclean. The sense of degradation and contagion that her "womanly weakness" worked upon her over the twelve years was no doubt oppressive. It seems clear that Jesus wanted to call attention to the fact that He did not shrink from ritual uncleanness incurred by the touch of the "unclean" woman. On several occasions Jesus rejected ritual uncleanness, and by immediate implication, rejected the idea of the "uncleanness" of a woman who had a flow of blood, menstruous or continual. Dramatically, and mercifully for women, Jesus altogether rejected the blood taboo, another of the traditional teachings that bound women.

Neither did Jesus limit woman's role to housekeeping. Jesus quite directly rejected the stereotype that the only proper place for women is in the home, during a visit to the house of Mary and Martha. (Luke 10: 38 ff) Martha took the typical woman's role, and was distracted with much serving. Mary took the supposedly "male" role and sat at the Lord's feet, listening to his teaching. Understandably, Martha apparently thought Mary out of place in abandoning the kitchen and choosing the role of "scholar and intellectual," for she complained to Jesus. Again, Jesus' response enriches our view of the good news of the gospel, especially for women. He treated Mary first of all as a person (whose highest faculty is the intellect, the spirit) who was allowed to choose her own priorities, and in this instance had "chosen the better part." She received Jesus' approval, and support: "It is not to be taken from her."

One cannot infer from Jesus' behavior that women should not be pastors or teachers. But certainly, if women have in fact been silenced by God, there should be no women pastors, teachers, missionaries, evangelists, etc. The basic argument on this issue stems from 1 Corinthians 14: 34-35:

"Women should remain silent in the churches: they are not allowed to speak, but must be in submission, as the Law says. If they want to enquire about something, they should ask their own husbands at home; for it is disgraceful for a woman to speak in the church." (NIV)

In his chapter, "Should Women Be Silent in the Church?" Charles Trombley raises several questions, the last of which he sees as of special importance to the proper interpretation of the passage: "Where and what is the law that underscores this restriction?" [10]

Trombley's answer to that question concurs with reliable scholarship: "The expression 'as also saith the law' refers to the Oral Law of the Jews, now called the Talmud." This was the very law to which Jesus referred when He said "You transgress the commandment of God for the sake of your tradition." (Matt. 15: 3 NAS).

Convincingly, Trombley points out that it was the Judaizers with their "Oral Law" who wanted women silenced. Historically, since then, the actions of the church fathers are even more reprehensible since, as followers of Jesus, they should have known better. Furthermore, even in modern times there is little change for the better in the attitudes of church hierarchies (with some exceptions). Katherine Bushnell, medical doctor and Hebrew and Greek scholar, in her *God's Word to Women*, written in the nineteenth century, shared insights which are needed now as much as ever, possibly more so:

> At no point is faith in the entire Bible being so viciously and successfully attacked today as at the point of the "woman question," and the church so far attempts no defense here of her children. It assumes that the interests of merely a few ambitious women are involved, whereas the very fundamentals of our faith are at stake. [12]

Briefly, for those who want to pursue further study with authors friendly to the idea of women's speaking in the church, or even teaching, let us look at Paul's advice to Timothy. "But I do not permit a woman to teach, or to have authority over a man; she must be silent." (1 Tim. 2: 12 NIV) Trombley argues that Paul cited Eve's fate in the creation order to refute and reduce the influence of the Gnostic women in Ephesus, but that he did not intend thereby to forbid all women for all times the privilege of public preaching when males are present. [12] Trombley's paraphrase of the passage, which should be read in the context of his entire chapter of scholarly discussion, is as follows: "Let a woman learn quietly, without interruptions and questions. Presently I'm not permitting a woman to teach anyone or exercise her sexual wiles to control a man, but to be reverent and peaceful. Because Adam was formed first, and then Eve. And it wasn't Adam who was deceived — Eve was thoroughly deceived and became a transgressor. Nevertheless, woman shall be delivered from the condition that requires her silence; she may someday be restored and able to teach. This is possible because childbearing, by producing the seed who destroyed Satan's power, balances the superior position of man established in the creation order. However, women can only be restored as they walk in faith and love."[13] He concludes, "Any idea that God could not or would not speak through a woman simply because she is female contradicts the whole New Testament teaching of Jesus Christ and the Apostle Paul. No person, male or female, is called by God on the basis of sex, but on the basis of commitment to Him. In Christ there is neither male nor female."[14]

In approaching Scripture with regard to women's equality, four principles should be kept in mind: First, *all relevant scripture must be used.* Too long the church has looked only at those texts which suggest (on the surface at least) the inferiority of women, while neglecting to give equal cognizance to such female-friendly verses as passages that present the equality principle: "There is neither Jew nor Greek, slave nor free, male nor female, for you are all one in Christ Jesus." (Gal. 3: 28 NIV)

There is also the oft-neglected reciprocity principle (1 Cor. 7: 3-5 NIV): "The husband should fulfill his marital duty to his wife, and likewise the wife to her husband. The wife's body does not belong to her alone but also to her husband. In the same way, the husband's body does not belong to him alone but also to his wife. Do not deprive each other except by mutual consent and for a time, so that you may devote yourselves to prayer. Then come together again, so that Satan will not tempt you because of your lack of self-control.

A second principle is that *close attention must be paid to historical context.* In Trombley's discussion of 1 Cor. 14: 34-35 and 1 Tim. 2: 12, when special attention is given to the historical context, the real meaning of the text becomes clear. The inferior status of women in Palestine according to the Oral Law is a factor of great significance in helping to sort the positive from the negative impact for today.

A third principle which figures large in my judgment, on many important matters is that *what is universal and eternal must be distin-guished from what is particular and timebound.* Theological principles must be taken seriously, but there are other pieces of advice which the church in general ignores quite happily. For example, the passage "Drink no longer water, but use a little wine for your stomach's sake and your frequent infirmities" (1 Tim. 5: 23) is ignored by tee-total churches."Greet all the brethren with a holy kiss" (1 Thess. 5: 26) is not compelling today's Christian men to engage in regular demonstrations of obedience. Contrariwise, Paul's opinion that a woman who prays or prophesies with her head uncovered dishonors her head (1 Cor. 11: 5) is a verse which in some modern Christian communities is laid on women with such seriousness as to suggest that some great eternal principle is at stake.

Whatever may have been Paul's intention in his declaration of equality of personhood in Galatians 3: 23-29, on the level of practical application, he did not succeed in implementing all the terms of his own ideal: "There is neither Jew nor Greek, there is neither bond nor free, there is neither male nor female, for you are all one in Christ Jesus." In this passage, he presents three paired types of people who, under the law and sin, have unequal relationships, but now in Christ have equality of personhood. Paul demonstrated by his life and ministry that old distinctions between Jew and Gentile were no longer valid. Nevertheless, though in *principle* Paul was true to his teaching in a large part regarding slaves and free men, or between men and women, he failed to carry through successfully on the last two. He never challenged the system itself in these cases, as he did when equality between Jew and Greek was discussed.

Take the case of Onesimus the slave, for whom Paul pleads. Onesi-mus is no longer just a runaway slave but has become a "son," "a brother beloved," a person to be received by Philemon, the master, as though he were Paul himself. Although the guiding spirit in Paul's efforts was love, and we presume that the end result was Onesimus' freedom, Paul did not challenge the slavery system of his day. To-day's church would not do less than stand against slavery, as traffick-ing in persons is seen to be a heinous crime. Perhaps, we in Christian churches should now note the parallel. Women generally have not yet experienced their full freedom which Jesus purchased at such great cost. We have some catching up to do!

Finally, the fourth of our principles is that *Jesus Christ must be the starting point*. Passive irresponsibility on the part of women is as contrary to His will as prideful domination on the part of men. If we dare to call ourselves His disciples, we must not ignore His words and actions.[15]

Consider what happened on the day of Pentecost and the consequences as spelled out by Peter, who was quoting Joel, "And it shall come to pass in the last days, says God, I will pour out of my Spirit upon all flesh; and your sons and your daughters shall prophesy, and your young men shall see visions, and your old men shall dream dreams; and on my servants and on my handmaidens I will pour out in those days of my Spirit, and they shall prophesy." (Acts 2: 17,18) "Yes, I will endue even my slaves, both men and women, with a portion of my Spirit, and they shall prophesy," says it even more clearly, and highlights God's gracious touch of mercy toward "all flesh." [16] As someone said to me who came asking support for a leprosy mission overseas, "Jesus said, 'Heal the sick, cleanse the lepers.' He mentioned the lepers especially so we would not leave them out." The prophesying to which Peter (and Joel before him) referred was not only the foretelling of events such as the return of the Lord, but also the proclamation (preaching) to the world at large of the glad tidings of salvation through Jesus Christ. Can any of us imagine to what extent the communication of the gospel has been hindered by the prejudices and non-Biblical traditions of men that have prevented enormous numbers of highly motivated women from following the Spirit in preaching the good news?

God said, "Go!" Church leaders in all too many cases said, "No!" Women have been rendered powerless in the decision-making processes of church bodies, and speechless in the public services of their churches by those who are often manifesting, not a liberating anointed view of what the Holy Spirit is doing through men and women, but an unreasonable devotion to their own sex with contempt for the other sex. That male chauvinism should parade itself as something godly, cloaking itself in Bible verses with intent to silence half the human race is sad indeed.

When Dr. Paul Yongii Cho invited me to be the evangelist for the

Spring Crusade of the Seoul Full Gospel Church, he was excited to think of the encouragement to ministry his women would receive through the fact that I, the guest speaker, was a woman. "A woman brought me the gospel when I was dying. My mother-in-law is my co-pastor. Two-thirds of my cell group leaders are women, and I find them loyal and faithful servants of the Lord, and responsive to my leadership," said Pastor Cho. Then he told me of his own awakening to the generally neglected ministries of women in the church. "As I was in prayer, the Lord revealed to me the plan for establishing the cell group system, which contributed in a large part to the phenomenal growth of the Seoul Full Gospel Church. But I had difficulty getting our men to commit to the giving of so much time and energy to cell group leadership, since they had their own business affairs to care for." Then said Cho, the Lord spoke to me, "Use the women!" I said, "No, Lord, this is Korea! We have our customs. The people will not receive women as leaders!" But use women he did, and with what phenomenal success! The call of the Spirit prevailed over the established traditions and customs of the culture, and the established church.

Fortunately for me, from the beginning I was privileged to see what a woman can do in speaking the wonderful words of life, when the two women who preached in our country school house were instruments for my enlightenment. Then, another mercy: the believers who nurtured me in my Christian infancy also believed women may be called to preach. When I was a teenager in Kelowna at Evangel Tabernacle, seeking God with all my heart and evidently anointed with the Holy Spirit, the pastor's wife, Mrs. Catrano, said encouragingly, "I believe you are called to preach!" John Lindahl, an elder in the same church, pointed to the visiting evangelist Evelyn Olsen and said, "Some day you will preach just like Evelyn, and even better." At the time the possibility seemed to me very remote.

But not everyone has been so fortunate. "Pastor, I would like to get involved in ministry," said one of the finest Christians I know to her minister. What she wanted was to participate in the soul-winning activities of the church, share scripture and lead in prayer. What she got was an introduction to the leader of the women's group, and from her an assignment, "You may bring the pickles next week."

Said she, "I am so tired of being told I may bring the pickles." In my capacity as pastor I was in a position to enable her to find her place in one-to-one soul-winning and discipling, and in the ministry of visitation. My plea on behalf of such women is that the leaders take responsibility, as the Scripture says they should do, to enable not only the men but also the women to fulfill their calling before God. "It was he who gave some to be apostles, some to be prophets, some to be evangelists, and some to be pastors and teachers, to prepare God's people for works of service so that the body of Christ may be built up...." (Ephesians 4: 11, 12 NIV)

Many women have sought my counsel as to how to find their way into fulltime Christian service. Of course, there is no one way. We do know however that before God women are equally responsible with men for their own life and service. My advice to earnest Christian women who feel they may be called to preach is first of all to work at serving your pastor and fellowship in a true spirit of submission, humility and sincerity. For what they have suffered at the hands of those who were their religious superiors, simply for being female, *multitudes* of women will at last receive special rewards for service, precisely because they took their frustrations and sufferings in a spirit of sweetness and grace for Jesus' sake.

Remember that if you have no burden for souls at home, you will not suddenly be transformed into a Catherine Booth merely by moving to another city, or going to college. If you have been to Bible College, and have a university degree besides, and still no openings, no pulpit opportunities, no chance to begin service on a pastoral team, you can either plant a church, or alternately seek a service opportunity with a parachurch organization (they serve missions and win souls also).

If you are persistently drawn to the preaching ministry, keep in mind that the same Holy Spirit who is calling you to ministry can also guide you into your proper place of service. Even Paul the apostle had to pray for doors to open, and rely upon the guidance of the Holy Spirit. The main thing is to keep your eyes on the Lord, and resist leaning on the arm of flesh which can only lead to disappointments, and, if you are not careful, to bitterness and rebellion. There is every indication in Scripture that increasingly, in the "last days" when God pours out his Spirit on all flesh, young men and women will prophesy (preach). (Acts 2: 18).

In these days believing Christians are in many ways in a position comparable to that of Simeon and Anna, just and devout persons who were waiting for "the consolation" of Israel. To Simeon the Holy Spirit revealed that he would not die until he had seen the Messiah, the consolation of Israel (v 26). When Simeon took the baby Jesus in his arms he exclaimed, "Now let your servant depart in peace, for my eyes have seen your salvation which you have prepared before the face of your people Israel." (Luke 2: 28-32).

Anna, a prophetess, a widow of 84 years of age, who served God with fasting and prayers day and night in the temple, arrived at the temple at just the right moment; on seeing Joseph and Mary, Jesus and Simeon together she also burst into praise, loudly proclaiming to those round about that looked for redemption that this child was the Messiah! Anyone, man or woman, could look for no greater ministry than to be in the Spirit at the right place, at just the right moment — to herald the coming of the King!

Notes

1   Judith Lushman, "Her Honour, Sir, Was Not a Person," *Weekend Magazine*, 14, 16 (date unknown).

2   Pauline Ashton, "Windy Nellie, The Canadian Woman's Best Friend," 18, *Weekend Magazine*, December 15, 1873.

3   Letha Scanzoni and Nancy Hardesty, *All We Are Meant To Be*, 12, Waco, TX: Word Books, 1974.

4   Catherine Booth, *Female Ministry: A Woman's Right to Preach the Gospel*, New York: The Salvation Army Supplies Printing and Publishing Department, 1975 (1859), 5.

5   Charles Trombley, *Who Said Women Can't Teach?*, Bridge: So. Plainfield, NJ, 1985, 74.

6   *Ibid.*, 19, 20.

7   Leonard Swidler, "Jesus Was a Feminist", *Catholic World*, January 1971, 178.

8   *Ibid.*, 179.

9   Trombley, *Ibid.*, 29.

10 *Ibid.*, 3.

11 Katherine C. Bushnell, *God's Word to Women* (1923) privately reprinted by Ray Munson, North Collins, NY.
12 Trombley, *Ibid.*, 179.
13 *Ibid.*, 184.
14 *Ibid.*, 185.
15 Lucille Sider Dayton, *The Feminist Movement and Scripture*, publisher unknown.
16 *New English Bible.*

15

FAMOUS VOICES

As the Sixties gave way to the Seventies my life, though very busy, had found a pleasant rhythm of its own. The Fraserview Assembly, the church Velma and I pastored, was outgrowing its facilities so that plans were on the drawing board for a new sanctuary in the spring of 1972. The radio ministry on CJOR 600, one of Vancouver's historic stations, had expanded to four and a half hours of open-line programming each Sunday. One of the dividends of the continuous investment of time, energy and love in several outreach ministries was the privilege of interaction with very interesting people, some local and some international.

RICHARD AND SABENA WURMBRAND

On occasion I have been powerfully moved by a book, in terms of impressions gathered, insights developed and convictions formed. Such was the case with Wurmbrand's *Tortured for Christ* which I read high in the jet stream en route to Toronto. Richard Wurmbrand suffered fourteen years of imprisonment, three years of which was solitary confinement, some for being a Jew, and some for being a Christian.[1] Sabena, his wife, bravely carried on as pastor of their Lutheran church after her husband was taken away for refusing to cooperate with the Communist authorities of Romania. Then she too was apprehended, enduring afflictions in prison camps, and inhuman harsh labor under severe winter conditions, as women too were forced to dig the Danube Canal. When the story progressed to the point where Richard and Sabena were reunited, I wept with them, and said prayerfully to the Lord, "If these people are real, if this is a true story of modern-day persons who were willing to be living martyrs for Jesus Christ, please send them this way so they can speak to our students at the universities." In two weeks, Godfrey Dawkins, a young Anglican minister to African students, leader of the Nairobi-based Trinity Fellowship, visited Vancouver. To my surprise, Godfrey, a good friend of the Wurmbrands, offered unhesitatingly to convey my invitation to Richard and Sabena.

My prayer was answered. Just as I had hoped, Richard Wurmbrand addressed hundreds of students in the Simon Fraser University Mall where at that time Mao Tse-tung's portrait hung in a prominent position. At the request of the students, he showed the scars of his many tortures under Communism. Along with Richard Wurmbrand's incisive witness on my radio open line, there was his exchange with Ed Murphy on Radio CKNW, and the city-wide meetings which I organized with other cooperating churches. I believe we must not forget our brothers and sisters in the family of God who suffer for Jesus' sake. The Wurmbrands came again and again to Vancouver with my complete cooperation. I felt myself honored to assist them, and consider myself a kindred spirit.

JACK BROWN

Jack Brown, junkie, con-man, convict and killer, kept my radio audience spellbound with the story of his life's misadventures and amazing transformation.[2] In studio with him was his faithful wife, Pearl, who, according to all that's reasonable, should have abandoned the fine-looking old dog years before. He knew the Birdman of Alcatraz, and Bonnie and Clyde before they knew each other, Machine Gun Kelly, and Al Capone. Jack himself spent four years on death row, as well as several years in solitary confinement. I was personally influenced by my encounter with the man who claimed that it was he who coined the phrase "monkey on my back."

Not that all of his story was gruesome and sad. I thank the Lord that his Christianity has not wiped out the sense of humor that helped him survive a near lifetime of harsh prisons. While serving time at Leavenworth, Jack volunteered to be a subject of research on drug addiction at the U.S. Public Health Service Hospital in Lexington, Kentucky.

"We'll give you all the dope you want, or can take. We'll see how much you can build a tolerance for and which kinds produce different effects," said the administrator. "Just one thing more. There comes a time when you have to go off it, cold turkey!" Jack continued at the CJOR mike, "Five chimpanzees and I made up the group for that experiment. For nine months I shot my limit, which some physicians have told me would be enough to kill fifty men if administered at one time to a normal unhooked system."

"My role in research was to show whether or not after being well-hooked, a smooth transition could be made to non-addiction, without terrifying effects. The experiment failed; the so-called merciful transition did not occur. There was only one thing left for me, and that was cold turkey .... sudden irrevocable withdrawal of the stuff that held my nerves together."

"We got very well attached to the chimpanzees. There were four males and a little female, Mary. Then the monkeys started dying and two old convicts who shouldn't have been on the program to begin with, conked out. Mary was the only survivor. We were over in the corner trying to die, both of us, rollin' around in our vomit and the doctor came by and saw us and said, 'I hope I don't lose these two.' I looked up to see which two he was talking about, and it was me and the last member of the monkey family. 'I hope so too,' I said."

"He wrote an article in one of the papers talkin' about me and Mary and kinda classified us together. As a matter of fact he very kindly said if we both survived he'd let us get married. But I told him, 'I can't commit bigamy, I'm already married to Miss Texas.' "[3]

Jack vomited, groaned and swore his way through his withdrawal and finally prayed to die. "By that time," said Jack, "I was helplessly nude so when an orderly came by to hose me down with warm water I begged him, 'Kill me! Kill me! Drown me! Oh God, please kill me!' "

Through it all Jack had not forgotten how to laugh, and now on the road sharing the secret of his deliverance through the gospel, he was thinking of men and women, old and young, hooked or being enticed to addiction. He saw himself on a rescue mission. Jack

Brown continued, "About three weeks later, huddled in a corner with Mary, the only female chimp in the group, again I heard the doctor tell someone, 'I hope these two don't die. The Lord knows they have fought hard enough.'"

His account of the torment of real life withdrawal was getting our full attention. I, an animal lover, could never forget his account of the sufferings of one other involuntary member of the research group: "I had just turned the corner down a patch which led me by one of the doctor's homes when I heard voices and a pitiful whining. I went around to the back yard where I discovered a doctor and two men working with a beautiful collie dog that had been used in research. He had been in confinement while kicking a habit but somehow escaped observation and got loose. His escape entailed scaling an extremely high fence which stood between him and the residence of the doctor who had been administering drugs to the animal. In his desperation for drugs he scaled the fence only to fall on the other side, breaking his back. In that condition, he crawled to the doctor's home where he lay at the back door, whining for the man to come and give him a shot of opiate."

"I shuddered as I walked away, remembering how recently I would have been willing to risk a broken back for a fix," recounted Jack.

Mary, the chimp, having gotten the "other monkey" off her back, turned out to be a role model for Jack. The doctor said, "We have tried to get her to eat fruit with narcotics in it, but she won't touch the stuff. Jack, I hope you do as well." But Jack wasn't as wise as Mary. According to his own account, though the sickness of withdrawal was unbelievable agony, he had gone cold turkey probably fifty times in his life.

The man who was in and out of eight prisons, addicted to heavy drugs for some thirty years, who survived four years in a four-by-seven-foot cell next door to the death cell and the electric chair, was now clean, clear-eyed and compassionate. He had had a meeting with God, and he knew how to talk about it. His conversion gave every despairing listener new hope, as he described his all-out commitment to God in prayer.

"I was pouring myself out in a conversation with a very real and powerful God. For an hour I confessed and asked forgiveness. I pleaded for cleansing and asked for a miracle." He, his dear old mother and his faithful wife had their miracle. He went on to write *Monkey Off My Back*, and witness to thousands of students, prisoners and ordinary citizens, including the congregation of Charles Spurgeon's former church in London, England. He began "It's a long way from a dirty cell just off Death Row in a terrible prison in America to this pulpit where Charles Spurgeon proclaimed the word ... but by the grace of God, I made it."

When Jack was with me in the CJOR studio in the Grosvenor Hotel in downtown Vancouver, I was glad to know him, and enjoy him as another of God's answers to prayer. I was satisfied we were communicating "hope" powerfully. I was also influenced to modify my view on capital punishment:

"Jack, what do you think of capital punishment?"

"I spent four years on death row" was his instant response, "and I'm against it." He was his own best argument.

MALCOLM AND KITTY MUGGERIDGE

"Mr. Muggeridge is the single living person about whom I feel there is nothing more for me to say of him by way of introduction and I am incompetent to say it," said William F. Buckley, Jr., as he prepared to interview Malcolm Muggeridge on Buckley's TV program, "Firing Line." There's some consolation for me, Bernice Gerard, in knowing that others, even famous media persons, were awed by Muggeridge. His career in journalism has spanned forty years and five continents; he has written for practically every newspaper, journal and magazine in Great Britain (as well as countless others elsewhere); he has been a reporter, interviewer, filmmaker, editor, and television personality, known to more people in the literate Western world than anyone in his intellectual class.

I had read *Jesus Rediscovered*[4] which Malcolm says is a collection of essays written by him, the iconoclastic seeker, over a period of years, but I could not have dreamed that one day both Malcolm and his wife Kitty would be in studio with me, drawing calls from delighted listeners. How I came to be blessed not only with their presence in the studio on three occasions, but also the enormous privilege of personal friendship, I will share in pages to come after this comment on broadcasting with the Muggeridges. Callers were quick to draw Mr. Muggeridge into a discussion of his books, the famous people he knew, and his personal faith.

CALLER: Am I speaking to Malcolm Muggeridge? (*Many people assume that the radio moderator has to hand the phone to the guest so the guest too may hear the question. In fact, the calls come amplified through a separate small speaker box and are heard by all in the studio*).

It is a great joy to hear your voice. Over the years I have been very much influenced by you, not only by what you said but by the way you said it. Malcolm, you have been associated with men like Bernard Shaw, H. G. Wells, Bertrand Russell and Beatrice and Sidney Webb; I have been influenced by them but I have discovered they have no message.

MUGGERIDGE: Quite, agreed.

CALLER: They have nothing to draw with and the well is deep. I wanted to ask you a question about Shaw. He seemed to be irritated by religion, and so very critical and yet when his wife died and was being buried, he stood beside the coffin and sang "I know my Redeemer liveth." How can this be, so much bitterness and then apparent capitulation?

MUGGERIDGE: I didn't know him well, but I knew quite a lot about him. I think he was absolutely haunted by religion all his life, and would have loved to be a religious man. But simply, I would say, there are indications of a real leaning in this direction but I think he was frightened of it, and always broke off to be funny. For that reason at the end of his life he was somewhat a melancholy person. In the case of H. G. Wells, of course, the collapse was total. I don't know if you ever came across the little book of his called *Mind at the End of Its Tether*. He was completely and absolutely broken, and turned his face to the wall. Wells and Shaw were classic examples of those precluded from grasping the reality of life by their fantastic egotism.

At that moment Kitty leant toward Malcolm with a written suggestion. Her aunt Beatrice Webb, founder of the Fabian Society with her husband Sidney, Wells and Shaw, was another classic example of a heart with a yearning for God and a head which turned away. Malcolm continued, "Kitty's Aunt Bea was a woman of initially strongly marked religious tendency, and it was Herbert Spencer ... who actually turned her off it. I think that her life too was a tremendous tragedy because she turned her back on what had so tremendously attracted her. They lived in the Embankment in London, and she in the early times always turned into Westminster Abbey for her prayers. They, all three, had in common that they never experienced the essential quality of humility. The ultimate is for the religious person to kneel down and say to God, 'Thy will be done.' That's what they could not do."

One of the interesting things about Malcolm is that he knows, or has known personally, writers, philosophers, artists, statesmen, politicians petty and otherwise, and people of electronic media fame, that students of higher learning and people like me have only read about. We studied Bertrand Russell and his philosophy, more or less meekly learning to take in and regurgitate his substance, at least for examination purposes. We who were Christians resisted with all our might his notion that in the end nothing would remain for mankind but unyielding despair. Malcolm commented that when he stood up against Russell, he experienced actual physical fatigue due to the conflict. My own stress in those campus debates in which some professors actually bullied the class was expressed in nightmares with a cosmic dimension. In my dream I would be falling, falling, or somehow in flight in the immense uncharted expanse of the universe.

Said Malcolm about a radio session he once had with Bertrand Russell, "I had spoken in praise of Christianity, and he rounded on me with unexpected ferocity, shrilly insisting that everything most cruel and destructive and wicked which had happened in the world since the end of the Roman Empire had been due to the Christian religion and its founder. I shouted back. It was an absurd and unedifying scene which nonetheless left me physically exhausted, as though I had been engaged in a physical wrestling match. I remember still with a lively sense of horror how, as Russell's rage mounted, a flush rose up his thin white stringy neck, like a climbing thermometer, to suffuse his human features, making of the great philosopher a flushed ape."[5]

With Malcolm Muggeridge in studio the broadcast actually touched greatness, as he, the master wordsmith, continued his confessions in somewhat the same vein as St. Augustine. Elsewhere he has written, "Words being my single pursuit, I have to accept my output of them as being, as it were, my gross personal product. And what an output! Millions and millions, on all manner of subjects and in all manner of contexts. ... Surveying now this monstrous Niagara of words so urgently called for and delivered, I confess they signify to me a lost life. Possibilities vaguely envisaged but never realized. A light glimpsed only to disappear. Something vaguely caught, as it might be distant music or an elusive fragrance; something full of enchantment and the promise of ecstasy."[6]

Throughout his long adventuresome life, he says, he had never really cared for the world or felt particularly at home in it.... "As though it were a foreign land and I a stranger, knowing no one and unable to speak the language." He was in truth to be numbered at last with those who like Abraham look for a city which hath foundations whose builder and maker is God. (Heb. 11: 10).

I had gone to the studio well-armed with certain of my favorite Muggeridge texts typed and ready, knowing that what touched my heart and fired my imagination would surely get to my audience in the same way. It was music to my ears to hear Malcolm at my request reading his own stuff:

"Despite the agnosticism of my home and upbringing," he continued, "I cannot recall a time when the notion of Christ and Christianity was not enormously appealing to me. ... I knew from a very early age — how I cannot tell — that the New Testament contained the key to how to live. I somehow knew it to be our only light in a dark world. Not just in my father's sense that Jesus himself was a good man, and his moral precepts greatly to be admired, even though his ostensible followers in the various churches ignored and perverted them ... He was God or He was nothing."

No, what appealed to me were the wild extravagances of faith; the phrases about God's wisdom being men's foolishness, St. Francis of Assisi rejoicing at being naked on the naked earth, the sublime paradoxes of *The Marriage of Heaven and Hell*. Surveying the abysmal chasm between my certainty that everything human beings tried to achieve was inadequate to the point of being farcical, that mortality itself was a kind of gargoyle joke, and my equal certainty that every moment of every day was full of enchantment and infinitely precious; that human love was the image vouchsafed us of God's love irradiating the whole universe; that, indeed, imbedded in each grain of sand was eternity, to be found and explored, as geologists explored the antiquity of fossils through their markings — surveyed this chasm, yawning in its vastness to the point of inducing insanity, tearing us into schizophrenic pieces, I grasped that over it lay, as it were, a cable-bridge, frail, swaying but passable. And this bridge, this reconciliation between the black despair of lying bound and gagged in the tiny dungeon of the ego, and soaring upwards into the white radiance of God's universal love — this bridge was the Incarnation, whose truth expresses that of the desperate need it meets. Because of our physical hunger we know there is bread; because of our spiritual hunger we know there is Christ.[7]

One of my listeners wrote afterwards "Thanks to God's grace and Malcolm Muggeridge, *Jesus Rediscovered* started me back into the family after many years in the wilderness." A secretary at Trinity Western University said it was Muggeridge whom God used to bring her to faith.

Unsolicited testimonials piled in one after another. Muggeridge, who described himself as an actor standing in the wings of the theater waiting for his cue to go on stage, only to find that his lines didn't fit the play, had at last found the play to which his lines belonged. To me he wrote, "Today, Sunday, is one of those rare sunny winter's days you get in England, and I'm looking out of my study window at the newly ploughed brown earth and bare trees against the skyline with great joy. Such a peaceful scene that it's hard to remember how all round about the world's in turmoil. I feel often like the Apostle Paul — that the time of my departure is at hand, and I truly have no other purpose than to employ what little remaining time there is in serving the Lord to compensate for some at least of the much more time spent in pursuing other empty purposes." (January 11, 1976)

People looked for Malcolm to declare himself as a twentieth-century Apostle Paul, giving us an account of a dramatic Damascus Road conversion. But no such statement has come forth. The truth is rather that Malcolm has been interested all his life in questions that are, at their heart, religious. It was the publication of *Jesus Redisco-*

vered that catapulted his name into world circulation as a spokesperson for the Christian faith. At about the same time, he became active in the right-to-life movement which is where I first met him. Later, in 1985 when I visited his home in Robertsbridge, Sussex, I asked him what difference to his Christian faith becoming a Roman Catholic had made? He answered, "No difference, really! I was a believer on Jesus Christ before I became a Roman Catholic." He went on graciously to point out that the army of the Lord has many different contingents, meaning communities of faith within the church universal.

PAUL YONGGI CHO

Perhaps the most dramatically supernatural of all the life histories that crossed my broadcast desk was that of Paul Yonggi Cho of Korea. From the moment I first heard him speak in Rio de Janeiro, I felt, "There is something special about this man," and wanted to hear more. Now in Vancouver, he was telling his story on the air.

> When I was 18 years old, after the Korean war, having suffered malnutrition because of our great poverty, I was struck down with an extreme case of tuberculosis. The doctor gave me three months at the most. Since I was born and raised a Buddhist, I naturally called on Buddha for help. With a three-month calendar on the wall, I chanted to Buddha, imploring him to help me get ready to die, even though I was frightened to die, and had a burning desire to live.
>
> People came and went from the shelter where I lay covered with a torn dirty blanket, some saying kind words but words without hope. One day when I was breathing with great difficulty I cried out to an unknown God, "God, if there is a God in the universe, please get me ready to die."
>
> In less than one week a young woman knocked on my door, and entered carrying a Bible. I was stunned for in our culture women are not forward, and men dislike being taught by them. Arrogantly I ordered her to leave but she cried, "I can see that you are dying; I want to tell you about Christ Jesus, my Savior."

Says Cho, "The doctor described my physical condition at that time saying 'The right lung is completely destroyed by tuberculosis, the upper part having collapsed and gangrene set in. The left lung is also tubercular. Malnutrition and hard work have caused your heart to enlarge and it cannot circulate the blood. There is no medical help for these things.'"

In many ways, the visitation of the mysterious young woman was as miraculous as any other element in the supernatural experiences of Paul Yonggi Cho. He cursed her, and threatened her, reminding her that with millions of tuberculous germs flying around, she too would become infected. To which she replied, "My Christ will protect me." When she left, he sighed, "Bless Buddha, she is gone!"

The following morning she was back again, this time to sing and read aloud from her Bible. Again says Pastor Cho, "I cursed her and called her a Christian dog. On the fifth day when she came, I asked why she continued to come and pray for me." "There is someone who constrains me to come here and pray for you," she replied. "Who is it?" he asked. "My Jesus," she answered, and the tears began to roll down her cheeks. "Suddenly," says Cho, "My obstinacy was broken, and I too began to cry, and said 'Your Jesus I want to know.'" Mysteriously, to this day, Pastor Yonggi Cho does not know the identity of the woman who brought him to his Savior and Healer. He simply remembers her as the woman with the shining face.

His trials were far from over, "Still I was carrying a high fever and coughing up blood, but in my heart I knew I was being healed. Before I was whining and crying, now I was rejoicing and praying."

Pastor Cho continued to share on Radio CJOR what I have not seen in print anywhere: the account of his personal struggle with sickness, and the submission to God of his own life. After his initial commitment, with which an Assemblies of God missionary to Korea also assisted him, he regained strength sufficient to permit him to return to his studies in medical school. His heart was set upon a career as a surgeon. "Then after about a year," says Cho, "I began to vomit blood again. I was terrified so I rented a small room and began to fast and pray to really know the will of God."

I locked myself in and began to pray, "Jesus, I want to meet you and have a consultation about my future." The hours dragged on until at 2:00 a.m. Cho lay down upon his bed in exhaustion. As he told it in our studio, "I felt absolutely powerless but I was very much awake. Instantly my whole house was on fire with smoke rolling about in the ceiling. I tried to shriek, 'Fire!' to call for help but my cry was barely audible. When I looked up someone was standing there with a white, white streaming robe, and I said, 'Oh, fireman, pull me out, pull me out!' but he was doing nothing. His face was bleeding and I saw some thorny things crushing down on his forehead .... Then suddenly all the fire and smoke disappeared and I could see only the person and the light shining out of His face, and I said, 'I am with Jesus.' Then the love began cascading into my soul, so that I was completely scorched under this shining love.... When I tried to speak no words would come; my tongue and lips were frozen.

"When I attempted persistently to say 'Jesus' in the Korean language, I realized the language I was speaking was not Korean, and I was frightened to death.... I really felt that my inner soul was released and love was flowing out of my heart like a river. Then Jesus spoke, 'My son, you have been looking for fame, money and the glory of this world to this time. Sooner or later you will lose every one of those things, and it will all be just ashes to you. You must make a decision for heaven or hell.... I raised you up to bring my message to this generation.' "

The audacious, world-famous pastor-to-be said, "No, Jesus, you know that I am not preparing to be a minister, as I still have an open cavity in my right lung."

Jesus replied, "Turn yourself over to me. I will help you."

Paul Yonggi Cho says, "I reached out my hand and as soon as I touched Jesus Christ, something like the electric power of lightning shook me through and through. I was so thoroughly shaken up that I fell on the ground as if dead; when I returned to consciousness it was early morning with the bright sunshine flooding my room."

Our program theme was "Experiencing the Supernatural." We had the real life evidence in the robustly healthy pastor Cho who was sitting at his mike across from me, his voice ringing out with clarity the truthfulness of his claims. We talked together on CJOR exactly twenty-three years after his miraculous healing. At that time he was pastor of a twenty-seven thousand-member congregation for which multiple services had to be held each Sunday in the ten thousand-seat auditorium which was patterned architecturally after the famed

Albert Hall in London, England.*

In the tremendous rapport that developed during our ninety minutes together communicating God's love, Pastor Cho told me about
the inspiration he had just received: "I invite you to come to Korea
to be the speaker for our spring evangelism crusade at the Seoul Full
Gospel Church. You will be such an encouragement to our women! I
will be your interpreter."

The Korean ministry visit was a spiritual highlight of my life. Pastor Cho spoke at five Sunday services, beginning at seven in the
morning and continuing through three in the afternoon. The crusade
for which I was a special speaker was a mid-week event, but I was
given five minutes at each of the five Sunday services to introduce
myself and tell of my expectations for the meetings to come.

Up to the high platform in the great auditorium Pastor Cho and I
would go, then after the service of typically fervent Korean worship,
the entire auditorium would empty completely so that the waiting
multitudes could have their turn. The pastor and I would go quickly
to a lower floor to a private reception room where we had Korean
soup, a banana and some ginseng. Then up again to another service,
abounding in prayer, praise and preaching until at last, at the end of
the day, we arrived at the bottom of the long, long stairway to find
sixty to one hundred elders lined up to bow and bid the pastor farewell for that day.

As I stood to preach in Pastor Cho's pulpit, four in-house TV
monitors revealed parts of the audience in overflow auditoriums and
hallways. Needless to say I was nervous, and prayed up a storm before I dared set foot in the place. Back home in Vancouver, I was at
that time spending many hours each week at City Hall where I was
serving as an alderman in a city of unbelief; thus the Korean church,
with people who truly believed God answers by fire, was a dramatic
experience in contrasts.

My first thought was, "What could I possibly say to these spiritually alive Koreans who suffered so much for the Master's sake when
they saw their homeland drenched in the blood of Christian mar-

* As of May 1988, the congregation numbers 530,000 persons.

tyrs." Pastor Cho had said on air in Vancouver, "When Communism came down, they destroyed more than two thousand churches and killed five hundred leading ministers .... under the Japanese occupation three hundred thousand Christians were martyred. Another source of sorrow is the knowledge that under the Communists, in addition to those killed, large numbers were captured and sent to Siberia."

But Grace, the wife of Pastor Paul Yonggi Cho, encouraged me to go ahead, saying, "Our people love you. When you stand in the pulpit they think of you as they do my mother, Sister Choi." Sister Choi, at that time Cho's co-pastor, had contributed greatly to Paul Yonggi Cho's success in the huge ministry God granted them. She was the powerful praying leader behind the Prayer Mountain where we found over a thousand people praying at mid-day.

Pastor Cho himself first gave me tips for my pulpit presentation. "When you speak, use short sentences. The Korean sentence must begin at the end of your English sentence; I can't start till you finish." Believe me, I tried. The interpreter has often been referred to as "an interrupter" both by the speaker and the audience. My previous experience in foreign lands allowed me to see that, even through an interpreter, communication can be effective, especially as both persons experience the liberation of the Holy Spirit. Later Cho said, "I feel comfortable with you beside me in the pulpit; you remind me of my mother-in-law, Sister Choi. I have had many guest speakers from America more eloquent than you, but I prefer your unadorned direct approach, and the spirit of your ministry." How good of him to take a moment to let me know.

Notes

1   Richard Wurmbrand, *Tortured for Christ*, Hodder and Stoughton, 1967.
2   Jack Brown, *Monkey Off My Back*, Zondervan Publishing House: Grand Rapids, Michigan, 1971.
3   Bernice Gerard's CJOR Encounter, June 24, 1973.
4   Malcolm Muggeridge, *Jesus Rediscovered*, Fontana Books: Great Britain, 1969.
5   Muggeridge, *The Green Stick*, 175-6.
6   *Ibid.*, 14.
7   *Ibid.*, 81-82.

16

AVENGING ANGEL

How did I get involved in politics in the Seventies, and with what effect? The following story filed by John Faustman for *The Vancouver Courier* was in many ways typical of the secular media's view of Bernice Gerard the politician. Whether the subject (or victim) of the report approved it in principle or in detail was, of course, immaterial.

AVENGING ANGEL IN "LOOSE CITY"

Two years ago, in a protest against the rising tide of moral turpitude, city Alderman Bernice Gerard took her infamous walk on Vancouver's nudist Wreck Beach. She's had one foot in the camp of the righteous and the other foot in the headlines ever since.

Today, after three years' service on city council, Miss Gerard's commitment to what she thinks is right is as strong as ever.

She is thinking of taking another Wreck Beach walk this year. "As far as Vancouver's concerned," she told me last week, "I don't like to see the beaches go nudist, and I connect these things with prostitution."

"Because we're so loose, we collect all the pimps from Alaska to San Francisco. There's a lawlessness here..." she adds, and then goes on to talk volubly about the erosion of standards, desensitization and the effect of pornography on our "young people."

It's like Bernice Gerard to cover a host of topics in a single burst of sentences. She discharges the moral shotgun of her speech at one particular demon, and whole legions of them fall.

In fact, Gerard talks like one of those articles in a Watchtower magazine — she titles each statement with some horrific lead-in: Is civilization doomed? Will illicit sex destroy us? Are drugs killing our young?, and by the time you get to the end of the story, you've forgotten what the question was. Not that it matters. The question is always answered in the title.

This is known as evangelism. Spreading the word. And that is precisely what Bernice Gerard has been doing since she was 13.

An orphan from the time she was just a few days old, Gerard was raised by a Canadian Indian family. It was a rough and tumble, very "irreligious" upbringing, and Gerard describes it briefly in her autobiography — an embarrassingly ill-written spiritual account called *Converted in the Country*.

Her early years with a drunken foster father stamped her irremediably.

"I saw enough liquor in the first little while, I determined I would never get drunk like that," she says.

Then, at 13 she went to school one day, and for the first time in her life she heard someone read from the Bible. She was born again. "I felt brand new and totally forgiven, and in love with the world," she says, describing her conversion.

Her teenage years were spent in one foster home after another, as she found herself a ward of the child welfare department.

"I am an example of what the government can do," she likes to say, and she describes how her guardian moved her from one home to another, in an attempt to wean her away from an excessive passion for fundamentalist religion.

Even at 15, young Bernice was convinced that certain churches were "wrong," and she writhed through Baptist services in a fit of guilt.

"My guardian decided I was too religious for my own good; that the best thing I could do was get broadened out. And I was narrow, no question about that," she admits. But no matter which home they placed her in, Bernice stuck to her beliefs. Though she had friends during high school, she never succumbed to the evils of drinking, smoking or dancing.

During her first job as a teacher in a small town in the Interior, Gerard teamed up with the McColl sisters — a pair of itinerant evangelists. The three of them toured the world for the next ten years, but 1959 found Gerard back in Vancouver, where she enrolled at UBC.

She wanted to be a writer, "but the creative writing people scared me to death," she says. "They were all taking their whiskey straight, and pulling the hairs of their beards while they pondered, and I thought: 'What could I write for those people?' " She took her master's degree in 17th century literature, instead, and wrote her thesis, appropriately enough, on Milton.

In the meantime, she was teaching courses at the Western Pentecostal Bible College, and during the summer she toured the province, preaching in an open-air tent.

The preaching never stopped, although today Bernice has managed to reach a larger audience.

She broadcasts a weekly religious show for CJOR, and she is the pastor of the Fraserview Assembly.

The particular form of her religion goes under the name of something called "charismatic renewal" — a down home blend of Christian redemption and optimism that has as its basis the converted souls of former junkies and reformed Las Vegas gamblers.

Personal testimony is the key to winning sinners for Jesus.

"It's good news. That's why I do it," said Bernice Gerard when I visited her in her basement suite office this week.

Aside from a wall full of books, and a table full of electronic tape-recording equipment, and a full-sized poster of Salvador Dali's *Crucifixion* on the wall behind her desk, her office had the air of a living room in Burnaby.

Her desk was littered with missionary pamphlets, there were photographs of her nieces and nephews lining the window, and a bright-colored quilt covered the one chesterfield in the room.

Gerard herself was dressed in a conservative flower print dress, with neat white pumps on her feet and a small gold cross at her throat.

She has a mannish, blocky presence. There is nothing reticent about her, and her opinions are as tight as her carefully set short brown hair.

She places her body distinctly in a chair, and once having settled, her hands seldom move from the prearranged position on her lap. You get the feeling that Bernice Gerard is prepared for anything — including the end of the world.

She peppers her conversation with words like "abstemious" and "redemption" and she quotes passages from the Bible, and at times her country background shows through, when she describes her life as "a big, long whomping journey."

She mentions other.evangelists, like Oral Roberts and Aimee Semple McPherson, and though she denies a tendency towards fire-and-brimstone preaching, she is capable of being instantly abrasive.

"The left-wingers on city council would tend to say that poverty is obscene. But I just received some dirty stuff in the mail from someone who wants to upset me. Now that's obscene. Pornography!" she says, "Heaven help us!"

From Gerard's point of view, the world out there is full of unscrupulous people, roping in the young, getting them on drugs, and into what she describes as "the sex scene." She sees herself as a bulwark against such tendencies. She welcomes her job on city council because it allows her a further chance to spread the word.

Her thin lips move towards a grin as she describes her working relationship with her more worldly council colleagues. You can sense her pleasure at being so different. "I noticed when I first went to council, different members were apprehensive about me," she says.

"I can recall Alderman Kennedy asking for a certain kind of liquor at Puil's house one night, and then looking over at me — as though he had to apologize or declare himself." She sighs. "Thank God we've got over that. Now I drink my orange juice and nobody comments."

She will hazard few comments about her role as an alderman, however, though she does find that "some of the more colorful people on council speak their minds." She describes Harry Rankin as "very colorful."

When it comes to colorful, however, few can approach Gerard. She sees the transition from evangelism to politics as a simple one, since: "...Every Christian should have a prophetic witness."

She laughs when I suggest she's becoming the avenging angel in Lotusland, but she does not deny that some of her prophecies have drawn a lot of attention.

Over the past few years she has repeatedly warned us that abortion is ruining us, that we have become the "Mecca for prostitution," and that the stage play *O, Calcutta!* might completely destroy what was left of our thin moral fiber.

"That play," she says, "would better have been done in one of those smut theaters."

A curious anomaly in a century approaching the 1980's, Bernice Gerard is following her own particular light. Many have disagreed with her, others have criticized her, but those who know her would never suggest she is not honest. At the height of her career, both as an evangelist and a politician, the thing Bernice Gerard fears most is that she will become a cariacature of herself. It may already be too late.[1]

My self-portrait would be very different from the one drawn by John Faustman in *The Courier*. From day one, after my election to Vancouver City Council, my political career was off to a noisy start. Weary from campaigning, I only reluctantly responded to the suggestion made by a BCTV reporter that I meet their crew in a local pornography shop. As it happened I did know where the pornography shops were. Our Citizens for Integrity group, founded with Pastor Bob Birch and patterned after the Festival of Light, was committed to keeping Judaic and Christian principles in law, and, with that end in view, had researched the porn industry in our city. Inside the Love Shop was literally tons of hard core pornography, violent sadistic literature showing women with their throats cut, or hanging spread-eagle by ropes. The owner of the shop ordered the television people out, and somehow I got locked in. BCTV made the most of the story.

Vancouver, world class city, gateway to the Orient, required that the mayor and ten members of Council at large be elected from the whole city, not from individual wards. As a pastor and broadcaster in the city, I had become increasingly aware of the lack of representation in city affairs of what was then called "the silent majority," and also of persons with deep Christian commitment who had something really worthwhile to contribute.

"Shame! You are bringing your personal morality into Council chamber," was shouted at me on more than one occasion. In that milieu, it sounded like a rational statement, but in fact the statement is absurd. We need good people to represent us at the civic, provincial and federal level, not people who leave their principles at home.

Doug Little, Vancouver City Clerk, who in the august chamber of the Council had spent years of his life seated just below the Mayor listening to Council proceedings had warned me not to run for election, adding "You are doing too much good the way you are." His concern was that too many Christians run for office with good intentions, then, like chameleons, blend with the foliage instead of showing their true colors. That certainly didn't happen to me, although everything else did. Somewhere towards the end of my first two-year term, I asked cautiously, "Doug, how am I doing?" He replied, "Just great! In fact, I am considering retiring early, and running for Council myself. I intend to act just like you do!"

But people who take stands lend themselves to cariacature. The individuals who make up the press gallery rarely found occasion to commend my hard work or competence, although the city engineer, Bill Curtis, told me, "You are a good alderman." My colleague on Council, Warnett Kennedy, said he understood somewhat of my motivation. In a personal note to me when I was defeated at the polls after four years on Council, he again warmly commended my general competence. Council's function is city planning, social services, financial planning, the levying and collecting of taxes, the construction and maintenance of bridges, streets, sewers, and water works, the allocating of funds for parks, civic theaters and art galleries, health and zoning concerns and a myriad of other things including garbage collection and dog catching. Ray Spaxman, the Vancouver city planner who has literally made his mark on our spectacular slopes and skyline, once in my hearing referred to City Hall as the "spiritual center of the city." "No, Ray," I replied, "Caesar's palace perhaps, but all too much of what goes on in our city hall demonstrates that the faith of the participants is 'that man lives by bread alone.'" The whole idea of participatory democracy is that all segments of life and thought in a community have equal opportunity to bring their best to the process of governing.

"But Christians have no right to impose their beliefs on others" is frequently put forth as a reason for Christians to be nonparticipants. I hope that in a free society we will take a "live and let live" attitude but we will always in an orderly society need red and green lights for direction of traffic, the yellow line down the middle of the road, and other similar restraints devised by consensus and shared responsibility.

For example, on Council's Community Service Committee, did I, a teetotaler, always vote down a liquor licence application? Some said, "As a Christian you should never vote yes to a liquor license." Granted, I know the horrendous damage done by excess of alcohol. But my view is that the alderman is not there to make up the laws on an *ad hoc* basis as he/she goes along. As a Council we have put by-laws in place. If the application meets the criteria for acceptance, my personal abstemiousness should not hinder the other person's business or personal interests.

But I don't underestimate the problem, either. At one point when I was judging these matters, there were enough liquor outlets in Vancouver for two-thirds of the drinking population to sit down together at one time. When there are too many proprietors of booze outlets competing with each other for customers, in order to get ahead of the competitors, certain places offer live sex shows, with nude women cavorting, whips in hand, to entertain male customers. On tour with other Council members who were investigating a certain hotel, I saw girls gyrating in the nude in front of mirrors before an audience of men who sat drooling into their beer at mid-day. Needless to say, I voted no every chance I got to these ugly, exploitive watering holes that trafficked in female flesh. My prayer was always, "Oh God, where are the reformers? David Livingstone, who fought the slave trade, we need you now to help set the captives free!"

It was a columnist for the *B.C. Catholic* who first suggested that I let my name stand for nomination to run for alderman with the Civic Non-Partisan Association. It seemed like the right time. Previously, I *had* considered running for Vancouver School Board, but discovered that provincial law barred anyone criminal, lunatic or clergy from taking elected office. By that time I was serving at the University of B.C. as chaplain, and among other things, was the first woman to officiate as the clergy person at the University's baccalaureate service. Subsequently, as the urge to seek a place on Council seized me, Premier David Barrett's government set new guidelines, thereby giving clergy equal access.

Also by this time women were increasingly visible in city politics. The story around City Hall is that once women got into Council, the plumbing in the washrooms had to be renovated. This provoked something of a political debate since it was suggested that the men's latrines near the Council Chamber not be taken out but merely covered over, and a temporary place made for fixtures more suitable to the female frame. It was not expected that women would last long in civic politics.

Since I had been on open-line radio for over thirteen years by this time, I was well known. In making my decision to run for office, more important to me than the urging of friends, or evaluation of favorable circumstances, was my own developing Biblical understanding.

I literally preached myself into politics, shocking as the idea may be to many conservative other-worldly evangelicals. Considerable negative comment came my way from those conservative evangelicals who imagined our witness would in some way be damaged. At the same time those non-believers who were apprehensive of "born again Christians" achieving political power, imagined that behind every born-again politician is a monolithic, oppressive, power-hungry church structure. My own church congregation was favorable, even enthusiastic about my venture in faith. To the official board I said, "Please pray about this. If you are opposed, I will defer to your judgment." The Rev. Tom Johnstone, who was in our church the morning I announced that I had received the nomination, commented on the extraordinarily positive response of the congregation, which spontaneously burst into applause.

Some of my Christian critics were particularly concerned that I, as a minister of the gospel in the political arena, would receive a great deal of persecution simply for who I was. More difficult for me to deal with was the fact that some people believed that ordinary believers in our metropolitan area, and particularly those in my own congregation would have to "take persecution" on my account. Their idea seemed to be that if we all keep reasonably quiet and inactive in community affairs, we will save ourselves a lot of trouble.

The truth is that Christians will be spoken against as evil-doers whether they deserve it or not, as Scripture says in 1 Peter 2:11,12, (NEB) "Dear friends, I beg you, as aliens in a foreign land, to abstain from the lusts of the flesh which are at war with the soul. Let all your behaviour be such as even pagans can recognize as good, and then, whereas they malign you as criminals now, they will come to see for themselves that you live good lives, and will give glory to God on the day when he comes to hold assize." Peter is confident of one thing: those that live godly in Christ Jesus will be spoken against. Jesus affirms the same. (Luke 12: 49-53) Trouble because one is faithful to God is only a short-term problem.

In preaching on *Exodus*, I took a long hard look at a fully developed prophetic ministry as demonstrated in the life of Moses who is cited in Deuteronomy 34: 10 as the greatest of Israel's prophets. We Bible believers today understand the urgency of the Great Commission, but are frequently guilty of taking an either/or approach when we should be saying, "Yes, let us preach the good news for the salvation of the lost, *and* explore every possible means to act and speak prophetically to our contemporaries." The promise of the Lord is for the Holy Spirit to be poured out on all flesh, "Even on my servants, both men and women, I will pour out my Spirit in those days, and they will prophesy." (Acts 2: 18 NIV)

Those who prophesy in the assembly of believers provide edifica-
tion, comfort and exhortation. The reaction of nonbelievers to the
ministry of the prophets shows that they dealt with sin and salvation,
wrath and grace: "But if an unbeliever or someone who does not understand comes in while everybody is prophesying, he will be convinced by all that he is a sinner and will be judged by all, and the
secrets of his heart will be laid bare. So he will fall down and worship
God, exclaiming, 'God is really among you.' " (1 Corinthians 14: 24,
25 NIV)

The prophet who foretells the future is easily recognized, especially if he or she predicts some future event such as the return of
Jesus the Messiah. But another equally important prophetic task is
"forthtelling," that is "telling forth the will of God for the situation."
With an understanding that this is for every believer, we move easily
into involvement with social and ethical concerns, right conduct and
right relationships.

If the prophetic ministry is only to be exercised with believers in
the believers' meeting, how is it that the prophets of the Bible received such a vigorous response from the unbelievers? Stoned, torn
asunder, slain with the sword, etc? (Hebrews 11: 37)

We gain an insight into our responsibility as Christians when we
realize that, because of the Incarnation, everywhere we go, Jesus
goes. We are indwelt by the Holy Spirit. Therefore, at the market-
place, the school, waterfront, bank, bakery, farm, fish cannery or
Parliament, our daily lives have a "prophetic" impact. Since our life
style is made up of various components, each of which reflects our
value system, whether we think of it or not, each of us is a prophetic
word to our contemporaries.

For example, should we or should we not drink alcoholic beverages? For some of us, to abstain is to emphasize that we choose
rather to be "high" in the Spirit. "Do not get drunk with wine, which
leads to debauchery. Instead, be filled with the Spirit. Speak to one
another with psalms, hymns and spiritual songs. Sing and make
music in your heart to the Lord." (Ephesians 5: 18 NIV) To abstain is
to identify compassionately with that large percentage of our society
known as alcoholics. We protest against all conditions, circumstances and social pressures that serve to keep people in bondage. We

don't insist that every person act in the same way we do. But society should recognize the legitimacy of our conviction.

Unfortunately, Christians often shrink from the prophetic task, and somehow see the "condemning of ungodliness" as embarrassing to themselves and their church, and as an end in itself whereas righteous living is a part of God's redemptive action and a proper expression of His love. (Ephesians 5: 6-11)

On this point the Apostle Paul did not equivocate.

> Let no one deceive you with empty words, for because of such things God's wrath comes on those who are disobedient. Therefore do not be partners with them. For you were once darkness, but now you are light in the Lord. Live as children of light (for the fruit of the light consists in all goodness, righteousness and truth) and find out what pleases the Lord. Have nothing to do with the fruitless deeds of darkness, but rather expose them. (Ephesians 6: 6-11 NIV)

A biblical example to be employed with great benefit is that of Moses who was born in terrible times, when Pharaoh had embarked on a program of genocide for Hebrews, or at least population control (Exodus 2). Moses had first to hear from the Lord before he had clarity about his own call:

> The Lord said, "I have indeed seen the misery of my people in Egypt. I have heard them crying out because of their slave drivers, and I am concerned about their suffering. So I have come down to rescue them from the hand of the Egyptians, and bring them up out of that land into a good and spacious land, a land flowing with milk and honey. ... I am sending you to Pharaoh.... (Exodus 3: 7-10 NIV)

The Lord told Moses, "I will send you, I am come down to deliver them." In reply, Moses pled personal unfitness. "Who am I, that I should go to Pharaoh and bring the children of Israel out of Egypt?" (3: 11) Understandably, he fears the unbelief of the people, and is aware of his own lack of eloquence. (4: 1, 10) Finally, Moses summons all his courage and cries out, "O my Lord, send someone else to do it." (4: 13) At this the Lord is angry with Moses for his audacity; nevertheless he provides Aaron who will be glad to serve as Moses mouthpiece. (v 14)

The parallels for today are convincing and compelling. Moses did not develop as a person for God all at once. Raised a member of the royal household, he was "moved with compassion" at seeing his own people in need, and personally experienced an identity crisis. On seeing an Egyptian striking one of his fellow Hebrews, Moses killed him and hid his body in the sand. (Exodus 2) When he fled Egypt after this, Moses went to the rescue of the seven daughters of Jethro the priest, whose flock was being driven by unfriendly shepherds from the watering troughs.

Moses' ministry as a prophet begins when, out of the compassion of his heart, he is forced to identify with the Israelites in their bondage: "By faith Moses, when he had grown up, refused to be known as the son of Pharaoh's daughter. He chose to be mistreated along with the people of God rather than to enjoy the pleasures of sin for a short time. He regarded disgrace for the sake of Christ as of greater value than the treasures of Egypt, because he was looking ahead to his reward." (Hebrews 11: 24-26 NIV).

"By faith he left Egypt, not fearing the king's anger; he persevered because he saw him who is invisible." (11: 27 NIV). Here perhaps is a clue to the *real* reason much of today's Christian public witness is weak and ineffective. You cannot forsake Egypt, if Egypt is all you have. The wrath of Egypt is indeed awesome if you have no pervading awareness of the might and power and glory of Him who is invisible.

We should not be surprised, as we study Moses, to find that the prophet's first task is to denounce all offenses against the law. With the power of charisma (anointing), the Holy Spirit awakens in each person that hidden moment when light is accepted or rejected. For example, Jesus in conversation with the woman at the well, first identifies her problem: "You have had five husbands and he whom you now have is not your husband." (John 4: 17,18) The revelation of her sinful condition was but a step toward her acknowledgment of Jesus as Messiah.

What distinguishes the prophetic lawgiver from ordinary representatives of the law is that the prophet does not wait to be notified of a case before pronouncing judgment on it, but exercises authority (without proper, formal authority or accreditation from men). What the text (the law) has not achieved, the prophet attempts.

Far out as all this may seem to some, the Holy Spirit works today in similar fashion through those who exercise the gifts of the Spirit as they are moved with compassion for persons in need. Today, there is a need for God's servants, for love of God and neighbor, to do all they can to keep the Judaic and Christian ethic in the law. One may expect opposition, even scorn, but with the power of his or her anointing, the prophet will awaken in each person that hidden moment when light is accepted or rejected.

King David wrote, after he had committed adultery with Bathsheba and then arranged the death of Uriah her husband, "Be gracious to me, O God, in thy true love; in the fullness of thy mercy blot out my misdeeds.... Create a pure heart in me, O God, and give me a new and steadfast spirit; do not drive me from thy presence or take thy holy spirit from me." (Psalms 51: 1,10,11 NEB).

It was only as Nathan, the prophet, confronted David, and roused him to righteous anger against the rich man who stole away and sacrificed the poor man's lamb, that David's moment of truth arrived. And Nathan said to David, "You are the man. This is the word of the Lord the God of Israel to you. 'I anointed you King over Israel, I rescued you from the power of Saul, I gave you your master's daughter and his wives to be your own, I gave you the daughters of Israel and Judah; and, had this not been enough, I would have added other favours as great. Why then have you flouted the word of the Lord by doing what is wrong in my eyes?'" (2 Sam. 12: 7-9 NEB).

We often hear it said, "They know they are doing wrong. No one needs to tell them." But did David know in the deepest sense, that he was the villain until under the inspiration of the Lord, Nathan presented the tender story of the poor man who had one little ewe lamb which had eaten of his own food, drunk of his own cup, and been cradled in his arms? Nathan's word pierced the King's heart like an arrow, and caused him to fall down in repentance toward God.

Notes

1   John Faustman, "Avenging Angel in 'Loose City,'" *The Vancouver Courier*, July 25, 1979.

17

WRECK BEACH — THE GREAT NON-EVENT

Doing all we can to keep the Judaic and Christian ethic in the law is a goal worthy of the best of us. However, in our society, even seemingly modest movements in that direction can cause a furor, especially if the media gets in the act on the side of the lawbreakers. The Wreck Beach controversy is an example from my own experience; Claudia Bain outlined the problem in a letter to the editor of the *Vancouver Sun* in 1977:

> For ten years our favorite walk as a family has been south of the university along the Fraser to where it joins Burrard Inlet; along tide-washed, log-and-rock-strewn beaches under overhanging willows and alders; at the foot of the cliffs below the university, the waves rolling in; in view all the while ships and ferries, tugs, barges, and sails, sunset, islands, and snow-capped mountains; on to the old guntowers, then up the trail and home. We took picnics and out-of-town guests to Vancouver's last natural beach. It is an artist's paradise! Now nudists have taken over the whole area from the Fraser to Spanish Banks.

Mrs. Bain asked that the Board of Parks and Recreation take action to reclaim the public beaches for regular families. At City Hall nobody except me was much interested in what I perceived to be part of a cultural revolution, a departure from family values.[1]

Alderman May Brown, who was more politically astute than I, commented, "That one is a can of worms." The City Council refused to even discuss officially the nudists' takeover of the super naturally beautiful beach, and left the Parks board to discuss the matter and

act if they chose. Rookie politician that I was, I had no idea what a
media event was about to descend upon me.

The debate over the nudists' takeover of seven miles of beach had
been firing up for some months. "Point Grey Beach Walk," as it was
called in *Vancouver At Your Feet*, was described as stretching from
Locarno Beach to Spanish Banks and around Point Grey to the west
boundary of Shaughnessy Golf Course. The authors advised,
"Allow half a day at least for the entire walk — more if you want to
explore."[2]

For my part the true story of our effort "to liberate the beaches"
began with citizen complaints, and the cavalier attitude of certain of-
fending media. One year earlier late in August, CBC had run an
early evening news story with pictures of frontal nudity on Vancouver's beaches, particularly Wreck Beach. Said the nudists, "We plan
to move into city beaches where it is more convenient, and not so
rocky." Many viewers who were unhappy with the flouting of community values by our tax-supported national network felt that their
telephone calls of protest were of little or no effect.

By the following July it was clear that something had to be done.
Now some citizens were arguing that it was silly to require the wearing of bathing suits in Vancouver's many city pools. Corky Day, a
counterculture figure of the Seventies who claimed to be "the original popularizer of Wreck Beach nudism," was busy working on his
"Free the Beach Defense Fund." He understood me better than
many who were to add their voices to the furor: "The well-known
evangelist, city councillor and talk show host on radio CJOR op-
poses what she considers the sinful and anti-family practice of social
nudism ... she argues that this uniquely beautiful natural beach so
close to the city should be made acceptable to those offended by nudity ... Gerard announced her plans on her morning and late night
talk-shows. If she can't stop nudism, she at least wants it confined to
the university beaches, or preferably only to private nudist parks."[3]

Though the media never mentioned the name of one other person
in the "battle for the beaches," I was by no means without allies and
advisors. Since we could not rouse City Hall either to show concern
or take action, our Citizens for Integrity committee, which included
Pastors Robert Birch and Allen Hornby, and Alderman Stella Jo

Dean of North Vancouver, decided that we would conduct a silent protest by going for a walk on the beach Sunday afternoon. Someone was to scout the territory earlier in the week to determine the exact instructions for the protestors who would join us. The scouting task fell to me. As it happened, Art Zapparosan, a pastor in Trail who was following me about that whole day, researching how one person handles city, media and pastoral responsibilities, got into the spirit of the effort, and accompanied me to the beach.

We parked at the extreme west end of Spanish Banks, descended a gradual 150 feet or so to the beach, and found that, though it was a cloudy day, there were a few dozen persons relaxing on the beach completely in the nude. Some men, trousers in hand, were simply walking about.

By Sunday morning at 9:00 a.m. I was in the studio at Radio CJOR giving the call for a "silent hike" beginning a few Sundays later at Spanish Banks west and following the historic Point Grey Beach walk. "Please, no placards, no tracts, or other literature, and no verbal exchanges with anyone on the beach!"

The mere mention of ordinary citizens appearing on the beach on Sunday afternoon for a "silent hike" provoked a storm of commentary. Allan Garr, also a talk show host on Radio CJOR, went on at length about the rights of the nudists, and proclaimed on air that he would be there in the nude to meet me. During the four o'clock tea break in the aldermen's lounge at City Hall, he challenged me loudly to meet him there in the nude ... not just him *but me also* in the nude! At that point, I fled the scene, desperate for peace and sanity. Needless to say when the big day arrived Garr was a no-show.

Christopher Dafoe, a *Vancouver Sun* columnist, rambled on at length in advance of the protest in an attempt to amuse himself and others at our expense. Bemused, he pondered our tactics, and then announced, "If the sun does shine ... it will be interesting to observe Alderman Gerard's tactics, and I plan to be there ... stark naked." Dafoe also suggested that we, the protesters, ought to take off our clothes: "Then at a given signal from Alderman Gerard, the protest group will begin to disrobe. Hats, shirts, trousers, frocks and all that properly goes underneath will be hurled to the four winds. The sensation will be electric, etc. ... The strip-tease of protest may have to go on all summer. But Alderman Gerard, think of the tan you'll get.''[4]

He didn't show up either, of course, but later wrote: "Several lovers of the ridiculous have called to express their disappointment over the fact that I failed to appear mother naked on Wreck Beach during Sunday's unspectacular anti-nudity protest sprint by Alderman Bernice Gerard and her little band of pilgrims from Citizens for Integrity. ... after all, I did say that I planned to attend and my failure to outrage members of Citizens for Integrity with a glimpse of my bare bum is regarded in some quarters as a kind of betrayal.''[5]

The walk itself was, as everyone knew, a symbolic gesture. Two hundred citizens walk silently on a Sunday afternoon to say, "This is public property. To be nude in a public place is illegal. We want the authorities to act against this disregard for the law." We wanted the citizens of Vancouver to express themselves and not simply to hand over the public beach to illegal users.

What was different about the walk was the scenery along the way: nude bathers and loungers were strung about the beach, and media people were everywhere. Peter Walls described the situation, story line as follows, "Gerard ... became concerned in recent months that the 'Judeo-Christian content of our laws' was being eroded by the gradual advance along a city beach of people who like to sun themselves all over. So she organized a group ... and announced that she planned to walk fully clothed among those dressed in their birthday suits to protest 'the psychological alienation' that people feel toward beaches littered with immodesty.

> Then, on a summer Sunday, she marshalled her followers who number perhaps one hundred [our people counted two hundred], and told the encircled media, hanging on her every word, that she wants every inch of every beach for every citizen because nudism on public beaches is a "cultural revolution" she is sworn to battle...
>
> Now Gerard didn't go more than about 200 yards (from Spanish Banks west) when she encountered her first nudists of the day. They had worked their bare behinds into a comfortable patch of sand amid pebbles and driftwood and were determined to get the most out of the overcast day. Gerard said nothing to them nor they to her, although they at least looked at her. They also stared with bemusement at this invading army dressed in Sunday finery which the sunbathers have abandoned.

Reporters, working the old reaction story gambit, scurried through the sand, and doing their best to exhibit worldliness, started asking the nudies what they think of all these clothes. Photographers jumped about like three-year-olds trying in obvious agony to reconcile what they wanted to shoot with what they can put before the public.[6]

The major theme of the media myth about Wreck Beach, which is the beach furthest from the city and the hardest to reach, was that we Victorian prudes were intruding needlessly on the idyllic innocence of the young and the beautiful. To my surprise, because I was a member of City Council, the reporters made it entirely my venture, and cast me in the role of villain. No amount of telling on my part could convince the reporters that I had *not* gone to Wreck Beach, that far-off idyllic haven; my whole point was that the nudists were spilling westward to Spanish Banks. Theirs was a spirit of civil disobedience; ours was against the alienation of the public beaches from the average citizen by a militant nudist minority.

The newspaper, radio and television reporters were having such a marvelous time creating their own myth about Wreck Beach where only the young and beautiful bare their bodies, that they actually came to believe their own fiction, and so did most of Vancouver. So convincing were they that I received letters of condemnation and commendation from places as far away as Oregon and Nova Scotia.

For example, from Halifax,

Dear Bernice,
I just saw you on T.V. I feel you should leave those nudists alone. There are many health camps in Canada and U.S.A. I have visited many of them. I saw nothing indecent, and when everyone is dressed the same there is nothing left to be desired. ... I feel people should be allowed to go down town this way if they wish. It is their body. You don't have to look at it. I do wish there was a place in Nova Scotia where you could let it all hang out and not be put in jail,
Belle Brady

Lester Halpin, a newspaper columnist for *The Oregonian*, writing for Portland and environs, titled his message "Ridicule Turns on Anti-nudity Group: Vancouver, B.C. — Canadians have not had much to laugh about recently ... but a confrontation here between unclad sunbathers on a *de facto* nudist beach and a procession of anti-nudists clothed in their Sunday best has been the best joke of the year throughout British Columbia."

Halpin continued his defense of the sunclad bathers on a *de facto* nudist beach, after identifying me as the villain of the piece. "Her secret weapon was to be silent, disapproving 'Shame! Shame!' looks at naked bodies, but a fifth columnist in her ranks suddenly removed his clothing to expose a well-tanned hide and began to shout traitorous insults at his zealous leader."[9]

There was not a grain of truth in Halpin's claim regarding the beaches being "*de facto* nudist," we did not walk to the famous little half mile of Wreck Beach; no fifth columnist among us disrobed and began shouting.

One might guess that in July 1976 Halpin had trouble working up his column in *The Oregonian* and so decided to serve up some fiction for fun, but he apparently wrote the best he knew and was seriously dreaming of the day when all public beaches would be *de facto* nudist. His final paragraph in a column one year earlier promises "In the 21st Century, which the writer will not see, athletes in the Olympic Games, if the games are still around, may perform naked like the athletes of ancient Greece."[10] Halpin's hope was constantly being deferred by what he saw as Mrs. Grundys who keep popping up here and there.

To finish the Halpin story, it's only fair to say that some of his commentary was correct: "Wreck Beach is a secluded strip of ocean shore which nestles within metropolitan Vancouver but lies outside the city limits at the foot of a bluff on which is located, high above, the University of British Columbia." Correct. But Citizens for Integrity and I walked only as far as the Tower, and thus the Wreck Beach myth was entirely balderdash.

I have never been to Wreck Beach but that was not important to reporters creating a story, or in this case, "building local folk lore." Halpin, for example, continues, "Ms. Gerard and her dressed defenders of decency proved perforce that they were physically fit when they scrambled through the underbrush down to the secluded beach while they were encumbered by layers of clothing." Why did the newspapers and other media fail to give an accurate presentation regarding the debate over the use of public beaches by the nudists?

Why did they choose to focus on nudity itself rather than on the issue? The real issue is who uses public beaches? Our law prohibits nudity in public places, yet for the most part the media presentations, with their strong influence on public opinion, were supportive of those who openly contravene the law.

While we were asking for West Spanish Banks and Marine Drive Foreshore Park to be returned to ordinary families, the press found "Wrath at Wreck Beach" best served their editorial purposes: "Really, Alderman Gerard, what's all this nonsense about 'liberating' Wreck Beach on July 10?"[11]

The Sun editorialists were particularly scornful of me: "Forget the silly protest, Miss Gerard. The hole in the knee of your swimsuit is showing." *The Province* urged that I get involved in a survey at a major downtown intersection, asking women who pass by whether or not they are offended at the sight of naked men. "Really Alderman Gerard, can you possibly believe that the average woman finds the sight of a naked man offensive even in public?"[12] There was no way to defend oneself, to put either the questions or the answers into context.

We were doing our symbolic trek to draw attention to the fact that a long stretch of easily accessible public space was being used as an unregulated nudist camp. Nudism is not legal at any beach, but it takes the B.C. Attorney General to act for law enforcement.

Through the *Vancouver Sun's* letters to the editor, I appealed to the public to stop and consider what was happening. My letter read in part, "Those who see nudism as something to be practised in the privacy of the home or in a licensed nudist camp had better speak now, or they will find themselves psychologically alienated from their own beaches and hiking grounds. As an elected public servant I am glad to join with Citizens for Integrity to raise the question. It is up to all of us to say what kind of community we want ours to be."

Now, with the clarity of hindsight, I see what a hoot the fictional Wreck Beach media event really was. Their fiction was so much more fun for them than our facts! Indeed, to this day, I am still under questioning: "You really did go to Wreck Beach didn't you, and then you wished you hadn't so you changed your story?"

And I reply truthfully, "No, neither I nor any of our group of protesters went to Wreck Beach. We were concerned about the lack of law enforcement on easily accessible city beaches." Again and again, the interviewer has looked at me in sheer unbelief. Mostly they are young journalists and they believe their own newspapers, and radio and television pundits. They actually *believe*! Even though truth is stranger than fiction, their own fiction often carries the day.

Interestingly enough, while some Christians were glad we were speaking out, others, hoping for greater respectability, intellectual and otherwise, felt my public prophetic image was no help at all. At Regent College, I had the opportunity to warn students that there is a vast difference between attitudes required for reading the Bible and those required for reading the local newspapers. The former must be read in faith, the latter with a good deal of healthy skepticism and discernment. As for the dailies, if you can believe all you read, you can eat all you see.

In fact, there was nothing trivial or foolish about the community discussion on the use of our beaches, and the acceptability or otherwise of nudism in public places. If nudity at public beaches is acceptable, why not in Stanley Park, on Granville or in the town at large? The problem we face is not about people dressed or undressed; rather, we are in a social war to determine what foundations will guide our society. Most of my really nasty mail came from militant homosexuals who evidently had staked out their territory on the beach, and saw our protest as directed against them. During that turbulent time the secretaries at City Hall never knew what they would find in my fan mail. The greater part was supportive, but I remember letters with pictures of the male anatomy plus crude remarks.

There were also unpleasant incidents such as a bomb threat at Radio CJOR studio one night with the message, "Bernice Gerard will not broadcast tonight!" One never knows if the writer is a lone fanatic or if he speaks, as he claims, for others also. After searching the old studio in the basement of the Grosvenor Hotel for a bomb, to air I went! If the writer expected publicity from me on the air that night, he was disappointed.

One crisp November evening, unexpectedly released from a City Hall meeting, I decided to attend the 100 Huntley Street rally with Rev. David Mainse at the Orpheum Theatre. From a distance I could see a crowd filling the sidewalk in front of the Orpheum; then at the entrance, I found myself in a marching crowd of about two hundred people, mostly young, carrying placards and chanting in unison, "Down with born-again hate! Down with born-again hate!" Just as I was adjusting to the scene, a young woman with a placard came alongside and shouted amid the din, "Are you Bernice Gerard?" I nodded, "Yes." With that she spat full in my face, her saliva streaking down the upper front of my jet black fur coat. In the crush of things, all I thought to say to her in reply was, "And what's your name?" At which point she gave me another mouthful!

Inside the foyer of the Orpheum I called the city police, requesting that they clear the theater entrance since the marchers were hindering people from making their way into the meeting. Later I found out that a false rumor had been spread that Rev. David Mainse had come to town with Anita Bryant, who was hiding in a hotel until meeting time. This was the protesters' focus. The truth was that David was as innocent as the flowers in May and totally unaware that he was being targeted as "the enemy," and so was I!

Inside the theater, I contemplated the street scene, trying to make sense of it. I was truly sorry for the frenzied young woman who carried such a burden of hate. As for me, there was no cause for self-pity; having cleaned off my coat I could now think of better things. My public profile as an active community-minded Christian made some of the gays try to cast me in an Anita Bryant role; but I knew that Gerard and Bryant were very different people. They needed a scapegoat but I resist being told by them or anyone else but the Lord what my calling is. However, there was a consolation in that street scene with all its strife and turmoil; the words of Jesus could be appropriated: "Love your enemies, and pray for those who persecute you, that you may be sons of your Father. He causes his sun to rise on the evil and the good, and sends rain on the righteous and on the unrighteous. If you love those who love you, what reward will you get?" (Matthew 5: 44-46 NIV)

Bible reading is challenging as well as consoling. It was during my private devotions, having just returned from the Orient where the "boat people's" plight was covered in the Hong Kong, Bangkok and Singapore English-language newspapers, that I was moved to get

mayor Jack Volrich to ask that we as a city do something about helping the refugees. He responded by appointing me chairman of the
Vancouver Refugee Committee, which coordinated and assisted all
the groups in the Greater Vancouver Regional District and beyond,
in their efforts to receive refugees and help them start a new life as
Canadians. This time around, the media, television, radio and print
went all-out for compassion. It was in many ways Vancouver's finest
hour, demonstrating that collectively we could act together to care
for people. Moira Farrow wrote eloquently on behalf of the dispos-
sessed; Laurier Lapierre at CKVU blessed me for "being a good
woman" and kissed my hand after the interview! He has not always
blessed me.

Out of my private experience of prayer have come personally compelling insights, deep concerns that touch on my relationship to fellow human beings and sometimes to all creation. Read the Bible and
ask "What does it say? What does it mean? What must I do about
it?" Read the daily newspaper and you may find the down-to-earth
present reality to which the Scripture's lofty principles are meant to
be applied.

CALIGULA

Even though my personal preference was to drift peacefully through
July and August, simply enjoying the summer of 1981, my first reading of *Sun* film critic Mark Andrew's report on *Caligula* disturbed
me greatly. What should be done by community-minded citizens
was clear. As for my getting into another hullabaloo like the *O Calcutta!* protest, I was thinking, "No way! If people want to go to hell
in a handbasket, what can any of us do about it? . . . . But what about
the young ones who as yet hardly know their right hand from their
left?"

In 1977, as a city alderman, I had tried to persuade City Council to
cancel the stage play *O Calcutta!* which had been scheduled by the
theater management to run in Vancouver's own civic theater, the
Queen Elizabeth, even though *O Calcutta!* was a focus of obscenity
trials in several parts of the world. I argued unsuccessfully that it was
foolish for the city to allow its tax-subsidized theaters to be rented to
just any theatrical group. "If *O Calcutta!*, with its group masturba-

tion, mass copulation and bondage sex is welcome in the theater, then anything would be welcome," said I.

People naturally asked, "How is it that you know so much about *O Calcutta!* if it is such a dirty play?" To which I replied that as a house guest of Malcolm and Kitty Muggeridge in Sussex, I was able to sit in on a meeting of the principals of the Festival of Light in Great Britain as they had an afternoon's discussion with Malcolm; *O Calcutta!* was of concern to them at the time. In Vancouver, the city aldermen including me, finally voted to ask the civic theaters board to impose an age restriction on the show. In my view it was a lame duck gesture since we could easily have acted decisively to uphold family values, especially in the face of teen problems multiplying around us: too many unwanted pregnancies, too many abortions, too much venereal disease. The fathers and mothers set the stage for the real-life play; the children only act out the parts.

Reluctant or not, it did not take long for me to realize that Citizens for Integrity must act on *Caligula*, or fold. Mark Andrews, the *Sun's* film critic, described opening night at the Towne Theatre. Clearly Vancouver was making history. "On hand in the lobby are B.C. censor Mary-Louise McCausland, who approved of showing the 17-million-dollar film in its uncut version, Bill Nowrie of Landmark Cinemas, the chain responsible for bringing the movie to Vancouver, and three members of the police force.

"And why all the fuss?

"Because Caligula represents the first hard-core sex footage to play in a commercial theatre in Vancouver. It is a brutal film which contains vivid and lurid scenes of brutal violence. ... Suffice it to say if you are offended by scenes of torture, rape, mutilation, necrophilia, and decapitation, you should avoid *Caligula*. Also you should know that the sex footage is very graphic; fellatio and cunnilingus scenes abound, and they are carried to their physiological conclusion. The human parts are real all right, and the juices flow on camera.

"In a way, producer Bob Guccione has made *Caligula* into a lavish extension of his magazine, *Penthouse.* The giant stone phalluses, as plentiful as Corinthian columns, represent objects of worship. The sex is two-dimensionally cold. ... The film seems to parallel sex with violence."

At one point, Andrews comments on the violence, and the obvious flagrant violation of the Criminal Code of Canada in this regard, "...But there certainly are scenes which mix violent and sexual acts (such as the one in which two nymphets rub themselves with blood from a freshly castrated soldier), a definite no-no according to the Attorney General." [13]

Mark Andrew's Saturday review of *Caligula* was sufficiently explicit to let all readers know that, as a city, we were making a landmark decision. Historically, the police after consultation with the Attorney General, had power to move in and close down such movies, and it was the Attorney General's duty to see that the law was enforced.

Frank Dorst, then youth pastor on the team at the Fraserview Assembly and Margaret Rosati, a high school teacher, went with me to see *Caligula's* early afternoon showing: one cannot effectively protest what one has not seen! We slipped quietly into a back seat over someone's big bucket of popcorn. The owner returned in a short time, looked down the row aghast, and said to Frank, "Isn't that Pastor Chapman? (it wasn't, it was Gerard). Is this a committee or something?" He confided to Frank that he had been brought up in Sunday School, our Sunday School! His wife, it seemed, did not like his attending these kinds of shows. We noticed he left early and failed to make even a dint in the popcorn. Apparently we and *Caligula* ruined his appetite.

Caligula was all Mark Andrews had said and worse. The film depicted the debauchery of the mad emperor with the addition of lurid scenes which could only have been added by a modern mind; for example, the mechanical method of decapitation at the games, and the circus merry-go-round of women abusing themselves sexually. We did everything we could to draw the attention of our busy elected officials to the fact that the first hard-core pornography was running in a Vancouver commercial theater. We called Mayor Jack Volrich, met with various citizens' groups, called Crown Counsel Sean Madigan, went to see Mary Lou McCausland, film classifier for B.C., and attempted in every way we knew to get the personal attention of Premier Bill Bennett and members of the provincial cabinet, especially Attorney General Allen Williams.

Convinced of the importance of the issue, and frustrated in our attempts to get a hearing from provincial authorities, we decided to call a press conference on the street in front of the *Caligula* marquee, and then picket the place. Alderman Stella Jo Dean and I, experienced as we were, should have known better than to call a press conference on Granville Street, since the whole point was to provide a forum in which *we* could get our message across to the politicians who tune into the evening news, and to people of concern and goodwill in our entire city. As it happened, Rev. Bob Birch and I, co-chairpersons of Citizens for Integrity, arrived a few minutes late to find our press conference already in progress, looking like a circus, and completely out of control as everyone on the street who was willing to talk, whether on our side or not, was being interviewed.

The first week of the picket line I received a telephoned death threat, and several obscene phone calls. Frank Dorst, leading the group of picketers, was physically assaulted so that he was bruised and his clothes torn. Ironically, though we were mocked by lewd talkers, others who milled about were moved spiritually by our presence on the street and right there requested prayer for themselves. Certainly we had not planned a Billy Graham altar call at the *Caligula* marquee, but that first day there were six definite decisions for the Lord.

No, *Caligula* was not closed down. The theater management decided to make the most of our opposition, and wrote in their advertisement, "Alderman Bernice Gerard saw it, and she said, 'I nearly up-chucked three times.'" On seeing the theater ad with my name in it, Velma Chapman, my co-pastor, almost did likewise. We admit our voices against it were, for some people, an encouragement to patronize it. But no one really knows who came or who stayed away and why; in this landmark case someone needed to give a warning.

The situation reminds me in some ways of a pending volcanic explosion. Just south of Vancouver, Canada, is Mount St. Helen's, the "Saint that Blew." Although warned of impending doom by scientists, many people illegally entered cordoned-off areas. Steve Graham of Portland summed it up best when he wrote, "For two months St. Helen's was fun to be around. We told volcano jokes and enjoyed the notoriety of living so close to a natural wonder.... T-shirt makers had a ball creating slogans. Silk-screened creations appeared with captions such as 'I survived the Mount St. Helen's eruption!' Entrepreneurs on the mountain slopes were offering genuine volcanic ash, or so they said.

"On Sunday, May 18, the fun stopped. The mountain without warning unleashed a blast of pent-up gas and volcanic material not unlike that of an atom bomb minus the radiation."

The editor noted, "All of a sudden the laughter died. It was snuffed out by a massive searing explosion of primordial death. Peaceful Mount Saint Helen's in southwestern Washington State had become a killer." [14]

For me, the situation in Vancouver was no joke either. It was impossible to see the first of the worst of the porn plague come to our beautiful city, and do nothing. When the full consequence of our collective failure of vision sets in, the young will ask "How was it that so few were concerned and why did it take them so long?"

To sum up, Eric Nicol of the *Vancouver Province*, put it all in perspective, minus the Bible verses:

> The film *Caligula* has been showing in Vancouver for 10 weeks now, and apparently no one yet has asked the police to lay a charge of obscenity. [We did, but the police refused to accept it.]
> This proves what a sophisticated city Vancouver is.
> When *Caligula* opened here, many of us feared that some citizen would demand that the cinema manager be arrested. Such action would ruin the city's reputation for being sophisticated. It would get into the papers, and people back east would read about it and nudge one another saying, "Har-de-har, Vancouver isn't that sophisticated after all." Striking Stanley Park into a petrified forest.
> But the Gods have smiled on us. The uncut version of *Caligula* has been allowed viewing, the good people of Vancouver accepting its main attractions — explicit sex and vicarious sadism — with the openmindedness that puts the city in the vanguard of Canadian urban sophistication. We stay ahead of Toronto, which never recovered from Ontario's banning a film called *The Tin Drum*. Vancouver remains close behind Montreal, in height of sophistication, Quebec City holding the edge only because it has savoir-faire which sounds even more worldly than sophistication.
> As a matter of fact, in French, sophistication means falsification. The

word relates to sophistry, which is deceptively subtle reasoning. The Quebeckers have spoiled a really neat word, probably because of the Jesuits. No wonder Trudeau doesn't understand our Western sophistication.

To Vancouver, sophistication means exhibiting intellectual tolerance. We see no sophism in restricting a historical cavalcade of sleaze to consenting adults with the price of admission. Is a film like *Caligula* less likely to influence the behavior of a healthy-minded under-18 than a mentally-disturbed adult? Well, our Vancouver kids are sophisticated enough to handle that. They know that it is the true sign of maturity: the right to view classified filth.

Naturally there are bound to be a few victims of our finely-experienced, aware, knowing and worldly-wise definition of sophistication. Not everyone can tolerate, intellectually or emotionally, unlimited broadening of the mind. That may be one reason why Vancouver has the nation's highest rate of alcoholism, suicide and crimes of sex and violence.

But you can't make an omelette, certainly not the suave, James-Barber omelette, without breaking eggs.

Broken lives are part of the sacrifice to sophistication. Every idol must be fed. The community is grateful to those who have paid the price. Maybe Vancouver should have a monument to the Unknown Sophisticate.

The marvelous thing is that the city has become sophistication's darling in less than a hundred years. A new world's record for having seen it all. It seems like only yesterday that the Vancouver motorist, coming upon the scene of an accident, stopped his car and hurried to lend assistance to the injured. Then we developed to the point where we merely slowed down for a look at the carnage. And finally today — the acme of sophistication — we honk at the car ahead that has slowed down to look at the mayhem and thus impeded our progress. That is real sophistication. The ability to care less, and do it with flair.

You newcomers to Vancouver may wonder how long it will take you to become as sophisticated as the rest of us. Be of good cheer. Although you hail from some relatively gross community, such as Armpit, Sask., or Ottawa, Ont., the sophisticated manner is quickly learned. Should anyone, for example, mention the name of Bernice Gerard, our moralistic ex-alderperson, you respond with a guffaw. This marks you as a sophisticate and offsets any amount of manure on your boots.

To be double sure, write a signed letter to the editor saying that you found *Caligula* rather dull but that censorship is even duller.

Very sophisticated.[15]

Notes

1   Claudia Bain, "Time to reclaim a Paradise from the Nudists," *Vancouver Sun*, May 31, 1977.
2   Soules, Gordon, *Vancouver At Your Feet*, Soules Economist Research, 355 Burrard Street, Vancouver, B.C.
3   Corky Day, Free the Beach Defense Fund, News release 6-21-77.
4   Christopher Dafoe, *Vancouver Sun*, June 22, 1977.
5   *Ibid.*, July 13, 1977.
6   Peter Walls, "Wreck Beach Nudies Eye Passing Parade," *Vancouver Province*, July 11, 1977.
7   Belle Brady, Halifax, undated.
8   Lester Halpin, "Ridicule Turns on Anti-nudity Group," *The Oregonian*, August 2, 1976.
9   "Wrath at Wreck Beach," Editorial, *Vancouver Sun*, June 29, 1977.
10 Lester Halpin, "Interpreting the View a Matter of Perspective," *The Oregonian*, August 2, 1976.
11 "Naked Averages," Editorial, *The Vancouver Province*, June 29, 1977.
12 "Average citizen loses in 'nudist takeover,'" *Vancouver Sun*, July 9, 1977.
13 Mark Andrews, "Caligula," *Vancouver Sun*, July 4, 1981.
14 *The Columbian Inc.*, Vancouver, Wash., U.S.A., 1980.
15 Eric Nicol, *The Province*, September 9, 1981.

18

FOR THE LIFE OF — ME!

Now the time has come to talk about my mother, about things I did not — could not — tell in my first autobiography, *Converted in the Country*. In that book I wrote, "I lost my mother." I knew her sad fate but felt completely helpless to do anything about it. She was "lost" to all her fearful children. Some things I did not know then, and so could not tell. At that time I had not even seen her. And, of course, what touched on my own identity and my relationship to her and my experience with my adoptive father Leo Gerard was personally painful to me. I judged the telling of it all to be of little benefit to others, in any case.

I have wanted my autobiography of a spiritual-intellectual pilgrimage to stand on its own in the tradition of Augustine, John Bunyan, and a multitude of lesser grateful writers, all of whom shared the intention of bearing witness to God's goodness. Now at this time of crisis in Canada over the "right to life," I see my statement "for life" as a duty, and privilege.

In me, from the beginning, there was an urgent need to know my origin. I now know that, had the pro-abortionists been in power at the time my mother was carrying me, I would never have seen the light of day. As it was, the authorities arranged that my birth take place at the Royal Columbian Hospital, just a few miles from the Essondale psychiatric institution where my dear little mother spent a total of nearly forty lonely institutionalized years.

How interesting and mysterious that some of us have a great need

to know our origins, and ultimate destination, and others seem not
to care. My thesis advisor, Professor Roy Daniels, held that only
some people had this sense of contingency, that is, from the start they
had a sense that there must be a great Cause behind all things in the
universe; creation speaks to them of the Creator. Others are simply
satisfied to say, "It all just happened, and so did I. It doesn't matter
to me from whence I came, why I'm here, or where I am going, if
anywhere!" My response to that is, "Maybe so, but I cannot believe
that such persons if they thought more deeply, could truthfully say
such things. To see oneself in this amazing universe, ourselves so
fearfully and wonderfully made, inspires awe and inevitably raises
cosmic questions, so it seems to me."

When my niece Jean lay dying at the age of 26, she became concerned with the question of her ultimate destination. In response to
her call, I went to her bedside, praying that spiritual growth would
come of our exchange. Thank God it did! Jean, in childlike faith,
cried out for God's mercy, and experienced the peace of God. On my
last visit she prayed with openness, sweetness and sincerity, as one
who had the witness of the Holy Spirit that she was a child of God in
right relationship with Him. (Romans 8: 16)

But beyond the question of her own peace of mind as she awaited
her death she had other important questions of the heart, in particular, "Why was everyone so secretive about Grandmother Nielsen?"
The question was hard to answer at any time, especially at the side of
a young person's death bed. What others may answer, I know not,
but I know why it took *me* so many years to establish a relationship
with my own neglected mother and I will answer it now: I was frightened. When fear takes over, we behave irrationally.

When I met Fred, the first of my blood relatives to come to see me
in Rossland, I was eager to learn of the entire family, especially
mother. Breathless with the excitement of it all, I hung on his every
word, as he described our sisters and our other brother. Finally, he
told me, "Dad owns a hotel in Dawson Creek, called the Mile
Zero...."

"Yes, but what happened to mother?" I asked, "How did she die?"
"She didn't die." "She didn't? Where is she?" Now I was getting
emotional.

"Mother has been a patient in the psychiatric hospital at Essondale all these years, even more years than you have lived. She was in
and out before she was pregnant with you, and in fact she was hospi-
talized even while she was carrying you." Fred told me all he could of
our family's life in northern British Columbia: Dad had been a tele-
graph operator, away from home a great deal, Mother bore six children in eight years, and with most of the deliveries she had only an
Indian midwife to help her. Life was harsh; the burdens and the loneliness were too much for Swedish-born Ada Nielsen to bear. That
night I cried and cried, and finally drifted off to fitful sleep weeping
for my mother.

God knows how I wanted to see her! My first attempted visit was
just as I was leaving British Columbia for what became a ten-year
absence. Packed up and on our way to Miami, Florida, to take up
permanent residence in the United States, Jean, Velma and I attempted what was to be a momentous visit for me. With old wives' tales
about mental illness cluttering my mind, bravely bearing my anxie-
ties, I arrived at the psychiatric hospital, and began the long walk up
the pathway to the big grey structure with its many barred windows.
Some patients were looking out, and I thought I heard some shouting. To this day all I remember then is that my stomach was churning
and it seemed impossible to go on; I was too frightened. I covered up
my defeat by saying, "Maybe it is better not to know. Maybe it is just
too sad, and no one can do anything to help," and we drove off to
live our new lives in the exciting United States of America.

Why did I not get to my mother's side sooner to kiss her cheek, pat
her hand, help her learn to read again, sing with her, pray with her
and comfort her? Because the monster of fear and ignorance that
plagued my understanding and hindered my compassion needed to
be unmasked. Ten years later, after I returned from the United
States, my old friend and social worker, Wini Urquhart, went with
me to see my mother. Small and gentle, very quiet, there she stood!
At last, I embraced my mother. By that time she was so thoroughly
institutionalized that she was more comfortable in her own familiar
surroundings than anywhere else. But in those brief years before her
death, the reality of knowing and loving my mother face to face, did
much to heal my inner person of the wounds of childhood. As she

went blind toward the very end of her life, it was again a time for tears. It was inexpressibly sad to see one so deprived for so long now shut in even from the light of day. At the very last, as the doctor called to say, "Your mother has pneumonia and complications," my last prayer beside her bed was, "Please take her home, Lord! She's yours, she's ready."

Her funeral, conducted by Rev. Velma Chapman and her husband Dick, was attended by her husband, all her children except one, and many of her grandchildren. It was for me a time of sadness, not only for Ada Nielsen, but for all the mothers who gave others life but were separated from the joys of motherhood by tragedy. She gave me life, but her circumstances were so very difficult. There is no question that according to all reasonable definitions I was an "unwanted" child, but never once have I wished that I had not been born. And, drunken and brawling as my adoptive family was, I do not think *they* ever thought I should not have been born. Now, strange as it may seem, "being unwanted" in our society is a crime punishable by death, and the "unwanted" have no right of appeal.

It was on a CBC television program, Vancouver "Citizens' Forum," that I first encountered those champions of the underprivileged and disadvantaged who were working night and day to see that we in Canada got abortion on demand, and even abortion before demand. In her "defense" of the unwanted child, a young social worker was arguing that the birth of the welfare children she worked with should not have been allowed. "The present social assistance allowance for the purchase of clothing is inadequate," said she, "and it really would be better if these kids had not been born." I noticed that it was the people who are already safely here who argue on grounds of economics, and grounds of any kind at all that others should be deprived of life.

Little wonder it felt so right for me to take my stand with the right-to-life people. It is good that a child be wanted, but the "wanted" criterion as a basis of the right to live creates a dangerous precedent: it presumes a child exists and has rights only because someone wants him or her. Each human being, including the extremely aged, the senile, the sick and those mentally and physically defective, has inviolable rights and dignity.

I first got involved in the formal pro-life movement when Dr. Heather Morris, president of the Alliance for Life of Canada, called to invite me to speak at the Festival for Life in Ottawa, in November 1973. The Alliance, which had affiliates across Canada, was presenting a petition on behalf of protection for unborn children. When we were all together in Ottawa, the speakers at the conference addressed the question of how best to persuade the country to reject abortion and other anti-life practices. British author-journalist Malcolm Muggeridge drew a standing ovation from the overflow crowd packed into the Ottawa Technical School's eleven-hundred-seat auditorium for his remarks in defense of the unborn child's right to live.

If society allows abortion, "we do so at peril of our immortal souls," Mr. Muggeridge warned. "If we accept a view of the world as a factory-farm in which we kill, in which we shape human life as we think it ought to be, the curtain falls on everything that is great and true and noble in our way of life. If we say, 'this is a good life and this life is bad!' — if we take that power into our own hands, believe me, an old man, we've come to the end of the road that began two thousand years ago. Men will again have to struggle out of darkness.

"There is not the slightest doubt that the next move in the game will be euthanasia (mercy killing). Already the signs are visible — in some British hospitals the notation NTBR appears routinely on the medical charts of persons seventy and older, meaning 'not to be resuscitated!' "

The distinguished author and journalist continued, "The decision as to which life will continue, and which will end is not ours to make. A fertilized egg might be Beethoven or might be an imbecile. But whatever it may be, it is another infinitesimal element in the workings of God's plan!" Mildred Jefferson, an American surgeon and then vice-chairman of the American National Right to Life Committee, termed abortionists the "new annihilationists." Dr. Jefferson, the first woman graduate of Harvard medical school, accused pro-abortionists of "encouraging doctors to give up their role as healers to become the new social executioners" and emphasized that "There can be no high quality of life, in a society where only the perfect, privileged and planned have a right to live."

Morris Shumiatcher, chairman of the Civil Liberties Section of the Canadian Bar Association, spoke of the pro-abortion movement as "part and parcel of the kind of society described by people like Aldous Huxley in *Brave New World* and George Orwell in *Nineteen eighty-four*.[1]

Last, and feeling very much least in that distinguished roster of speakers, came I, to speak for the unwanted child. As delegates fanned out to lobby over one hundred members of Parliament, I made my way to the office of Grace McInnis, Member for Vancouver East. In response to my asking for her support to stop the killing of the unborn, Grace looked at me in all sincerity and said, "If you had been destroyed in the fetal stage, you wouldn't know anything about it." My reply, which I fear did not move her at all, was, "According to your views, if someone walked in here to your office, aimed a gun and took your life, you wouldn't know it tomorrow either. But I don't feel this is a good argument for murder."

"You have your view and I have mine. There is no point in our going on with this discussion," was her somewhat abrupt but nevertheless polite dismissal. Between her and me, on this particular issue, there was a great gulf of misunderstanding.

"We believe that every life is of infinite value and that this value is not significantly diminished by the circumstances of life's beginning." For me this statement of the Right-to-Life credo formed a part of a litany of the joy of life, but not for Grace and a multitude of other Canadians who saw the issue very differently. In 1972 almost 40,000 babies were destroyed; British Columbia's abortion rate was 22.4 abortions per 100 live births, which made us guilty of destroying proportionally more lives than any other province in Canada. In 1972 alone, the abortion juggernaut destroyed approximately as many little Canadians as the total of Canadian losses in World War II.

Dr. Heather Morris, president of the Alliance and herself a gynecologist and obstetrician who delivered thousands of babies in her Toronto practice, had asked the pro-life forces for a petition to be presented to the Prime Minister and the government of Canada, to get the government to provide legislative protection for unborn children. The text was as follows:

Parliament's most basic duty is to protect innocent human life. The scientific evidence now puts it beyond reasonable doubt that a new life begins at conception, yet our laws permit the widespread practice of abortion in Canada. Therefore, we the undersigned, call upon Parliament to enact legislation providing the child conceived but not yet born the same protection provided for any other person. We also urge Parliament to show leadership in fostering a life-sustaining society.

In Ottawa, May 9, 1973, the Minister of Health, Marc Lalonde, and the Prime Minister of Canada, Pierre Elliot Trudeau, received from Dr. Heather Morris the signatures of 353,652 Canadians. The P.M. was not impressed! Said Trudeau, "The pro-choice people could easily get 1,000,000 signatures." Whereupon the Right-to-Lifers launched another petition, this time gathering 1,000,000 signatures, which they presented in 1975. It was the same Trudeau who was Justice Minister in August 1969 when the Criminal Code was amended so that abortion could be performed in Canada if in the opinion of a hospital's therapeutic abortion committee the continuation of the pregnancy would likely endanger the mother's life or health. This provision was interpreted to mean abortion on request. Trudeau was not moved by the million votes-for-life to stop the killing!

On the basis of the 1969 legislation Canada moved rapidly toward implementation of the new provision for abortions. Since the state of modern medicine is such that a pregnancy rarely constitutes a threat to the mother's life, nearly all the abortions performed have been done on the grounds that the pregnancy threatened the mother's health. Unfortunately, the Criminal Code gave no definition of the word "health," leaving it to the psychiatrists and medical doctors to stretch the meaning of the word to the point of absurdity. As a result, according to a paper presented by Dr. William Allemang, senior staff obstetrician and gynecologist at the Toronto General Hospital, at the National Canadian Conference on Abortion at St. Michael's College, May 25, 1972, the word "health" had already gradually come to mean any unwanted pregnancy.

Moreover, according to Dr. Allemang, once an abortion was performed under these broader indications, any subsequent refusal to terminate an unwanted pregnancy was seen as discriminatory and a contravention of the rights of the individual. This then became a "necessary medical service," insurable under the provincial health insurance schemes. In fact, the stage has been achieved, at least philosophically speaking, of "free abortion on demand." For obvious reasons, the medical profession finds the term "request" preferable to the implied threat of "demand."

Since the war against the child continues unabated, it is of value to note the haste with which both the United States and Canada set about to implement the death ethic expressed in the U.S. Supreme Court abortion decision of 1973, and the Canadian abortion amendments of 1969. Seattle attorney Kenneth VanDerhoef who contributed six "friend of the court" briefs in the U.S. watershed case, *Roe vs. Wade*, today describes that judgement as "having little to do with abortion and everything to do with life." VanDerhoef, who knows more about the critical right-to-life cases which face the courts in America than almost anyone, says, "Early advocates of legalized abortion admitted that abortion was only the first step in creating a society where 'useless' lives might be disposed of. ... The idea that the preborn can be destroyed is now applied at the other end of the life continuum to individuals who are comatose, that is, in a stage of prolonged unconsciousness. In various legislative actions and judgments of the courts it has been proposed that these patients have no meaningful existence and are therefore worthy of removal. But they won't die! A committee of the American Bar Association described them as the 'biologically tenacious!' Usually these people do not receive treatment for their condition, but are given food and water, often called 'comfort care.' The move now is to redefine food and water as treatment which can also be withdrawn."

VanDerhoef continues, "It's a natural extension of non-personhood. It is in fact active euthanasia since food and water do not treat the coma; starvation and dehydration are not natural. Such a withdrawal is to take a positive step to assure that a person will not survive. Most nursing personnel are not willing to supervise a starvation. The dissenting opinion in a recent court decision asserted that the lethal injection is more humane than starvation." This noted lawyer who has given twenty years of his professional skill and energies to the pro-life movement, looking into the future, says, "It would not surprise me, if within five years, facilities will be licensed to give lethal injections to these non-persons, so called." [2]

Looking back over the phenomenal increase in the number of abortions in North America in less than two decades, in which the death toll of preborn children in Canada rose to more than 60,000 annually, and in the United States to 1,000,000 annually, it is easy to see that, as Ken VanDerhoef says, we are no longer in the debating stage, or the deciding stage; rather we have moved to total implementation of the death ethic. Moreover, having begun by killing the child in the womb, society has now moved to accepting the practice of surrogate motherhood in which the child, who now has no right to life on his or her own, is seen as a commodity, an *item* to be bought and sold.

Finally, no better summary of the new ethic for medicine and society to which I have been referring as "the death ethic," can be found than that given in an editorial in *California Medicine*, the official journal of the California Medical Association, September 1970: "The traditional Western Ethic has always placed great emphasis on the intrinsic worth and equal value of every human life regardless of its state or condition. This ethic has had the blessing of the Judeo-Christian heritage and has been the basis for most of our laws and much of our social policy. Reverence for each and every human life has also been a keystone of Western medicine and is the ethic which has caused physicians to try to preserve, protect, repair, prolong, and enhance every human life which comes under their surveillance. This traditional ethic is still clearly dominant, but there is much to suggest that it is being eroded at its core and may eventually be abandoned. This of course will produce profound changes in Western medicine and in Western society." [3]

After discussing "certain new facts and social realities" which seem certain to undermine and transform the traditional ethic, the editorial goes on to discuss "the process of eroding the old ethic and substituting the new which has already begun."

"It may be seen most clearly in the changing attitudes toward human abortions. In defiance of the long-held Western ethic of intrinsic and equal value for every human life regardless of its stage, condition or status, abortion is becoming accepted by society as moral, right and even necessary. It is worth noting that this shift in public attitude has affected the churches, the laws and public policy rather than the reverse. Since the old ethic has not yet been fully displaced it has been necessary to separate the idea of abortion from the idea of killing, which continues to be socially abhorrent. The result has been a curious avoidance of the scientific fact, which everyone really knows, that human life begins at conception and is continuous whether intra or extra-uterine until death.

"The very considerable semantic gymnastics which are required to rationalize abortion as anything but taking a human life would be ludicrous if they were not often put forward under socially impeccable auspices. It is suggested that this schizophrenic sort of subterfuge is necessary because while a new ethic is being accepted the old one has not been rejected."[4]

The editorial does not, as we might hope, urge doctors to reject the death ethic and get back to "reverence for life," but to get ready to take on the responsibilities of "birth control and birth selection" which will be "extended inevitably to death selection and death control."

The final sentences in the editorial have the most skilled and technologically advanced healers the world as ever known taking us forward into the Brave New World — and backward to Nazi Germany where in the name of science the medicalization of killing proved to be the boundary line between civilization and barbarism: "No other discipline has the knowledge of human nature, human behavior, health and disease, and of what is involved in physical and mental well-being, which will be needed. It is not too early for our profession to examine this new ethic, recognize it for what it is and will mean for human society, and prepare to apply it in a rational development for the fulfillment and betterment of mankind in what is almost certain to be a biologically oriented world society."[5]

As the California doctor-prophets of 1970 visualized it, we are moving forward to "a quite new social emphasis on something which is beginning to be called the quality of life, a something which becomes possible for the first time in human history because of scientific and technologic development."

Contrariwise, a host of other modern-day prophets see the argument for quality of life when used against "life" itself as moving us backward to Auschwitz, or at the least assisting in the creation of psychological conditions conducive to evil. A Jewish-American psychiatrist, Robert Jay Lifton, author of *The Nazi Doctors*, was concerned with ethical, social and political questions about the forces of destruction in our world. Though he is anxious that the Holocaust not be trivialized, he nevertheless sees its lessons as relevant for our times and says, "No other event or institution can or should be equated with Auschwitz; nor should we deny ourselves the opportunity to explore its general relevance for genocide and for situations of a very different order in which psychological and moral questions may be considerably more ambiguous."[6]

When Lifton, after nearly ten years of interviews with former Nazi doctors and Auschwitz survivors, tells what was at the Nazi enterprise, we should surely see danger signals for our own society. Says Lifton, "In Nazi murder, we can say that a barrier was removed, a boundary crossed: victims (as of Jews in pogroms) on the one hand, the systematic genocide in Auschwitz and elsewhere on the other. My argument in this study is that the medicalization of killing — the imagery of killing in the name of healing — was crucial to that terrible step. At the heart of the Nazi enterprise then, is the destruction of the boundary between healing and killing."

Lifton continues, "Medical killing can be understood in two wider perspectives. The first is the 'surgical' method of killing large numbers of people by means of a controlled technology, making use of highly poisonous gas. ... But there is another perspective on medical killing that I believe to be insufficiently recognized: killing as a therapeutic imperative." At this point, Lifton quotes the words of a Nazi doctor as remembered by Dr. Ella Lingens-Reimer. Pointing to the chimneys in the distance, she asked a Nazi doctor, Fritz Klein, "How can you reconcile that with your [Hippocratic] oath as a doctor?" His answer was, "Of course I am a doctor and I want to preserve life. And out of respect for human life, I would remove a gangrenous appendix from a diseased body. The Jew is the gangrenous appendix in the body of mankind."[7]

His answer, at least in a measure, shows how physicians trained as healers became killers. In the Nazi "biomedical vision," mass murder was committed to "heal" the racially "diseased" body of the German nation. The central belief was that the Nazis had a moral obligation to purify the *Volk*, a term which meant not only "people" but also conveyed for many German thinkers "the union of a group of people with a transcendental essence." [8] We can hardly fail to notice the parallels with our own era when so many millions are destroyed by saline solution and curettage, allegedly for the sake of quality of life for other individuals.

Dr. Carolyn Gerster of Phoenix, Arizona, who practices with her husband, Dr. Josef Gerster, specializing in internal medicine and cardiopulmonary diseases, is another who sees today's society as moving toward a greater and greater acceptance of the death ethic reminiscent of Nazi Germany. At a pro-life meeting in Vancouver, years ago, she recalled that as a young officer in the United States forces in Germany, she met and subsequently married Josef Gerster who had served with the Hitler Youth. Through the years, she related, "I would ask him how such terrible practices came to be accepted in Germany. How could a community of scientifically progressive healers turn into mass murderers? How was it that the Holocaust ever happened?"

Says Carolyn, "Until lately my husband was at a loss to adequately describe the process by which it all came to pass. Now he says, 'It was there in pre-war Germany as it is here in America at this time,' and he points out the acceptance of the death ethic, the willingness of physicians and other authorities to participate in the bureaucracy of killing.'" Asked why she spent so much of her time and energy traveling and speaking for the "right to life" movement, when she had a husband, five sons and a professional career to absorb her interests, Dr. Gerster replied, "When my grandchildren ask, 'How did all this killing begin? Where were you, Grandmother?' I want to be able to reply, 'I was in there fighting for the right to life, every inch of the way!'"

What, in fact, does the future hold for the human family? I believe that it will be seen that the greatest tragedy of our times was the decision for death — death by the millions of our own flesh and blood! The darkest possible scenario for the child in the womb is to be abandoned to the whims and fancies of a me-centered society. Ruled against by the highest courts in the land, used as a political football by the elected leadership of our nations, condemned to death by decision of its own mother and father, what defense remains for the innocent preborn child?

Ultimately, the first and last defense against injustice and even death, indeed the offensive against those who offer violence as a solution to society's woes, is love itself. As long as our justice system does not require that women abort their babies, as in present-day China, each woman has the freedom to choose life for her baby. Thus, the most critical issues of the decision for or against life will ultimately continue to be made in the hearts and minds of mothers and fathers. The fight for life must go on, as every life saved is a victory won for civilization and the human family!

Notes

1 Vivian McDonald, "Thousands Hear Anti-abortion Speakers," *The Citizen*, November 5, 1973, 45.
2 Kenneth VanDerhoef, excerpts from a speech at the Lawyers' Inn, Vancouver, April 29, 1987.
3 *California Medicine*, official journal of the California Medical Association, September 1970, Vol. 113, No. 3, 67-68.
4 *Ibid.*
5 *Ibid.*
6 *Ibid.*
7 Robert Jay Lifton, *The Nazi Doctors: Medical Killing and the Psychology of Genocide*, Basic Books Inc.: New York 1986, 5.
8 *Ibid.*, 16.
9 *Ibid.*, 14.

19

THE BLOODY FACE OF HISTORY

There is so much more to human existence than meets the eye. At first, like newborn puppies, we do not have our eyes open at all, and then as we reach maturity we become more keenly aware, not only of the physical world around us, but of spiritual forces and counter-forces, the war between the sons of darkness and the sons of light.

And so I close this book with one of the clearest examples of this warfare. Though it came late to my attention, the Holocaust, which involved the deliberate annihilation of six million Jews, shocks and grieves me to the very depths of my soul. There is much in our modern world to burden the conscience of humanity, but the Holocaust stands beyond the most evil imaginations of men, a demon-inspired event that casts a pall over modern man's every pretension to the good and noble. Even now, before the world has fully understood the enormity of Hitler's attempt to annihilate the Jews, "Holocaust denial," as typefied by the Keegstra affair, has become an ugly phenomenon of our times, another evil to be resisted by every person capable of thought and love. Especially should Christians resist falling in line with the antisemitism of our own day. To stand against the defamation of Israel and its people today is as good an opportunity as one can find to do what Albert Camus thought suited us best. Said he, "The world expects of Christians that they will raise their voices so loudly and clearly and so formulate their protest that not even the simplest man can have the slightest doubt about what they are saying. Further, the world expects of Christians that they will eschew all fuzzy abstractions and plant themselves squarely in front of the bloody face of history. We stand in need of folk who have determined to speak directly and unmistakably and come what may, to stand by what they have said." [1]

The late John Howard Griffin, author of *Black Like Me*, addressing a pro-life audience at the 1977 Festival for Life in Ottawa, pointed out that the tragedy is that people often do not become sufficiently concerned in time. When he was a senior medical student in Paris during the War he joined the Resistance Movement. In addition to being called out at two or three in the morning to attend to wounded troops, he was part of a team that smuggled German and Austrian Jews across France to England.

> One night I had the task of going to the rooms in cheap little boarding houses where we had hidden the Jewish families that we had moved there for safety, and explaining that ... we didn't know how to forge papers, and were not going to succeed in moving them any further. ... They said, "We know it is finished for us. We know the Nazis when they find us will ship us back to Germany into the concentration camps." And then, invariably, they would ask, "Can you take our children?"

"And suddenly," recalled Griffin, "sitting in those rooms that night, I began to realize what it was all about. I was sitting in rooms, cheap little rooms where unspeakable human tragedy was taking place. The tragedy of parents who loved their children and who were giving their children to a relative stranger so at least their children could escape the camps, the gas chambers and the crematoria. And it seemed to me, that formed me in my vocation. I spent the rest of my life sitting in rooms like that. ...

"Two things were made clear to me that night, first my immense shame that we had treated racism as an intellectual preoccupation, and even had heard arguments for and against it. The second, even more astonishing, which has always been confirmed in my subsequent life, was the realization that I could go outside of those rooms, I could go down the streets, and I could find the majority of people — decent intelligent human beings — knowing nothing of the tragedy that was going on in those rooms. There were even men quibbling, rationalizing, justifying the very racism that led to the tragedies inside those rooms." [2]

Griffin subsequently spent many years living in the inner city ghettos in the Sixties and investigating atrocities against the black people in the Deep South of the U.S.A. He had never intended to spend his life fighting racism; he intended to go back to the U.S.A. and become an academic, spending the rest of his life doing scholarly research. But once he began to perceive these patterns of injustice, he found he could never turn his back on them. He described it as walking on a string toward a goal you thought you had, a vocation that you thought you had, but always finding people lying wounded in the gutters and never being able to pass such people.

Griffin's most famous book, *Black Like Me*, told of his unique experience in the segregated American South of the Fifties. A white man, he had taken a potion to cause his skin to turn color so that he would be taken for a black. His book did much to raise my own consciousness of the enormous suffering racial prejudice produces. Similarly, after nine and a half hours of *Shoah*, the oral history of the Holocaust, I was again irrevocably moved to a higher level of understanding and commitment to resist such evil, in whatever guise it appears. Simone de Beauvoir, commenting on *Shoah* (annihilation), says, "After the war we read masses of accounts of the ghettoes and the extermination camps, and we were devastated. But when, today, we see Claude Lanzmann's extraordinary film, we realize *we have understood nothing*. In spite of everything we knew, the ghastly experience remained remote from us. Now, for the first time, we live it in our minds, heart and flesh. It becomes our experience." [3]

At the première benefit showing in Vancouver a few hundred Jews and a sprinkling of Christians encountered, on screen, a full range of witnesses, persons *now* living who give first-hand accounts of their experiences with the Holocaust: the S.S. officers who served in the death camps; the Polish villagers who tilled their fields within yards of the crematoria; the Germans who resettled occupied Poland, moving into the houses of Jewish people who had been sent to their death; the state employees who sold Jews half-fare excursion tickets to the camps — one-way; Western scholars of the Holocaust.

These living witnesses of today are joined by actual survivors of the death camps, most of whom speak under great duress as Lanzmann gently but firmly urges them, saying "You have to tell it. You have to! Go on! Go on!" Their eyewitness account must be recorded in the annals of history, to honor the dead and to save the living from venturing into such madness ever again.

Most vivid in my memory of *Shoah* is the account of the Polish barber, Abraham Bomba, describing the way in which he and other Jewish barbers were forced to cut the hair of women completely naked and about to be gassed. Bomba breaks down as he begins to tell of a friend of his — "He was a good barber in my home town — when his wife and his sister came into the gas chamber ... I can't. It's too horrible. Please." Lanzmann urges him on. "Please, we must go on." Bomba continues, "The women tried to talk to him and the husband of his sister. They could not tell them this was the last time they would see them, because behind him were the German Nazis' S.S. men, and they knew if they said a word, not only the wife and the woman, who were dead already, but also they would share the same thing with them. In a way, they tried to do the best for them, with a second longer, a minute longer, just to hug them, and kiss them, because they knew they would never see them again."

Filip Mueller, a Czech Jew, and survivor of five liquidations of the Auschwitz "special detail" (those who did slave labor inside the death chambers, and were themselves slated for death) was only twenty years old when he found himself at gunpoint inside the crematorium, ordered to undress the bodies of the dead, and load them into the ovens. Mueller has a particularly good face. I kept thinking as I heard him speak, "Dear God, he seems such a good human being. How could they do it to him, and how did he survive, his humanity so perfectly intact?"[4]

At Auschwitz, he had his own moments of complete despair, one particularly dramatic when he saw a large group of his own countrymen being herded brutally into the gas chamber. The following are his own words, "As soon as they left the vans, the beatings began. When they entered the 'undressing room,' I was standing near the rear door, and from there I witnessed the frightful scene. The people were bloodied. They knew where they were .... They were in despair. Children clung to each other. Their mothers, their parents, the old people all cried, overcome with misery...

"Yes, the violence climaxed when they tried to force the people to undress. A few obeyed, only a handful. Most of them refused to follow the order. Suddenly, like a chorus, they all began to sing. The whole undressing room rang with the Czech national anthem, and the *Hatikvah*. That moved me terribly, that ... was happening to my countrymen, and I realized that my life had become meaningless. Why go on living? For what? So I went into the gas chamber with them, resolved to die with them. Suddenly, some who recognized me ... They looked at me and said, right there in the gas chamber ... 'So you want to die! But that is senseless. Your death won't give us back our lives. That's no way. You must get out of here alive, you must bear witness to our suffering, and to the injustice done to us.' " [5]

The witness of *Shoah* and other similar documentaries, of which there are many in Israel, is needed in our time because it is a powerful answer to "Holocaust denial," and teaches lessons from the past to save our future. Regrettably, audiences in Vancouver were a mere sprinkling of the total population. Even survivors and children of survivors find it impossible to listen to the story (so some say). But I feel that standing up for the survivors who bear witness, against every evil revival of the spirit of the Holocaust is good, for our own souls' sake and for the future of our civilization.

My first in-depth experience with the Holocaust documentary and memorial known as Yad Vashem in Jerusalem, when I was leading a Holy Land tour, left me horrified. As the crowd of visitors moved slowly and silently from chamber to chamber, gazing upon unlimited suffering and death, I was aware that many among us were themselves survivors. Some had lost every single one of their loved ones. We all cried together, though all were bravely fighting back their tears. Awareness of the passing of time vanished completely.

Later, as I joined our group in the sunshine, who were by now eating ice cream at the refreshment stand, I felt suddenly guilty at the very thought of indulging in such treats so soon after viewing the tragedy of slain millions. In particular, the sadness of the little boy with the large brown eyes, dressed in a greatcoat, hands raised over his head in the face of the Nazi officer's gun, lingered on in my thoughts.

Then came an altogether different thought, "(There is) a time to

weep, and a time to laugh, a time to mourn and a time to dance."
(Eccles. 3: 4) Surely this is also a time for rejoicing. After all, the forces of evil did *not* triumph; Israel lives. We were in Jerusalem, the city of David! God keeps His promises.

Ever since that first visit, as we have led groups of Christian pilgrims through the land of Israel, and inevitably to Yad Vashem, I have seen the task of raising people's awareness of human history's darkest hour as an important part of our pilgrimage. At the same time, we can point out to people the promise of our glorious future in God's redemptive plan.

The truth is that God's promises to Abraham have been kept; indeed they are being kept even now. The Lord had said to Abraham, "Leave your country, your people, and your father's household and go to the land I will show you. I will make you into a great nation and I will bless you; I will make your name great, and you will be a blessing. I will bless those who bless you, and whoever curses you I will curse, and all peoples on earth will be blessed through you. (Genesis 12: 1-3 NIV) Significantly, in the original call, Abraham hears not only that a great nation (Israel) will be made of him but that in him "shall all the families of the earth be blessed." This is a promise for Gentile believers in particular, and more broadly for humanity in general.

Moses, looking across to the Promised Land, envisioned also the possibility of Israel's disobedience to the commandments and unfaithfulness to the Lord, and prophesied the dire consequences of rebellion: "You will be uprooted from the land you are entering to possess. Then the Lord will scatter you among all nations, from one end of the earth to the other." (Deut. 28: 63, 64 NIV)

Possibly, there is nothing more basic than these promises to Israel. We see today the demonstrations of God's faithfulness in the meticulous detail of present-day fulfillment: "When all these blessings and curses I have set before you come upon you and you take them to heart wherever the Lord your God disperses you among the nations, then the Lord your God will restore your fortunes and have compassion on you and gather you again from all the nations where he scattered you." (Deut. 30: 1, 3 NIV) Moses makes clear that the people scattered to all nations will return to "the land that belonged to your fathers." (Deut. 30: 5 NIV)

The Jewish people *have been dispersed* as the Lord had said through His prophets they would be. "I dispersed them among the nations, and they were scattered through the countries...." (Ezekiel 36: 19 NIV) And they *are being restored* to the promised land as He said, "For I will take you out of the nations; I will gather you from all the countries, and bring you back into your own land." "I will sprinkle clean water on you, and you will be clean; I will cleanse you from all your impurities, and from all your idols. I will give you a new heart and put a new spirit in you; I will remove from you your heart of stone, and give you a heart of flesh." (Ezekiel 36: 24-26)

Jeremiah predicts the day when the Lord restores His people to their ancient heritage: "See, I will bring them from the land of the north and gather them from the ends of the earth. Among them will be the blind and the lame, expectant mothers and women in labor; a great throng will return. They will come with weeping, they will pray as I bring them back..." (Jer. 31: 8-9 NIV) "He who scattered Israel will gather them, and will watch over his flock like a shepherd." (v 10) "They will sorrow no more. Then the maidens will dance and be glad, young men and old as well. I will turn their mourning into gladness; I will give them comfort and joy instead of sorrow." (v 12, 13 NIV)

Every visitor to the land of Israel can see with his own eyes that God is keeping His promises. For He said to Israel, "On the day I cleanse you from all your sins, I will resettle your towns, and the ruins will be rebuilt. The desolate land will be cultivated instead of lying desolate in the sight of all who pass through it. They will say, " 'This land that was laid waste has become like the Garden of Eden; the cities that were lying in ruins, desolate and destroyed, are now fortified and inhabited.' " (Ezekiel 36: 33-35 NIV)

It all ties in together; God's faithfulness to them means God's faithfulness to us. Isaiah writes of Messiah who is to sit on the throne of David — our Messiah. "For to us a child is born, to us a son is given, and the government will be on his shoulders. And he will be called Wonderful, Counselor, Mighty God, Everlasting Father, Prince of Peace. Of the increase of his government and peace there will be no end. He will reign on David's throne and over his kingdom, establishing and upholding it with justice and with righteousness from that time on and forever. The zeal of the Lord Almighty will accomplish this." (Isaiah. 9: 6, 7 NIV)

There is no hope like that inspired by the knowledge of God's faithfulness, and the promise of Messiah's return. "He will judge between the nations and will settle disputes for many peoples. They will beat their swords into ploughshares and their spears into pruning hooks. Nation will not take up sword against nation, nor will they train for war any more." (Isaiah 2: 4 NIV)

The darkness is defeated. God is light and in Him is no darkness at all. "But if we walk in the light, as he is in the light, we have fellowship one with another, and the blood of Jesus, his Son, purifies us from all sin." (1 John 1: 7 NIV)

We believers will know more certainly when we see Messiah at His coming; meanwhile, it is appropriate, as the Holy Spirit inspires us, to use the same confident language as the Apostle Paul, and others of Bible times:

"For I am convinced that neither death nor life, neither angels nor demons, neither the present nor the future, nor any powers, neither height nor depth, nor anything else in all creation, will be able to separate us from the love of God that is in Christ Jesus our Lord." (Romans 8: 38, 39 NIV)

Notes

1 Albert Camus, *The Art of Godmanship*, xii, quoted in *The Post-American*, Vol. 1, No. 1, Fall 1971, 1.
2 John Howard Griffin, published transcript of talk at Festival for Life, Ottawa, May 1977.
3 Claude Lanzmann, *Shoah: An oral history of the Holocaust*, Preface by Simone de Beauvoir, Pantheon Books, New York, vii.
4 *Shoah*, 117.
5 *Shoah*, 164-165.

Bibliography

Booth, Catherine, *Female Ministry: A Woman's Right to Preach the Gospel*, The Salvation Army Supplies Printing and Publishing Department: New York, 1975 (1859).

Brown, Jack, *Monkey Off My Back*, Coward-McCann, Inc.: N.Y., 1968.

Bushnell, Katherine, *God's Word to Women*, (1923), privately reprinted by Ray Munson, North Collins, N.Y.

California Medicine, official journal of the California Medical Association, September 1970, Vol. 113, No. 3, 67-68.

Lanzmann, Claude, *Shoah: An oral history of the Holocaust*, preface by Simone de Beauvoir, Pantheon Books: New York, 1987.

Lifton, Robert Jay, *The Nazi Doctors: Medical Killing and the Psychology of Genocide*, Basic Books, Inc.: New York, 1987.

Lythgoe, Mariann June, *The Baptism of the Holy Spirit: A Study of the Meaning of Religious Experience*, Master's Thesis, University of British Columbia, 1969.

Muggeridge, Malcolm, *Jesus Rediscovered*, Fontana Books: Great Britain, 1969.

———. *Chronicles of Wasted Time I: The Green Stick*, William Morrow and Co.: New York, 1973.

Scanzoni, Letha, and Hardesty, Nancy, *All We're Meant to Be*, Word Books: Waco, TX, 1974.

Swidler, Leonard, "Jesus was a Feminist," *Catholic World*, January 1971, 177-183.

Trombley, Charles, *Who Said Women Can't Teach?* Bridge: South Plainfield, NJ, 1985.

Wurmbrand, Richard, *Tortured for Christ*, Hodder and Stoughton, 1967.